Forever Changes

Living With English County Cricket

by

Dave Allen

Moyhill Publishing

First Published in 2016 by Moyhill Publishing.

A CIP catalogue record for this book
is available from the British Library.

ISBN 9781905597680

Printed in the UK.

Front Cover
*Centre photo is of Spencer Codling at the Ageas Bowl, 17 August 2015,
surrounded by cigarette cards of county cricketers from the 1930s.*

The papers used in this book were produced in an
environmentally friendly way from sustainable forests.

Moyhill Publishing,
Suite 471, 6 Slington House,
Rankine Rd., Basingstoke, RG24 8PH, UK

Dedication

To Spencer Codling
and all the other young people who will shape cricket's future

Contents

Preface

I will soon embark on my 57th season watching English county cricket. When I started there were only three-day County Championship matches played mostly for some years on uncovered pitches between 17 teams in one division, plus occasional non-competitive first-class games. This book describes the frequent and often significant changes that have taken place in county cricket in the years since then – changes far in excess of anything in any other professional spectator sport in the same period.

Many of those changes have had positive effects, to some extent keeping county cricket alive, but the book will also question the culture of endless change, which has led to some less happy consequences and continues unabated. There will be more changes next season, not least to the tradition of the toss, but looming ominously is a further reduction in County Championship matches which has been the major motivation for writing and publishing this book.

Linked to my concern with these proposals, and the England and Wales Cricket Board's current preoccupation with so-called 'white ball' cricket, is a broader worry that when I started watching and playing all those years ago cricket was embedded in English culture in a way that is no longer the case. Now, it is far more a niche activity for a minority of the population. That, too, will be a central theme of this book, albeit one which I have attempted to explore in a very particular way, linked to my professional life in the arts.

In addition to being a county cricket life-member, I am the Hon. Archivist at Hampshire and I intend this book to be the last of a few cricket publications over the past 20 years. The others were all concerned with Hampshire's cricketing history, whereas this is far more general, but there is here an occasional Hampshire 'bias' since I have much of that information readily available and I use it where it enables me to make a more general point. For example, I list by name the many Hampshire towns and villages that the county's cricketers visited in the 1950s, with Club & Ground and Benefit XIs. I am sure this was true of other counties and I hope that readers from outside my county can make the connection or preferably, carry out and publish their own findings.

My title refers to 'English' cricket and throughout the book that is generally the term I use, in the same sense that ECB refers to the England *and Wales* Cricket Board. The focus is on county cricket, including Glamorgan, and to a lesser extent Test Matches, so it is very much about the English game, although I have sought throughout to place that English game in a broader British social, economic and political context. There are occasional references to women's cricket and club cricket and I suspect that any revision of this book in a few years time (albeit improbable) would need to pay more attention to those topics.

The dedication is specifically to my young friend Spencer and, more generally, to all those young people who, like him, are the future of cricket. I hope I might have a few more years enjoying it, but whatever happens to me, it is the young people of today who will shape the game of tomorrow, and while I have no concerns for Spencer, who seems very well supported in his love of our game, as a former schoolteacher I am concerned for the game's future unless we can engage many more young people. In that respect, while I am arguing for the importance of the County Championship, there will be no case here against the development of the shorter forms of the game, which have attracted new followers and done so much to revive and sustain the professional game on-and-off the field.

I have spent pretty well my whole life living and working in two cities, Portsmouth and London. I am still an inner-city boy and one of my greatest concerns is the way in which through my lifetime, cricket has become predominantly a game of the suburbs and rural areas. One solution to that problem lies with specific projects designed to promote inner city forms of the game for the 'kids' who can no longer stick a dustbin in the middle of the street and defend it with a lump of wood. One of those projects is 'Cage Cricket', created in my home city of Portsmouth, and so any profits from this publication will go to their charitable arm, Cage4All.

I do not pretend that the younger members of my audience will find this lengthy book an easy read, but I hope that some of them at least might stay with it, perhaps revisiting it from time-to-time, and thereby coming to understand better how the English county game has arrived where it is today.

I was a schoolteacher and then subsequently an academic, so I am familiar with the conventions of writing and publishing books like this, which draw extensively upon secondary sources. I have avoided using conventional referencing in the text in order to facilitate a relatively easy read for what I assume will be principally a 'non-academic' audience. I believe, however, the references are clear through the text and can be matched with the list of significant sources at the end, although I have avoided including titles such as *Pickwick Papers* where they are merely listed to make a general point in the main body of the text. I have drawn extensively on *Wisden* and the monthly and annual publications of *Playfair,* and since what follows is principally a chronological narrative, those sources should be obvious.

Otherwise, I believe that many of the sources can be pursued quite easily online, an increasingly valuable resource for anyone engaged in cricket research. While I do intend this to be my final cricket publication, I shall maintain my cricket blog[1] and will happily pursue discussions and debates on there about any issues in the book. I have no desire to see the end of book publishing, but the internet and social media have opened up extraordinary opportunities for cricket lovers to share ideas and opinions and my experience as a 'blogger' has been an almost wholly positive one.

Other than on the cover, there are no photographs in this book. As a former teacher of art, design and photography I hope I have some understanding of the significance of visual images, but this is a book of historical events, ideas and opinions. In addition, I hope it might be read fairly widely, even by those 'reformers' who see me and those who share my views as 'old, and in the way', and so I have chosen to emphasise the written word and keep the costs as low as possible.

Dave Allen

Portsmouth, Spring 2015

---

1. hampshirecrickethistory.wordpress.com

Introduction

I was born in Portsmouth in 1949. Ten years later, during the glorious summer of 1959, I played my first game of organised cricket (at school) and went for the first time to see Hampshire's cricketers play at the United Services Officers' Ground in the city centre. Hampshire, runners up in the County Championship the previous year, met the great but ageing Surrey side, who after seven consecutive County Championship titles, were about to relinquish their crown to Yorkshire.

I understood very little about that particular match when I watched it then, but in the decades since I have followed cricket – in particular county cricket – very closely. This book will argue that the county competition I first encountered, which had changed very little over the previous 50 years or more, has since then been subject to endless changes, some good, some bad, but *forever changes* – with more looming. In addition, the English game I first encountered, despite facing significant economic problems at county level, was more deeply embedded in English culture than it is today. Over those years it has become a fully professional participant in a global domestic and international game, dealing often in huge sums of money. In some parts of the world, particularly the Asian sub-continent, cricket plays a central role in society, but in England it has become an increasingly niche activity, played, watched and followed by an often devoted yet diminishing percentage of the population.

I did not grow up in a cricketing family, although by the late 1950s we would sometimes watch Test Matches when they appeared on our newly installed television. My mum was increasingly aware of my fondness for cricket, and in late August 1959 she was quite happy to pack me off for the day to the ground just a few hundred yards from my school. I went on my own with no clear idea what I was watching, although by the start of the following season I was ready and willing to watch regularly, and in 1961 I became a junior member, celebrating my team win its first County Championship title.

My mum had been a librarian, and keen to encourage me to read, would often find books about cricket for my birthday and at Christmas. As a consequence, I very soon encountered the writing and broadcasting of John Arlott and HS (Harry) Altham. Altham was the President of my county club but also, with Arlott, one of the authors of Hampshire's history in 1957, which came to me as one of those presents. It did not take long to discover that he had also written a major history of the game. In the years since then some of the best cricket historians have challenged aspects of Altham's histories, but he remains a figure worthy of respect for so many contributions to the game throughout his life, as a player, writer, administrator and, crucially, for his encouragement of young cricketers. Given their natural Hampshire 'bias', he and Arlott became 'mentors' to this boy who very quickly discovered a fondness for the history of the game, alongside the playing and the watching. I read and re-read Arlott's writing and Altham's histories during those formative years and I am grateful to them for starting me on this path.

This is not however, merely a history of the 50-plus years of English county and Test Match cricket since that first visit, for the specific motivation to write it was the latest set of proposals that emerged in 2015 to cut the County Championship again. These proposals are seen as 'progressive' while those of us who love the Championship are seen as impeding progress but as we shall see, change is not necessarily synonymous with progress. During the 2015 season I took a number of opportunities to argue against a further dismantling of the four-day game and found considerable support from fellow supporters. I do not presume to write on their behalf but this book is for all those who share my love of County Championship cricket.

There is I hope a second and perhaps more important audience. Reflecting on my first visits to cricket and the valuable role of the early publications I encountered, I decided to write for a similar audience of young people coming to cricket for the first time. This is a fairly long book, packed with all kinds of facts, ideas and opinions and I do not assume that younger readers will immediately engage with, or understand, everything that is written here. Rather, I hope they might return to it from time-to-time as a point of reference, while searching out other accounts to learn more of how we have arrived where we are, which if history is any judge will probably be a brief stay! Perhaps in 50 years time, one or two of my readers will be 'writing' their updated histories of the game, although what form publishing might take in 2065 I hesitate to speculate.

That first trip to watch county cricket was on Monday 17 August 1959. As I was beginning to plan this book, I realised that Hampshire were due to play a home 50-over match v Lancashire on the precise anniversary – Monday 17 August 2015 – although not, sadly, in Portsmouth. Rather than write this book for an imaginary ten-year-old – an 'everyboy' or 'everygirl' – I thought I might find a particular individual to have in mind while working on it. On my first visit in 1959, I had paid my 'shilling', sat on the grass by the boundary and was ignored by everybody for the rest of the day. Nobody bothered to check whether I was enjoying myself, or perhaps more importantly whether I might come back. I did, of course, and they have had more than their money's worth from me since then, but it was all a matter of luck. On the other hand, in August 2015, Hampshire Cricket's community wing invited, as usual, a couple of the county's club sides to bring their Colts to play on the outfield before the match and then watch the professionals in action, so it was easy for me to ask Greig Stewart, who heads up that organisation, to find someone to bear in mind while I was writing.

Having requested a boy or girl around 10 years of age and preferably one who had never seen a county game before, I was taken to meet the adults from East Woodhay Cricket Club from the north of the county. In turn, they were happy to help, and immediately identified a boy called Spencer as the ideal candidate. So, there he is, on that day in August 2015, on the front cover. I required nothing special of him or his parents, who were with him on that day, beyond the willingness to let Spencer be my imagined focus. I think they were intrigued by my idea, seemed entirely happy to agree to my proposal, and after I met Spencer, his father confirmed this visit was his first county match and wrote down a few details, including his date of birth.

That was an extraordinary moment, because entirely by 'chance', it transpired that Spencer and I shared precisely the same birthday, so on his visit to the Ageas Bowl in 2015 he was, *exactly, to the day*, the same age that I was on my first visit in 1959. I suspect that Carl Jung might have a view of such a 'coincidence', but suffice it to say I was clear that the cricketing gods had conspired to enable this meeting and that the book was a project I must pursue. So I did, and I have, and here it is, specifically for Spencer and his peers, my fellow members and supporters and everyone else who loves English county cricket, and cares for its future.

1959 was one of the warm and sunny English summers of the 20th century, ranked eighth by Philip Eden in his *Wisden* survey (2000). There was a certain irony in the fine weather that summer since, for the first time, the English County Championship experimented with the covering of pitches. Almost inevitably, the covers were rarely used and batsmen flourished as they rarely had during that decade, although the first significant event I saw was Surrey's John Edrich trapped lbw for nought by Derek Shackleton, the leading bowler in the County Championship throughout the 1950s and 1960s. As a Hampshire boy, 'Shack' became my first great hero – the archetypal English craftsman cricketer of what is now a bygone era. He took 100 first-class wickets over 20 consecutive seasons. No other bowler has ever done that, and now none ever will.

Apart from an occasional adjustment of the points for first innings lead, the covering of pitches was the first significant change in English county cricket since it had resumed after the war in 1946, when Yorkshire had also won the title. Indeed the County Championship was in many respects much the same as it had been at the start of the 20th century when Yorkshire had also succeeded Surrey as County Champions. I knew absolutely nothing of the history of cricket on that first visit in 1959 but it was my introduction to a great English sporting tradition, which unlike many other city-based sports was still rooted in the counties, which had once been the political and social power-centres of the country. Despite English cricket being a *county* competition however, it was increasingly played in city and town centres, which were best able to provide the paying audiences that could keep the game alive. Most of the counties' main grounds were in towns and cities and at the higher level, every Test Match in England in 1959 was played in one of its major cities: London, Manchester, Nottingham, and Leeds, while in 1960 Birmingham would have its turn.

Despite that concentration in the urban areas, we shall see that first-class cricket in the 1950s had strong links across the counties at other levels, with professional cricketers often drawn from their counties' schools and clubs and in their early years appearing frequently at the local club grounds representing the county's Club & Ground and beneficiary's sides. County Championship matches too, would take place at a number of grounds within their borders taking cricket to their supporters, as Hampshire did in Portsmouth on that hugely influential day in my life.

One thing I had no idea about in 1959 was that it was the first season of a brief experiment with covering pitches against the elements. Variations in cricket's playing surfaces have an impact on the performance and outcome of every cricket match far in excess of any other professional sport. As I write this in late 2015, we have just learned that in next year's County Championship the visiting side will be allowed to choose to bowl first, and only if they decline will a traditional toss take place. This is entirely to do with negating the preparation of pitches to suit home sides – particularly their quicker bowlers – and as such, is the latest attempt to improve the lot of the county spin bowler, an endangered species in county cricket. It might work, and it might not. If it does not, we can be sure that something else will be tried. That is the theme of this book; that the one constant in English cricket since the year I started watching it, has been *change*.

Across the years since 1946, indeed to a large extent since 1895 when my county Hampshire were first admitted to the expanded County Championship, the counties had played each other with teams consisting mostly of Englishmen, over three days on uncovered wickets. The number of games they played varied, the number of balls in an over did not settle on six for a few years and the points awarded for winning and taking first innings lead changed every now and then. Apart from that and a much-discussed new lbw law in the 1930s, things seemed to be much as they had always been until 1959. But since then, change has been pretty well constant and that seems likely to be the case in the near future.

But if continuity was the case in English county cricket prior to 1959, the world-at-large was a rather less certain place. Two world wars had wreaked havoc showing seeds of uncertainty, now compounded by the 'Cold War' and the threat of a nuclear holocaust. Britain was granting independence to the former colonies and was said to have lost its Empire in the fiasco of Suez in 1956, while a young American, Elvis Presley was getting younger people 'All Shook Up'. Cinema and variety audiences were in decline as television became a fixture in many households; the motorcar took families to previously unexpected locations, and further afield, two weeks of Mediterranean sun was an enticing alternative to a Blackpool boarding house. Everything was changing, for better or for worse, and as if to acknowledge this, from 1959, English cricket started changing, too.

There is a view that sport reflects the culture and society it inhabits, locally and globally. The story is more complex. Sport is not merely a mirror *to* society; it is a part of it. It participates in the culture. If everything was changing, it was reflected in English cricket but it was also in some small way because English cricket began changing too. This change may have been less immediate or apparent than in for example, television, popular music or technology, but it was certainly at a greater rate than in most other spectator sports. On the surface at least the reason for that was almost entirely economic. In 2015, Stephen Chalke published a marvellous history of the County Championship, and he reported on one season when it was "deep in the doldrums" with rumours that a number of the counties might go under. As a consequence, "the reformers" came up with a variety of solutions about the length of games, the pitches, and the days best suited to attract spectators. That season was not 2015, but 1911. It was ever thus.

County cricket has always led a precarious existence, and almost every major change by these reformers is an attempt to make the game more 'exciting' in the hope of attracting its 'potential' audience. Sometimes those changes are wholly for the best and to be celebrated, but too often the pursuit of people who *might* come and watch takes for granted cricket's more loyal and committed supporters. Sometimes the changes go further, dismantling the forms of the game of which they are particularly fond.

Given these thoughts, this might seem likely to be a book written by an old bloke about the 'Good Old Days', and it will most certainly offer an argument against the further dismantling of the County Championship. Indeed it will go farther, arguing that a degree of reinstatement is long overdue because all those who run cricket have a duty to preserve the great traditions of the game as custodians for future generations. It is not however a polemic *against* the various forms of limited-overs cricket which have varied in length from 20–65 overs and which have certainly reinvigorated the game over the past half-century. Also, while setting out to describe and challenge the endless obsession with *change* in English cricket, it will acknowledge that the period when I first encountered county and Test Match cricket was in many respects a depressing and worrying one, both in economic and playing terms.

When I first watched county cricket it was certainly no new 'golden age' in English cricket, while many of the changes since then have been for the good of the game. But that is not true of them all, and we now find ourselves in a situation where globally, Test Match crowds seem to be shrinking, where the County Championship is dominated by batsmen and medium pacers, where county spectators rarely see the best English or overseas cricketers, where Test Match cricket is no longer seen live on British terrestrial television, and where very few English state school or inner city children encounter cricket in the kind of sustained way that leads them to play it and follow it into adult life. There are many other points to be made, no least about the global governance of the game, but this book will examine principally the way the English game has been transformed over the years since 1959.

Chapter One: Towards 1959

The main theme of this book is the almost continuous change in English county cricket since 1959. There is another thread, concerned with the ways in which cricket, once embedded in English social and cultural life and often taken for granted as such, is now less obviously a common element of what might defined as 'Englishness' or the English way of life.

I have said that I did not grow up in a cricketing family, my dad preferred tennis, but there was always encouragement, and in the world beyond our lower middle-class home with two parents, plus my sister and me, cricket in the 1950s seemed simply a part of being English, particularly for men and boys. When we walked around the seafront parks near our Southsea home, boys would be playing improvised games, and further along the esplanade towards Eastney there was the rather delightful St Helen's cricket ground, which every August staged a club Festival Week. Across the city, towards the HM Dockyard, Hampshire visited in most months of the first-class season including their own weeklong festival in August, and while my grammar school was proud of its cricketing achievements and occasional county players, around the corner from my home the local secondary modern had nets in the playground throughout the summer. In the late 1950s, cricket was covered extensively in the local and national newspapers while the BBC had begun regular broadcasts of England's home Test Matches on radio and television.

However, this 'embedded' cultural sense of cricket went beyond those who played with their school or club or watched the professional game. It could be found in many aspects of popular culture, encountered by many who would not consider themselves cricket lovers. When the West Indians beat England at Lord's in 1950, the Trinidadian singer Lord Beginner wrote and recorded perhaps the most famous 'English' calypso with its memorable refrain "Cricket Lovely Cricket" – familiar to many people for whom cricket was simply a passing interest. In this first chapter I shall consider a variety of ways in which cricket once appeared in popular fictions, films, television programmes and imagery, while suggesting that if this was fairly common then, it is now all too rare. Cricket is still popular, but its popularity is far more a specialised interest rather than an embedded element of English life.

In a very simple sense, we can hear this in the way that far fewer people today use metaphorical terms like "it's not cricket", "hit for six" or "playing with a straight bat" than was the case 50 years ago while, if the recently deceased are often described still as having enjoyed a "good innings" that may be simply because they come from a generation that grew up with cricket. My particular focus in this chapter, however, will be less on spoken language and rather more on examples of cricket in fiction, images and film, especially where it appears in a natural way within a broader narrative rather than the central theme. In that sense, we can see cricket as a more common and widespread social activity rather than the relatively specialised and separate minority interest it has become. A similar study of cricket in India would reveal many recent fictional films that have cricket as a focus or a key element – but not so in the British film industry today, where a title such as *Bend It Like Beckham* is more believable than 'Bash It Like Ballance', or, 'Crack It Like Cook'. In 2012 the British film *The Best Exotic Marigold Hotel* showed a retired High Court judge playing cricket, but in a street in India, with local boys.

From the formation of a number of county clubs in the mid-19th century, and the uncertain beginnings of the County Championship through to the unhappy and unnatural 'break' in county and Test Match cricket that came with the first world war, county cricket was sometimes the main focus of an English season. There was not then a Test Match touring side in every English season, but cricket at various levels was taken up and played extensively by most sections of society – albeit mostly but not exclusively by men. In that period, Test Matches were played only between England, Australia and South Africa – including an ill-fated 'triangular' tournament in 1912. Between the two wars, West Indies, New Zealand and India began competing on the Test Match stage, with Pakistan joining them in the 1950s after the war and partition.

From the Victorian and Edwardian periods, there are many examples of cricket appearing in popular fiction – including many boys' stories, annuals and readers in which the cricket was usually of the public school variety. For example, EW Padwick's extensive bibliography of cricket identifies more than a dozen items from 1920 through to the 1950s by one of the more prolific writers, Hylton Cleaver. The cover of his 1920 collection *The Harley First XI*, shows a distinguished senior boy in with striped cap and jacket over his whites, standing nonchalantly, hands-in-pockets, surveying a game being played in the shadow of the school and chapel, which bears a marked resemblance to Cheltenham College.

By the 1930s and the proliferation of 'talking pictures', cricket in literature was complemented by the new feature films some of which incidentally used cricket to set a context and develop characters. A good example might be

Charters and Caldicott in Alfred Hitchcock's thriller *The Lady Vanishes*. The narrative is not in any sense dependent upon them wishing to know about the latest Test Match score, but it adds humour to what is basically a spy thriller and helps to establish our sense of them as quintessential Englishmen of the period – not least when they return to England and learn that the match in Manchester has been washed out.

References to cricket in literature, theatre and cinema in imaginative works that are not cricket-focused suggest a sense of its place in wider society. If cricket appears in these broader narratives, it is generally understood; it exists; people care about it; celebrate it; or even enjoy ridiculing it. It signifies something to a popular, rather than a specialist audience. That is the case with the proliferation of cricketing references in recent Indian films, and the same idea can be explored through popular advertising. In the 1950s, one of the nation's heroes, Denis Compton, was famous for his photographic advertisements for *Brylcreem*, while John Arlott, always sporting his Hampshire tie, promoted pipe tobacco. Fashions for hair cream and pipe smoking come and go, but the choice of those 'celebrities' of the 1950s was intended to win an audience beyond the avid cricket follower. Arlott's unique, unmistakable voice appeared in later advertisements for lawn mowers, while Ian Botham once featured in television advertisements for a breakfast cereal. Each time this occurs there is an implication that cricket is a recognisable cultural activity beyond its own dedicated supporters. The appearances of Phil Tufnell and Andrew Flintoff in television quiz shows and so-called 'reality' television, function in much the same way, as do the winning appearances by Darren Gough and Mark Ramprakash on *Strictly Come Dancing*. But, while these are cricketing 'personalities', the depiction of the game of cricket in popular representations of today is surely far less common than it once was. While cricket has become increasingly globalised, televised and lucrative, in England at least, it is no longer a key player in the popular fictions and narratives – in short, it is merely one more activity appealing to one more niche audience, whereas it once appeared regularly in many popular fictions and documentaries as a part of English life, as a signifier of English identity.

In the mid-19th century as the county sides were moving tentatively towards formal constitutions and an organised competition, a number of novels and stories by Charles Dickens included however incidentally, references to cricket. Dickens appears in the first edition of Padwick's research among no fewer than 1,131 references to "Cricket in Literature" with nine novels by Dickens that include mentions of cricket – probably most famously in *Pickwick Papers* (1837) but continuing through to his final unfinished work, *The Mystery of Edwin Drood*, published when Dickens died in 1870. More generally, the books in this literature section are further subdivided under various topics. Of particular interest here are publications featuring "Cricket as Part of the English Scene" and "Fiction with Incidental Cricket", since it is in those areas that we can uncover cricket as an identifiable element of broader English life rather than as a specific focus for the informed reader. In the first of those sections there are 41 entries, including publications by Edmund Blunden (1932), Mary Russell Mitford (1824–1832), and JB Priestley (1973). Most of the entries are from the 19th or first half of the 20th century, and even Priestley's contribution came towards the end of the life of a man born in the reign of Queen Victoria.

The 127 entries under "Fiction with Incidental Cricket" come largely from a similar period. The few more recent titles include *Take a Girl Like You*, by Kingsley Amis, from 1960 and also the television-linked Raffles series from 1977. Similarly, in 2015, ITV's *Arthur and George* recounted a real event in the life of Sir Arthur Conan Doyle and his secretary, AH Wood, both of whom played first-class cricket. But even in the modern world, television versions of Raffles (EW Hornung) or Conan Doyle, rather like the cricket match in *Downton Abbey,* feed a market for nostalgia – keep calm and keep mentioning cricket. Indeed, it might be argued that by depicting cricket as they do, they identify it as from the past rather than anything significant for a contemporary context.

Padwick lists other notable authors, including Hugh de Selincourt, EM Forster, John Galsworthy, James Joyce, AG Macdonell, Wolf Mankowitz, Iris Murdoch, Siegfried Sassoon, Dorothy Sayers, CP Snow, WM Thackeray, Anthony Trollope, HG Wells and PG Wodehouse, but he offers hardly more than half-a-dozen titles since the early 1960s, although there is an interesting connection with the present in the title of Christopher Hollis's *Death of a Gentleman*. Padwick also lists an extensive section on "Children's Fiction" including, of course, Thomas Hughes' classic, *Tom Brown's Schooldays,* one of a number of these titles that have been produced for the cinema throughout the 20th century.

Another publication is Sir JM Barrie's book *The Little White Bird* (1902) including a chapter titled "The Cricket Match". Barrie was an enthusiastic, if limited, cricketer and in the last years of the 19th century formed an authors' cricket team, the Allahakbarries. They continued to play through to 1913 and included such illustrious names as Arthur Conan Doyle, AA Milne, Jerome K Jerome and PG Wodehouse – Kevin Telfer recently recounted their story in his book *Peter Pan's First XI*. One author not listed in any of the Bibliographies is Virginia Woolf, and there is no reason to suppose we have missed any references to cricket in her writings. Nonetheless, in 2015 Marion Whybrow published an account of Virginia Woolf (born 1882) and her sister, the artist

Vanessa Bell (1879) spending early summers in Cornwall with their parents and other siblings. The family leased a house in the town, visiting each summer until the death of the girls' mother in 1895 when Virginia was 13. For the front cover of her book, *A Childhood in St Ives,* Whybrow has chosen a posed picture of the two girls, Vanessa playing a straight-batted forward defensive, albeit with something of a gap between bat and skirts, while Virginia stands holding the ball as though she has just held one at slip 'off the edge'. Inside, is another shot of Virginia keeping wicket while youngest brother Adrian bats, and later in the book is a fine sepia photograph of an artists' cricket team – a parallel to Barrie's writers XI perhaps?

All these examples suggest that cricket played a part in the popular imagination at least through the Victorian 19th century and the first-half of the 20th century. It is important however, to be cautious in terms of the claims made for the audience for such publications and for cricket itself. As a young journalist in London, Dickens once suggested that the great city's "masses" showed relatively little appetite for the game adding, even if they had been interested, the admission of 2/6d (12.5p) to Lord's would deter them. Dickens commanded various overlapping audiences, including those who attended his public readings, those who read his fiction in serial form, and those who purchased and read whole books. But it was not until Forster's great Education Act of 1870 that the British Government ensured the formal education of all children aged between the ages of 5–13. It was an education rooted largely in the '3Rs' and simple design, ensuring the hand-eye coordination needed for factory work. However, even if, after 1870, there was greater literacy, we must not assume yet a mass readership, although access to literature was greatly enhanced following the Public Libraries Act of 1850. Writers and readers of the Victorian and Edwardian periods nonetheless had cricket as one common reference-point: it fulfilled a recognisably 'English' role in the Empire. In addition, the newspapers of the day would carry reports on a great range of matches – county games to be sure, but also on local clubs, schools, services games and others.

While the vast majority of authors and publications that Padwick lists under "Cricket in Literature" are from the period up to the second world war, there is one notable title from just after, by Leslie Poles (LP) Hartley. *The Go-Between* brings us into the 1950s, but simultaneously offers a recollection of 'minor' cricket at the turn of the century, as the Victorian Age is about to become the Edwardian 'Golden' period in English cricket. It is perhaps particularly fascinating since Hartley wrote it in his late 50s looking back at local cricket in his earliest years, while publishing the book at a time when England's Test Match team dominated the cricket world captained significantly by its first professional, the Yorkshire batsman, Len Hutton.

Hartley wrote *The Go-Between* in the year that the fearsome Fred Trueman destroyed the batting of the touring Indians and it was published in the following summer of 1953, as the English hero Denis Compton hit the runs that brought the Ashes home for the first time since the 1930s, and with Surrey winning the second of their seven successive County Championship. But Hartley's 'other country' of the summer of 1900 was certainly very different.

HRH Queen Victoria, until very recently our longest reigning Monarch, died in January 1901 living through just one 20th century cricket season, although we cannot suppose she paid it much attention. In that season, an undefeated Yorkshire won the 15-team County Championship, while Hampshire came last with no victories. The two great Sussex amateurs, Prince Ranjitsinhji and CB Fry, were the leading batsmen, and Wilfred Rhodes took 206 wickets for Yorkshire, but there were no Test Matches. The West Indians sent a touring side but they were not yet accorded Test Match status, after Australia had won the Ashes in the previous English summer. Ten thousand people watched each of the first two days of the University match at Lord's where RE Foster – of whom more later – top-scored for Oxford with 171 in a total of 503 from three balls less than 130 overs. Incidentally, this was in the season when, for the first time, each over consisted of six balls having previously been four. With the exception of 1939 (eight balls), it has remained as such *in England* since that point. As there were no Test Matches, the County Championship was the focus of top quality cricket, although there was a host of other major matches played by a wide variety of sides.

The Go-Between, can be read as a novel about class in English society at the end of Victoria's reign. Leo, an old and somewhat embittered man returns to a village where he spent a formative summer, and he looks back over half-a-century to recount the tale of a holiday that began gloriously but ended in the tragedy that would transform his life. Leo's story focuses on an illicit love affair between Marion Maudsley, who lives with her upper middle-class family at Brandham Hall in Norfolk, and a tenant farmer on the estate, Ted Burgess. Their relationship is dangerous, not merely because Burgess is socially not worthy of Marion, but because her family, benefitting from growing wealth and pretensions, expect her to marry Lord Trinningham, descended from the local nobility who once resided at Brandham Hall. The marriage will bring the Viscount back to his ancestral home and provide Marian with a title. To further complicate matters, his Lordship arrives to stay during the summer, having returned from the Boer War bearing heroic but disfiguring facial scars.

Leo, boarding at a private prep school with Marion's younger brother Marcus, is spending the summer with him at the family's invitation. This proves something of a challenge for Leo who is only middle-class – his deceased father was a bank manager – but he manages to conceal his status from the family. When Marcus is quarantined in bed with measles, Leo spends his days alone and becomes a messenger, the eponymous Go-Between, carrying love letters between the two illicit lovers without knowing their details or implications.

None of the narrative details need concern us greatly except to say that it is in many respects a book which reflects not only the period about which it was written, but also perhaps the years when it was being written, the early 1950s, when class was certainly significant following the relatively 'democratic' efforts of the British to defeat fascism in the previous decade. To some extent, perhaps we need to see it as a book about how the early 1950s thought about the end of the Victorian Age, and we might wonder, since 1952–1953 saw the birth of the 'New Elizabethans', whether the horrors and social disruption of the first-half of the century nurtured a certain nostalgia for that time, or at least, a version of that time.

The particular interest in *The Go-Between* for this book is in a cricket match between the great house and the village, an event in which Leo becomes a fielding hero. But even before that point, the book offers other references to cricket, placing it clearly close to the heart of English culture in 1900 – and perhaps it was still there in 1953? In that respect we might ask whether any contemporary novelists ever use a cricket match and sayings derived from cricket, as important narrative or thematic devices. I suspect not, and if not, that may reveal a good deal about the differences in the status of cricket in our world today and those of 50 and 100 years ago. Today, cricket is a highly professional, lucrative and global sport, but it operates in a hermetically sealed world and is much less embedded in English culture and society. Despite this, *The Go-Between* continues to be one of a number of period dramas that are the source of popular representations of the period in cinema and contemporary television – a new version of *The Go-Between*, for example, was broadcast on BBC television in September 2015, and the most recent cinema version was directed by Joseph Losey with screenplay by the cricket-loving Harold Pinter in 1971.

At one point in the story, Marcus, confined to bed, suggests that if everyone at the house catches his measles, the cricket match will have to be cancelled. He then adds somewhat ominously that this annual event helps to keep "them" quiet. Despite an initial sense of late-Victorian idyll in the story, there is at least a hint here of potential social unrest at a time when workers were growing better organised. In 1900, Keir Hardie was one of the first two Labour Representation Committee MPs elected to Parliament. In 1906 this increased to 29 and in February of that year Hardie was elected first leader of the newly formed Labour Party. At the same time the campaign for Votes for Women was becoming more prominent. In 1903, Emmeline Pankhurst founded the important Women's Social and Political Union, which *the Daily Mail* dubbed the Suffragettes. After often fiercely militant campaigning, women over 30 were given the vote in 1918 and 10 years later this was extended to women and men following their 21st birthday.

The class distinctions in Hartley's fictional village are depicted clearly in the cricket match. Lord Trimingham captains the XI from the great house but of necessity his side mixes 'upstairs and downstairs', as English county cricket has always done. Elsewhere, too, there are references to cricket and to class. When Leo meets Ted Burgess, the latter explains he is "not what you call a gentleman farmer, I'm a working one" adding he does not "have much to do with those grand folks" at the Hall – with the exception, of course, of Marian. As the cricket match looms, Leo is astonished and thrilled to be nominated as twelfth man for the Hall XI. He walks to the ground with the other players in his team and notes how day-to-day differences disappear, so that he feels as one with the butler, the footman, the gardener, and others. The Hall XI arrive appropriately dressed in white flannels, but the members of the village team are wearing an array of ordinary clothing, and Leo feels this gave his side an immediate edge. In one delightful passage, Trimingham goes into bat, and Marcus's older brother, Denys, an opinionated snob, suggests that his cover drive is worthy of a county player and, indeed, that perhaps not even RE ('Tip') Foster of Worcestershire can play a late-cut to rival his.

Foster was a great figure of the period and in so many ways, a typical amateur cricketer. He was one of seven brothers and the finest sportsman among them. After Malvern College and Oxford University he played for Worcestershire and, in 1899 Worcestershire's first year in the County Championship, he and his brother Wilfrid, both scored centuries in the two innings v Hampshire at Worcester. Fortunately for Hampshire, this was RM Poore's great year and his century enabled Hampshire to save the game. 'Tip' Foster captained England at football and cricket, and in December 1903 at Sydney, his Test Match debut innings of 287 was at the time the world record Test Match score.

Despite these achievements, for business reasons, Foster could not always be available to play for his county or his country. In the three seasons, 1899–1901, he played 70 first-class matches but never again in one season more than the 16 he played in 1907. In this respect, his career was similar to that of RM Poore, the professional soldier, who had a relatively ordinary season in 1898 in which he played 15 first-class matches, followed by his record-breaking 1899 in which he played 12 times for Hampshire and the Gentlemen. But in the next 11 English seasons he played just 16 matches after which he appeared just twice in India and retired. In a career of 22 seasons he played in just 55 first-class matches. It is difficult to imagine the great amateur achievements of such cricketers in the modern professional game.

In the novel, we are told that Trimingham takes what was then an unusual middle-and-leg guard, but despite scoring only a few runs, Marian applauds him enthusiastically on his return, leaving Leo to conclude that being a woman she knows very little about cricket. The Hall side fares rather poorly until Mr Maudsley appears and, with a careful half-century, sets a reasonable target for after tea. For the village, Ted Burgess replies in kind but Leo perceived his innings of brute force to be the opposite of Mr Maudsley's cunning. He suggests that comparing the two was not even a matter of the obvious class difference between the Hall and the village but was even more a struggle between "order and lawlessness", respect and opposition to tradition, and even "social stability and revolution". These are echoes of the political unrest that is generally latent in British society but which had been common across much of Europe through the 19th and early 20th centuries. It offers too, somewhat stereotypical depictions of the Gentleman cricketer's refinement up against a view of the raw power and relatively uncouth approach of the working man as Player.

These dichotomies are familiar, of course, and they continue to appear in various guises because they are convenient – simple oppositions that do not demand too much effort of thought. If we consider some of the great English amateur cricketers who were drawn from the upper and upper-middle classes, we can see in many the flamboyance and carefree gaiety expected, although others were rather more cautious, perhaps like Mr Maudsley. But few of the great craftsman professionals of county or England cricket were particularly like Ted Burgess. Many of those men would have been deferential in the dealings with the hierarchical world of English cricket and they were pragmatists both in the matter of winning cricket matches and in building careers, keeping them and their families in reasonable comfort – at least, once the benefit had come. There was no revolutionary fervour in their cricket; their efforts were all for the bat and ball. It is perhaps only with the broader social changes of the 1960s, the abolition of the amateur/professional divide and the formation of the Professional Cricketers' Association (PCA) that a more general change began to occur in the attitudes of county cricketers.

Since *The Go-Between* is a fiction, we cannot be surprised that the author arranges for Leo to field substitute late in the game, or that he holds a fine catch to get rid of Ted Burgess and thereby secures victory for his side. After the match everyone goes to supper at the village hall, continuing the sense of the great occasion, since for many the day was not merely one more match in the season but *the* match of the season. Later we hear Ted Burgess tell Leo that he must oil his bat for it will be needed next weekend, so, perhaps the village side plays regular fixtures? But at the Hall there is no indication that anyone else plays regularly or was tempted to go and watch them – nor even perhaps Norfolk in the Minor Counties Championship of 1900, during which season they played eight matches, including four home games at Lakenham's County Ground against Northumberland, Durham, Hertfordshire and Cambridgeshire. There is a sense in *The Go-Between* that this is a very special day for most of the participants, and a special match serving a variety of social purposes beyond the outcome of the match or of the individual performances. It is not easy to see how such feelings can be preserved in the modern world of media bombardment, professional sport, big business, even league cricket and top age-group sides.

At the supper, it seems briefly that there might be no entertainment, as the pianist is indisposed and Leo reflects the pessimistic mood in asking what a cricket match or a supper could possibly be "without songs". This, too, has echoes of the great nights of wine and songs with The Hambledon Club at the Bat & Ball Inn more than a century earlier. Eventually, Marian rescues the evening with her piano skills and Ted Burgess and Leo both sing – Leo to great acclaim. On returning to his seat he is complimented and asked whether he might like to be a professional singer, to which he replies that he would rather be a professional cricketer. It is interesting that Leo specifies precisely a *professional* cricketer, perhaps betraying his relatively impoverished circumstances, for generally in those days, a young man at prep school, with friends like Marcus aiming for Eton, would desire a cricket career rather more like Foster's or Poore's – playing as an amateur when able, with another, better source of income. But Leo specifies the professional route.

At the end of the great day, Marcus and Leo return to the Hall and they resume their habit of poking fun at each other. The camaraderie among the team that overcame class on the walk to the game dissolves entirely as Marcus remarks on the "stink" in the village hall from "the plebs" and implies a sense of relief that having done their duty they are now rid of the village until next summer. The next morning when a servant approaches Leo to congratulate him on his achievements, Leo sees his team-mate of yesterday in his previous rank.

Sometimes in *The Go-Between*, cricket is simply used as an obvious way of explaining or exploring broader social or moral issues – it is common speech in the way that "it's not cricket" is occasionally used to challenge poor behaviour in any walk of life, or "hit for six" used as a metaphor for a victory of whatever kind. In 1900 church attendance would be expected each Sunday and Leo, questioning the centrality of guilt and repentance in Christian services, begins to assert his independence from God's authority by suggesting that this levelling of sin was rather like a cricket match played in drizzle, where everyone might have a "dull excuse" for poor performances. Elsewhere, he considers that behaving correctly in particular social circumstances is akin to 'walking' upon recognising you are out. In recent years, one or two international cricketers like Adam Gilchrist and Jos Buttler have done this – while Stuart Broad notably did not – but they are often considered unusual, and even foolhardy for doing so. The issue was even explored recently in an edition of *the Archers*.

These attitudes, and the kind of cricket depicted, are simply one English kind of the game in 1900, although the way in which everyday discourse might include references to the game is now far less likely. Indeed, cricket was probably *the* English sport in the Edwardian years to a degree that is perhaps difficult for us to comprehend in these days dominated by football but with a plethora of other sports to play, watch and support, competing in turn with a broad range of entertainments. In part, cricket's status was explicable through the exploits and popularity of the first great English sporting 'superstar' WG Grace. He had played both his final Test Match and last county match for Gloucestershire in 1899, but he enjoyed a few more seasons playing for other first-class sides, not least London County, his new team, who played their matches at Crystal Palace. They did not compete in the County Championship but generally played against other counties and selected some of the leading players of the period such as CB Fry, Gilbert Jessop, Len Braund, Albert Trott and Charles Townsend.

There is a wonderful cartoon of the ageing and rotund 'WG' celebrating the awarding of first-class status to his new side, in David Frith's appropriately named *Pageant of Cricket*. Meanwhile, the growth of photography as a commercial proposition coincided almost exactly with the start of Queen Victoria's reign, and it developed alongside the increasing formalisation of the English game at Test Match and county level, thereby enabling not merely a documentary record of matches in progress but perhaps more significantly the portrayal of the stars. Iconography is central to the creation of celebrity in all aspects of the modern world of entertainment, and sport is no exception. Even today, more than a century later, anyone with the slightest interest in cricket can conjure an image of 'WG'.

In 1899, CB Fry began his weekly publication of *a New Gallery of Famous Players*. At the cost of 6d (2.5p) per week, cricket lovers could purchase these large photographs and brief biographical notes, building to a fine collection, which was subsequently published as a collection in hard covers. For some years after 1868, the magazine *Vanity Fair* published caricatures of famous cricketers while the English artist Albert Chevallier Taylor produced his portraits of the great players as well as one of the most evocative action paintings of a match between Kent and Lancashire at Canterbury in 1906. A century later, with Kent experiencing serious economic difficulties, the Marylebone Cricket Club (MCC) purchased the painting from the county. In the early 20th century, these various and increasing number of images were important in establishing certain cricketers as popular personalities.

Frith's fine book offers a range of images from the turn of the century. There are cartoons, caricatures and paintings but mostly, photographs, and these include team photographs and posed action portraits, although relatively few head-and-shoulders images, while the action shots in the days before long lenses, offer a rather distant view. Despite the gradual disappearance of WG Grace, Frith nominates this predominantly Edwardian era from 1899 as "The Age of Gods" or a period of "glorious richness".

Frith shares with us the wonderful photograph of Victor Trumper on the drive; the tragic Albert Trott; Hampshire's great soldier, RM Poore; two of the Foster brothers; perhaps the greatest 'all rounder' CB Fry; the awkward genius, Sydney Barnes; Australia's Monty Noble and Clem Hill; Bill Lockwood of Surrey, and Gilbert Jessop posing an uncharacteristically tentative defensive shot. The image of Jessop is unusually in colour but there is another from that period of Lord Hawke and his Yorkshire team, County Champions in 1900, 1901 and 1902. Four of the 12 in that line-up were amateurs, but the great professionals, including Hirst and Rhodes, are there too.

Those are images of some of the finest Test Match and county cricketers of the time, but there are others, including a 'daft' photograph of the Music Hall comic Dan Leno at practice in his back garden, and the three Cambridge University centurions who contributed most to their score of 703–9 v Sussex in 1900. There is a group of school children on their way to an afternoon of games and a charming reproduction of a painting, "Playing Out Time in an Awkward Light" by Frank Batson. It is probably a country house match on a ground surrounded by trees with a marquee and a reasonable number of spectators watching in the distance as we are offered the scene through the eyes of the facing batsman. The painting is now at Trent Bridge. Of its time it would have been considered a contemporary scene with a treatment that echoes the growing influence of Impressionism on this side of the Channel, but today it is of interest partly by evoking a sense of nostalgia and also because it reminds us again of the variety of cricket played at the time.

In 1953, the year that *The Go-Between* was published, there was much to celebrate in England including the Coronation; the conquering of Everest; Stanley Matthews' Cup Winner's medal, and England's cricketers winning the Ashes at the Oval for the first time since the 1930s. The second world war and its political aftermath, had led to a growing desire for democracy and opportunity in the country, and major initiatives like the Mass Observation project encouraged an increasing focus on everyday lives and 'ordinary' people in the 1950s by a new generation of creative individuals in the various arts. In part, too, this meant a turning against some of the established members of the 'old guard'. In the theatre, one playwright somewhat unfairly dismissed as 'old-fashioned', was Terence Rattigan who was felt to produce 'drawing room' dramas about upper-middle-class issues, notably relationships between older men (fathers, teachers) and boys (sons, pupils), whereas from the mid-1950s, the new generation in theatre, film and painting moved from the drawing room (if there was one) and the public school, to the kitchen sink.

This is not the publication to pursue that debate. For our purposes, it is interesting that Rattigan had been a useful schoolboy cricketer, opening the batting for Harrow v Eton at Lord's in 1929 and used cricket references in his work, notably in *The Winslow Boy* which includes, as the family solicitor and frustrated suitor, the character DWH (Desmond) Curry who we learn during the play had taken a famous hat-trick for the Gentlemen v Players at Lord's in 1895. Later, when 'Master' Ronnie Winslow has to be photographed sympathetically by the press, it is suggested he wears his cricket whites, as a costume "that would say both youth and England". What might he wear today to signify the same themes?

In 1953, Rattigan provided the script for the feature film *The Final Test*. He wrote it initially as a television script tribute to Donald Bradman after his famous last Test Match appearance at the Oval in 1948, then in 1953, turned it into the script for the feature film version, starring the popular British character actor Jack Warner as Sam Palmer, an ageing professional batsman playing at the Oval in his last Test Match. While this is a significant moment in Palmer's career, his young son Reggie, rather than watching his father's last match, prefers poetry to cricket and pursues instead an audience with one of his favourite poets, Alexander Whitehead (Robert Morley). This is a disappointment to his father, but when the great writer discovers Reggie's identity he insists the pair of them forget poetry and go to the Oval to watch the match, for he is a cricket lover.

The film is made more 'realistic' by the participation of a group of England cricketers who play themselves in the dressing room, including the professionals Len Hutton, Denis Compton, Jim Laker, Cyril Washbrook and Alec Bedser. To add to that sense of a 'real' match, the Director, Anthony Asquith, cut in footage from the Ashes winning Test Match between England and Australia that year and added fictional commentaries by John Arlott. As a film about cricket, it is very much the world of professional Test Match player, and while they are accurately depicted as living lives closer to ordinary folk than might be the case today, unlike the cricket of *The Go-Between,* it is very much a world in which the few of exceptional talents perform for the many (with a full house at the Oval).

As well as contrasting the interests of the aesthete and the athlete, the film uses a bewildered American Senator to poke gentle fun at the English attitude to cricket. The film's trailer announces, "There are some things an American will never understand", and we see the senator, wearing a large Stetson at Waterloo Station, alarmed to overhear conversations about how "England's finished, she ain't got a ruddy chance", while a daily newspaper warns, "England May Collapse Today." Fearing political and economic disaster, he learns the truth from a station porter and decides to go to the Oval to discover what cricket is all about. There he sits next to a well-spoken, middle-class spectator (Richard Wattis) and the Senator asks him whether he might see some "excitement", to which the rather dry Wattis remarks, "I hope not." The Senator pursues this line of enquiry remarking on the four previous games in the series and the five days devoted to each, before asking whether the view that, hopefully, there will be no excitement, would be a "fairly general one" among the 30,000 spectators, to which comes the reply, "Well yes, if they're English."

Despite the humour, there is a poignant core to the film in that its central theme is the imminent retirement of a once revered sporting star, and the anxieties in those days that the modest remuneration even for the best players may not be adequate for an uncertain future. What will be next for Reggie Palmer?

In 1956, John Arlott's 'commentary' could be heard again with another group of England cricketers, Godfrey Evans, Frank Tyson and Colin Cowdrey in an episode of BBC Radio's popular series *Hancock's Half Hour* in which Tony Hancock dreams he has been invited by the chairman of the MCC to play against Australia. Sid James plays the chairman who, having selected Hancock, bets on Australia to win. Hancock is suitably inept throughout the match, managing to concede 800 runs in an unfinished over but ends up the hero, as the winning four from a ball by Lindwall deflects from his ear. It is nonsense, of course, and even the presence of the real cricket figures is not intended to add 'authenticity', but it does offer the feeling that 60 years ago cricket was recognisably a key element in British cultural life, not least since, following the Oval triumph of August 1953, Hutton, Tyson and the others had gone to Australia (1954–1955) and retained the Ashes.

Cricket offers sufficient idiosyncrasies to be exploited by comedians and there were a couple of later examples on BBC television. One featured Fred Trueman in an episode of *Dad's Army* in November 1970, when Trueman bowls one ball in a challenge match for the Wardens against the Home Guard but then leaves the field injured and the Home Guard win by one wicket. One of the regular characters in *Fawlty Towers* is the retired and somewhat senile Major Gowen. The episode featuring the German visitors (October 1975) opens with Basil taking his wife, Sybil, to hospital for an operation on an in-growing toenail. On his return he encounters the Major in the Reception, and opening a typically bewildering conversation, the Major tells him "Hampshire won", to which Basil replies "Did it? Oh, isn't that good. How splendid."

Those two examples are more recent than those from the 1950s, but even so are from 40 years ago, with the first depicting the period of the second world war, and the second, a cricket comment from an elderly man. How often since then has comedy considered cricket sufficiently relevant *culturally* to provide a narrative context for its humour, and if it does, is that generally in a contemporary context? It is perhaps unsurprising that cricket has featured in the somewhat old world 'charm' of the Inspector Morse series.

During the 1950s there was a decline in paying spectators at English grounds although as we shall see this was somewhat offset by an increase in county members. Cricket was not alone in this, as football, dance hall and cinema attendances also decreased following their swelling during the immediate post-war euphoria. One of cricket's challenges was that all major matches lasted either three or five days during a period of full employment, but no great wealth. People had to choose carefully where and when to spend free time, with many workers still on duty on Saturdays. Through the 1950s, cricket lost some of its power to entertain and suffered by comparison with some competing sports and leisure activities.

The importance of entertaining the public in county cricket was one of the themes of a short story and the only published work of fiction by John Arlott. It appeared first in the *Lilliput Magazine* shortly after the mid-1950s period it depicts, and tells the story of a somewhat dour Yorkshire-born professional opening batsman, George Kennett, approaching the end of his career, struggling for runs and enduring criticism from his amateur captain KE Tallis who demanded his team adopt a more enterprising approach. Arlott sets the story in a late season match at Portsmouth for Kennett's fictional 'Norshire' against the real Hampshire side and he includes Roy Marshall who first played in the County Championship in 1955 and Hampshire's captain EDR Eagar who retired in 1957. But Neville Rogers who retired in 1955 is not playing, so in the 'real' world, it can only have been situated in August 1956 or 1957, which will become significant.

Arlott knew the world of county cricket well, so his story has the authentic ring lacking in some cricket fiction. In particular, he had close friends in the Hampshire side including Rogers and the Hampshire wicketkeeper Leo Harrison who had made his debut before the War, served in the RAF, and returned to the county as a batsman and fielder before settling into the role of wicketkeeper. Like many senior professionals, Harrison was a pragmatic and philosophical man. Arlott's story went out first under the title "A Cup of Cold Tea" which was George Kennett's preferred refreshment between innings, as he padded up. But the recurrent catch phrase in the story came from the 'real' Leo Harrison, commiserating with yet another batsman as he succumbed to the wiles of Shackleton, Cannings and the other Hampshire bowlers. Not unkindly, Arlott had Harrison remarking, "it ain't half a blooming game", although when the story was republished in an anthology in the 1980s, blooming had become bloody and "Ain't Half a Bloody Game" was the new title. In 2014, when Leo Harrison attended a ceremony at the Ageas Bowl to rename and dedicate part of the new pavilion as the Arlott Atrium, the ceremony included the reading of extracts from Arlott's story. The performance concluded with Harrison himself performing the last line, from which we learned, perhaps for the first time in public, that even "bloody" was not the real adjective!

In the story, Kennett learned that some team-mates had already been offered new contracts, but not him. He pondered his future – perhaps umpiring, perhaps coaching, or "at worst, some sort of labouring job" – and then he was battling against Hampshire's "quiet, hard side". After a cheap first innings dismissal on the first evening, the captain avoided any conversation and Kennett, deciding against the sociability of the hotel bar, took his supper in a local Italian restaurant. On the next morning "he savoured" the cricketer's relatively late start to the day with the hotel and dining room breakfast. Overhearing a conversation he realised he was to be dropped – this might be his final match.

Norshire were all out at tea on day two, and with showers around, the pitch would "do a bit". Hampshire were dismissed in turn on the third morning leaving a victory target of 167. There were, typically for these years, midweek and in poor weather, a "few scattered spectators" watching as George Kennett began the reply with his partner Stevens and the orders from his captain to "get on with it before the rolling wears off". Kennett paid no attention, dug in as he would always do, and watched wickets fall regularly at the other end. The instruction to "hit" came with each new batsman but to the annoyance of his captain, Kennett battled on. During lunch he enjoyed the cold tea but shortly after, at 106–5, the captain joined him. He played one or two shots but then declined an easy sixth-ball single; "Kennett looked down the wicket at his captain and knew the man was frightened" – he was trying to avoid facing the tall, young pace bowler, Malcolm Heath – "Tallis looked back defiantly, knowing that he knew".

Harrison soon stumped Tallis, while Kennett reached 50 with a single off Shackleton. He laughed at one of the spectators, "trying to start a slow handclap" as a ball from Shackleton crushed his fingers on the bat handle. Another wicket fell, but the runs came gradually until Kennett hooked Heath and the four brought victory as it is perhaps bound to in fiction. Back in the dressing room he prepared to shower and change, once again feeling part of the team, before opening a letter that had been delivered from his former captain offering him a post with his works side as a grounds-man, coach and probably Minor Counties player. In the bar, his captain congratulated him, bought him a drink and revealed that today's innings had him reconsidering his view that Kennett should be released. Kennett was grateful but with security guaranteed, revealed "I've made up my mind to retire at the end of the season, but I'd like to see the season out with the side". He lifted his glass and alongside him Leo Harrison observed, "It ain't half a bloody game."

With *The Final Test* and Arlott's short story, we have strayed somewhat from the idea of cricket embedded in broader narratives, to two examples that take cricket as their primary theme, although the first was shown in the country's many cinemas and the second published in a popular men's magazine, not a cricket publication. The intended audience is beyond the specialist and in both cases, the ageing professional at the heart of the story is an ordinary Englishman with normal anxieties and hopes.

I have suggested that post-war writers and film makers were increasingly inclined to take the lives of 'ordinary' people and 'ordinary' life as their subject matter and that this may have reflected, in part, the increasing post-war focus on democracy. These 'ordinary' people had voted for the benefits of the Welfare State and now they were being represented in a range of publications and broadcasts. It may also have owed something to the now familiar desire of younger generations to sweep away the favoured images and ideas of their predecessors, which in the 1940s and early 1950s were often unadventurous, middle-aged and middle-class – or perhaps nostalgically historical.

In film, the young director Lindsay Anderson made a documentary about the English at play in 1953 called, *O Dreamland,* shot at Margate's amusement centre and funfair and, while it is not wholly celebratory, it would be the first production in a series of films that were identified and often shown under the banner of British "Free Cinema". *O Dreamland* was one of three films shown in the first public screening in 1956, accompanied by a manifesto that proclaimed "the importance of people and the significance of the everyday". Anderson's fellow "Free Cinema" directors included Karel Reisz and Tony Richardson. Their new approach to documentary films led them, in the 1960s, to direct a group of British feature films including *Saturday Night and Sunday Morning, A Taste of Honey, This Sporting Life, Tom Jones, If …* and the film version of the ground-breaking 1950s play *Look Back in Anger.*

Factual accounts of major cricket matches would appear in cinema newsreels, and from the late 1950s all Test Matches in England were shown by the BBC. One of the next occasions in which cricket appeared on the cinema screens would have been in 1959, with a 50-minute documentary by Reisz, shot the previous summer, *We Are the Lambeth Boys.* This shows young people spending evenings in a London youth club on the south side of the Thames. It was screened for the first time, just along the road from its location, at the National Film Theatre in March 1959. The documentary had been shot over six weeks during the previous summer, sponsored by the Ford Motor Company as part of a cinema series of supporting features called *Look at Britain* and directed by Reisz.

We Are the Lambeth Boys offers an intriguing account of inner-city English teenagers in the summer of 1958, with Teddy Boys on the wane and just prior to the emergence of the first Mods, as popular culture exercised an increasingly ubiquitous influence on life across the country. The Lambeth teenagers are seen mainly in the organised, secular surroundings of a local council youth club. These clubs provided social spaces for young people to interact and mature in a relatively 'safe' environment. For example, while all but two of the Lambeth boys (and girls) have left school and are in employment, we do not see them in pubs, drinking alcohol or mixing socially with adults. By contrast, just one year later, Reisz's feature film, *Saturday Night and Sunday Morning* shows a young rebellious factory worker sharing social spaces with much older people, drinking copious quantities of alcohol and pursuing an affair with an older woman. In these respects, the Lambeth youngsters anticipate more accurately the discrete social groupings of young people, separating themselves by choice from their elders, which would have such an impact in the 1960s and beyond.

While Free Cinema pursued new attitudes, and *We Are the Lambeth Boys* records a new youth-oriented world, we now can see much of that world has significantly changed. The film opens with some of the young people walking towards the youth club on a bright summer's evening. Others join them, and we soon see the boys starting their summer evening by bowling and batting to each other in an outdoor cricket net while the 'Lambeth girls' stand around chatting. Almost without exception the boys and girls dress smartly on their night out and there is a sequence where the boys engage in an earnest discussion about clothes and in particular, the cost of quality suits.

In 1958, Lambeth appears to be almost wholly white and working class. Halfway through the film we see two girls walking towards the club past three younger boys in short trousers, including one who is black, but it is a fleeting moment. They appear to be playing happily together but in that same late summer there were extensive disturbances in the streets of north London, characterised as 'race riots'. Similar problems occurred in Nottingham and the protagonists were mainly young, white working-class hooligans intent on trouble. There are two passages in the film that hint at the possibility of gang violence, which the popular press would cover over the following decades. In the opening minutes we see 'Harry and his gang' dressed more like Teddy Boys and preferring to smoke and 'hang about' than join in with the cricket nets. Later, during a work-place sequence, we overhear a discussion about 'Smithy's mob', which may be threatening trouble.

Apart from Brian and Johnny who are still at a single-sex secondary modern school, the Lambeth boys and girls have apprenticeships or work in a variety of places including a butcher's, a post office, a dressmaker's, a factory and an office reception. This is a period of full employment and, while it is not mentioned, at least some of these young men will be among the first to escape being called up for National Service, thus tasting a social and economic freedom not experienced since the start of the war, 20 years earlier. Nonetheless, we are reminded of the significant class divide in Britain at the time with the boys' annual trip to Mill Hill (public) School for an afternoon of cricket, swimming and socialising. While these educational divisions still exist in contemporary Britain, young people today share a more common popular culture, which in 1958 was hardly widespread and appears not to have touched the public school at all.

The Mill Hill cricket sequence ends with a number of poignant 'portraits' of the boys, perhaps inviting us to ponder on their future and the future of Lambeth and Britain. Reisz then cuts to a far more boisterous truck ride home, replete with light-hearted shouting at pedestrians and territorial songs, which again perhaps hints at the looming threat of the football gangs who would be one of the less attractive developments of the 1960s. While the Lambeth boys enjoyed cricket at their youth club and in their visit to Mill Hill School, the film offers plenty of other evidence of them engaging in newer forms of popular culture, which were making a considerable impact on the lives of young people in the mid-to-late 1950s. Back from Mill Hill they joined their peers for the modern version of the singing in *The Go-Between*, with dancing at the club to the Mickey Williams Group (2/6d) a young rock & roll act featuring guitar and tenor saxophone. We see most of the Lambeth boys and girls jiving to the group's version of "Putting On the Style" which had been a number one hit record for British skiffle 'king', Lonnie Donegan, in June 1957 – just as Peter May and Colin Cowdrey worked out how to defeat the wiles of Lord Beginner's "two little pals" 'Sonny' Ramadhin and Alf Valentine in the first Test Match at Edgbaston, and the BBC broadcast ball-by-ball commentaries on the radio for the first time.

Donegan's hit was the last record to be released solely in the 78rpm format to reach the top of the British charts, and in no time the jukebox friendly and less fragile seven-inch 45rpm 'singles' would take over. Donegan had been the banjo man in Chris Barber's traditional jazz band but developed a very English form of skiffle – part folk, part blues – and enjoyed significant success. Although the craze itself was short-lived, its influence was huge. It is said that in Liverpool a skiffle group called the Quarrymen made a home recording of "Putting on the Style" on the day that two of its members, John Lennon and George Harrison met a young guitarist called Paul McCartney for the first time. Skiffle was a musical form in which young people with modest 'talent' could entertain their peers with no consideration for the standards or conventions of their elders and 'betters'. Skiffle hardly survived but the attitude did, and not only in music. In his social history of Britain, David Kynaston cites an amusing polemic by EW Swanton about the young players contesting the Varsity Match of 1955. Swanton described the "shoddy" appearance of many of the spectators and criticised the tendency of some players to discard their traditional caps and sweaters, asking whether the young "gentlemen" were "cocking a snook at the past". If they were, they were not alone.

Donegan's success began in 1956 as American rock & roll created a stronger foundation for a guitar-based sound that would challenge and to some extent replace the older dance bands. While skiffle was briefly the British challenger, it would not take long for rock & roll to become established here. If we imagine, as suggested, that Arlott's fictional game at Portsmouth did take place in August 1956, then just a few weeks later and about five minutes walk from the ground, Britain's first touring, professional and recording rock & roll outfit, Tony Crombie & his Rockets appeared for the first time anywhere as the headline act in the city's Theatre Royal – the 'birth' of British rock & roll.

Crombie was a leading jazz drummer who had played with Ronnie Scott and others but saw the chance to earn rather more money on the 'pop' scene. His band's name clearly owes something to Bill Haley & his Comets, by then enjoying chart success in Britain and Crombie's agent, having booked the Rockets into the London Palladium, sent them on a warm-up week to Portsmouth. The show is a fascinating example of the changing times in the world of British light entertainment, for this was not a night to resemble the rock & roll 'package' tours featured in films like *Rock Around the Clock* or *The Girl Can't Help It*. Rather, it was a traditional variety bill with an unusual final act carrying with it a sign that the times were definitely changing.

Variety was already suffering from the competition of television, not simply because people were content to stay at home to be entertained, but also because too many performers had very limited acts and once seen on television they struggled to attract live audiences to watch the same thing again. Variety Shows had grown out of the older tradition of Music Hall and in the days before television they competed with cinemas, dance halls and the 'pub' for punters who wished to go out in the evenings in search of entertainment. Music Hall and Variety Shows had been the staple of British light entertainment through the first-half of the 20th century, and while the presence of a rock & roll act was a complete novelty, there was always a star act on every bill with a plethora of supporting performers. The Portsmouth bill that launched British rock & roll included the Scottish compere Andy Stewart billed as "TV's New Funster"; comedian Johnny Dallis; mime act Ross & Howitt; dancers Nick & Pat Lundon; pianist Billy Wyner with two singers; Maxine Daniels (sister of Kenny Lynch), and Don Fox – the last two would accompany the Rockets on their subsequent tour of the country with their agent telling the *Melody Maker*, "the Rock and Riot Boys Don't Worry Crombie".

The Portsmouth show was well reviewed by the local *Evening News* under the headline, "Rock and Roll Greeted with Cheers", but having played a central role in giving birth to the new phenomenon, the city handed it on and returned to its traditional seaside holidays, football, occasional county cricket and Her Majesty's Dockyard, Royal Navy and Royal Marines. Similarly Tony Crombie, after a brief cinema spot with his Rockets and a modest hit record, realised that rock & roll was not for him and when he next appeared in Portsmouth and elsewhere, he had returned to the more familiar styles of the dance bands and modern jazz ensembles. His problem was essentially that the young ones wanted stars from their own generation, and about a month after the Rockets took to the road, a young merchant seaman called Tommy Steele displaced them in the hearts (and charts) of British fans. Shortly after that came another young man called Cliff Richard plus Wilde, Fury, Power, Eager, Pride, and even Gentle.

Perhaps county cricket was rather similar through the late 1950s. Aside from Arlott's fictional tale, we know that in the 'real' world, just one month before Tony Crombie and his Rockets appeared in Portsmouth, Hampshire started a match against Essex in Portsmouth on Wednesday 15 August – a game they would lose by 37 runs. On the first day, 37-year-old Vic Cannings was the only man in the match to return five wickets in an innings while 30-year-old Doug Insole, with 75, helped Essex to 241 all out in six hours of batting. On Thursday, another 30-year-old, Jimmy Gray carried his bat for 118* in a total of just 208 before Hampshire reduced Essex to 42–6, just 75 ahead – a day of just 250 runs, albeit 16 wickets. On the final morning, overnight rain without sun created a placid surface, and 'young' Bill Greensmith (the day after his 26th birthday) and Insole added 99 and Essex declared seven down setting Hampshire a target of 185 in 150 minutes. At 81–1 and 136–3 they looked well set, but needing 48 in 38 minutes they engineered three run outs, and lost.

On the next morning (Saturday), an England 'star', Frank Tyson, came to town although Northamptonshire batted first, closing on 125–6 because of rain and a gale so strong the umpires dispensed with the bails. There were more interruptions on the Monday as the visitors' innings ended on 178, and Hampshire reached the close on 151–5. On Tuesday morning Tyson took three wickets and Hampshire lost five for just 15, finishing 12 behind. Northamptonshire batted again and were all out for 148, after which there was just time for Hampshire to score 9–1 in 18 balls. The *Hampshire Handbook* called it a "most depressing match" and suggested the second Northamptonshire innings "incurred the displeasure of the spectators".

That, then, was the Portsmouth 'Festival' Week of 1956. Many locals – especially from the main employers at the Dockyard – would have booked leave to sit on wooden benches in damp and windy conditions with a cheese sandwich and warm beer watching some very slow scoring and while one of the games had an exciting finish, a defeat would not satisfy the home support. But the same week would also have attracted the holiday trade who would "Come to Sunny Southsea" for the beach and the end-of-pier shows as well as, or increasingly instead of, the cricket. During the course of that week in 1956, holidaymakers in Southsea might have danced to Johnny Dankworth's Orchestra or Roy Richards' Mayfair Orchestra at the seafront's Savoy Ballroom, while George Formby was starring in "Too Young to Marry" at

Southsea's King's Theatre. But the younger generation might have been more tempted by a visit to the Gaumont Cinema that was showing *Rock Around the Clock* as the Northamptonshire match was in progress. In Portsmouth they were lucky; elsewhere across the country about 80 local councils banned the film.

By comparison, the match was perhaps all too much like the variety shows, with a series of acts that had been seen before with often only subtle variations on a theme, for any but the connoisseur. In the second match, only Northamptonshire's Desmond Barrick (also 30 years old) reached a half-century – during that ponderous second innings – and while Tyson was the star, his only top order dismissal was Roy Marshall for 48. Spectators and home supporters in particular did not like seeing Marshall dismissed.

The Tony Crombie show brought live rock & roll to Britain around the time that households were receiving a new and less reverential second television channel. In addition, the local palais might now be a bowling alley; the coffee bars had froth on the top and 'Coke' for the kids; wages were improving, and the prime minister would soon tell the British people that things had never been better. Crucially, there was the greatest panacea of all – choice. Maybe some people were turning away from county cricket because it was dull, although it was not always like that match at Portsmouth. Perhaps cricket found it harder to acknowledge that people were going elsewhere simply because they could.

By 1960, the end-of-the-pier shows in Southsea and elsewhere were also struggling to find and keep an audience, just as live variety shows and, to a lesser extent, cinema had. But television was thriving and so was the 'youth market' especially in popular music and fashion. When that most elegant of batsmen Tom Graveney died in November 2015, *the Times* obituary suggested he gave "enjoyment" to spectators through the 1950s and 1960s, at a time when cricket "could be an attritional sport". That approach might be fine for the master craftsmen plying their trade but it was unlikely to attract the mass audiences of the 'swinging sixties'. In 1960 I began watching the county game regularly and played cricket at school throughout the summer term, but very soon I became aware that the game I was growing to love faced an uncertain future.

Chapter Two: 1959

Over about 100 years, to the end of the 1950s, English cricket saw the emergence of the properly constituted county clubs and the formal County Championship. Then, through the second-half of that period, came a rapid increase in the number of Test Match teams and the amount of Test Match cricket played. While the USA and Canada had met in what we believe to be the first international fixtures, the history of Test Match cricket identifies the first match as between Australia and England in 1877. The final Test Match before the first world war between South Africa and England ended in early March 1914 and was number 134 in the series – a total that covered 37 years, or an average of just under four games per year.

Test Match cricket resumed in December 1920 with Australia meeting England, and the next wartime break came after the West Indies played England at the Oval in late-August 1939. That was Test Match number 274, so 140 Test Matches were played in the inter-war period of 19 years, increasing the average to seven per year and the number of Test-playing nations from three, with the addition of West Indies, New Zealand and (all) India. After post-war partition, Pakistan became the seventh Test Match side from 1952.

In March 1946, New Zealand played the first post-war Test Match against Australia, and over the next 15 years, concluding with one of the greatest series of all time between Australia and West Indies, there were 231 Test Matches, an average in excess of 15 per year between the Test-playing nations. That figure, increasing all the time, is far greater today, to which must be added all the one-day internationals (ODIs) and Twenty20 (T20) internationals. As I write this in the last days of 2015, England are playing the first Test Match of their series in South Africa, having recently concluded a three match series against Pakistan, following the World Cup in the spring and three other series against West Indies (three Test Matches), New Zealand (two) and Australia (five) – 14 Test Matches, various 'white ball' games, and a major international tournament in one calendar year.

Other than the change in the lbw law in the 1930s, and the post-war increase in Test Match time until all were played over five days, the first-half of the 20th century was a period of few changes in English cricket. After one season of two-day matches in 1919, Worcestershire returned in 1920 and Glamorgan came into the County Championship in 1921. In 1939 there was, for that one year, an experiment with eight-ball overs. Thereafter, there were no significant changes in that competition until the first brief experiment with covered pitches in 1959. The glorious weather of that summer made that change fairly irrelevant and after a couple of more years the counties reverted to the 'uncovered' regulations for two more decades.

Meanwhile, Yorkshire who had won the first three titles in the 20th century had continued their dominance in the inter-war period and even when Surrey won their seven titles from 1952–1958, it was usually Yorkshire who threatened their supremacy and provided a significant number of England Test Match cricketers. One of English cricket's major figures, Sir Pelham Warner, wrote an account of *Cricket Between the Wars* in which he offered accounts of each season from 1921, chapter-by-chapter. His focus was on England's Test Matches and the County Championship but for most seasons he added the matches between Eton v Harrow and Oxford University v Cambridge University. His choices are indicative both of the range of what was considered 'important' cricket of the period and also his interests as an amateur cricketer, county captain, Test Match selector, senior administrator and writer on the game – for which he received his knighthood. For example, he devoted 13 pages to cover 1928, opening with Learie Constantine and the touring West Indians, the MCC side to tour Australia, and the first sight of Bradman. The first six pages ended with a tribute to the MCC's manager, Sir Frederick (FC) Toone, who he calls with familiarity 'Fred' and who had died shortly after returning to England, after which Warner turned his attention for the second half of the chapter to the Players victory over the Gentlemen at Lord's ("I saw every ball"), and the "exciting" finish to the University match which had the Headmaster of Eton waxing poetic in *the Times*.

The latter's school side beat Harrow in a late and close victory and then Warner noted that Lancashire had won the County Championship, while Kent were second, thanks not least to Freeman's 291 wickets. In this account, "Freeman" was not ascribed his popular nickname 'Tich', whereas when Warner described captaining an MCC team to Holland he listed his amateur side with full initials, of course. Finally, and of some specific interest to me, he devoted a page-and-a-half to the "first occasion" on which the MCC had played against the Royal Navy and Royal Marines at Portsmouth. MCC triumphed with a side that included four professionals – each identified only by surname. Elsewhere, we learn there were Admirals, Generals, Captains, Lords, and Major EG Wynyard, once of Hampshire and England. The MCC won the match but Warner described also the formal social events in some detail, including this passage, which seems so indicative of its time:

> Admiral Watson, the President at this time of the Royal Navy CC, was anxious that the professionals should be invited to the dinner and there is no doubt they were better Englishmen for their experience.

This was written with no hint of self-consciousness and leaves us in no doubt as to ways in which the world has changed since then.

Interestingly, issue 12 (Autumn/Winter 2015) of the *MCC Magazine* carried an article on Warner by Derek Pringle. He noted that Warner lived from 1873 to January 1963 but that while this was "an age of huge change" in the wider world, "cricket remained largely unaltered during his time" which Pringle added was "just how (Warner) liked it. Change often gives the illusion of progress, which is why he tended to indulge neither". Warner died in his 90th year but had he reached his century, one wonders what he might have made of all the changes to Test Match, first-class and club cricket over those next 10 Years. On the horizon were the introduction of a 'one-day' knock-out cup and then a Sunday League; the abolition of the distinction between amateurs and professionals; the automatic registration of top overseas players by counties; Sunday county cricket; the reduction in the number of matches played in the County Championship and the expansion of club league cricket across the country. The 1960s 'swung' in parts of the UK as a social and cultural 'revolution' of sorts occurred around a reforming Labour Government, but in some respects it was a short-lived period. By contrast, English county cricket did not run out of steam; change became the norm and remains so today.

One key difference with today can be found in the make-up of the county sides. Around 1960, the vast majority of county cricketers were Englishmen, and at most counties a reasonable proportion were from that county, most obviously at Yorkshire whose players were then all born within their boundaries. The relatively few overseas county players in 1959 included from New Zealand: Ray Hitchcock (Warwickshire); from Pakistan: Khalid 'Billy' Ibadulla (Warwickshire); from the Caribbean: Donald Ramsamooj (Northamptonshire); Carlton Forbes (Nottinghamshire); Ron Headley (Worcestershire); Peter Wight (Somerset); HL Johnson (Derbyshire); and Roy Marshall & Danny Livingstone (Hampshire); from South Africa: Denis Foreman (Sussex); Terence Barwell (Somerset); Joe Milner (Essex) and Stuart Leary (Kent); from Australia: Ken Grieves (Lancashire); Colin McCool and Bill Alley (Somerset); and from Ceylon: 'Laddie' Outschoorn (Worcestershire). That is an average of one player per county, and some of these men played only a handful of matches and were never established, capped professionals, while a few such as Marshall, Ibadulla and Alley, were key members of their teams, and Grieves and Marshall captained their respective counties. Between them, they played in very few Test Matches – they were good professionals, seeking a career in the best-paid and most secure competition in world cricket. To do so, they were required to 'qualify' by residence and turn away from further chances of playing Test Match cricket, although in 1973 Headley played for West Indies in an emergency. By then the regulations had changed, while his son Dean Headley later played for Kent and England.

In 1959, the first match I saw was very much in the 'old' tradition. Hampshire, a side with a modest record in the competitive County Championship, met one of the 'great' professional teams, Surrey. Some historians date the start of the County Championship back to the 1860s or 1870s but if we accept the significant changes in calculation dating from 1890, then in the 25 years before the break in the Great War, only Yorkshire with nine titles exceeded Surrey's seven. Kent won four times, Lancashire twice, and there were single successes for Middlesex, Nottinghamshire and Warwickshire.

When the competition returned in 1919, Yorkshire resumed their dominance although Middlesex won in 1920 and 1921. Lancashire enjoyed five titles between the two wars and Nottinghamshire and Derbyshire one each, but between 1919 and1939 Yorkshire finished first on 12 occasions. Surrey were no longer one of the strongest sides despite some fine players, and after the next war, Yorkshire won again in 1946, Middlesex in the glorious summer of 1947, and to everyone's surprise, Glamorgan in 1948. Along with Derbyshire and Warwickshire, they seemed to be unexpected 'one title wonders', with Glamorgan clinching their success through a fine victory over Hampshire at Bournemouth despite the worst efforts of the weather. In the event, both Glamorgan and Warwickshire repeated their success in later years – and both more than once.

The seasons of 1949 and 1950 were unusual in that two sides shared the title: Middlesex and Yorkshire followed by Lancashire and Surrey. The four 'big' counties were back at the top and after a second success for Warwickshire in 1951 Surrey returned to pole position. In the late 1950s, their captain Peter May was one of the finest post-war English batsmen, a product of the batsman-friendly pitches at Charterhouse and Cambridge University, but their success was based principally on a tremendous attack, built around one of the finest English fast-medium bowlers Alec Bedser, off-spinner Jim Laker and left-arm spinner Tony Lock (who could hardly be described as 'slow'). In 1955, another fine year, those three men all bowled more than 1,000 overs and took more than 100 wickets each as they amassed 438 wickets for the county. Bedser's opening partner and Surrey's fourth Test Match bowler, Peter Loader, 'only' managed 88 wickets in his 588 overs and those top bowlers all finished with averages under 18 per-wicket. Alec's twin brother Eric added 41 off-spun wickets while their captain in the early triumphant years, Stuart Surridge, offered some support and also turned Surrey into one of the finest of all close-catching sides.

One of the most extraordinary examples of Surrey's supremacy in the 1950s serves also to illustrate the significant difference between the County Championship of the 1950s played on uncovered pitches, and the modern game. In late August 1954 at a damp Oval, Surridge won the toss and when play started after 2pm he invited Worcestershire to bat on a drying pitch. In less than six overs, Lock took 5–2 and in the 29th over, Worcestershire were all out for just 25. Surrey knew that victory would bring them the title and after 24 overs by 5.30pm they had reached 92–3 when Surridge declared, to get at Worcestershire again that night. Two wickets fell quickly but the game went into the second day when, in the 36th over, Worcestershire were all out for 40. In around 65 overs Worcestershire lost 20 wickets for 65 runs and Surrey's 92–3 declared gave them the innings victory and the County Championship before lunch, and in less than one whole day's play. In *the Daily Telegraph,* Michael Melford described "much cheering and a speech to a crowd of 3,000" who had watched about one hour's play. In the previous season at the Oval, Warwickshire dismissed Surrey for 146 but the Champions still won by an innings *in a single day* with Warwickshire all out for 45 and 52, Alec Bedser taking 8–82 and 4–17. Even Bedser's match figures of 12–99 did not match Malcolm Heath's 13–87 for Hampshire v Derbyshire at Burton in August 1958 when Heath bowled unchanged with Derek Shackleton (7–88) to dismiss Derbyshire for 74 & 107, despite which Derbyshire won by 103 runs! Only Derbyshire's Derek Morgan (46) reached 20 on either side; such games are simply unimaginable today.

While 1955 and 1959 were unusually fine summers, 1954, 1956 and 1958 were awful and with counties playing on a variety of grounds on uncovered wickets, conditions often favoured the bowlers. In 1958, Kent for example, played 14 home matches at eight different venues, while in that same season, Surrey dismissed Lancashire at Old Trafford for 27 and Middlesex at Lord's for 89, while at the Oval, Warwickshire went for 63, Lancashire 83, Glamorgan 92, Nottinghamshire 106, Somerset 66 and Yorkshire 70 & 116.

In 1958 Surrey did not have things all their own way against Yorkshire. The London team travelled to Sheffield and dismissed Yorkshire for 138 (Laker 4–56), an innings that took 75 overs and one ball. But by close of play, Surrey had slumped to 53–7 and the next morning Trueman (4–39) soon had them out with a deficit of 44 runs. In the two first innings no batsman on either side reached 40, but in their second innings with Laker injured and unable to bowl, and Lock not playing, all the top six reached 30 for Yorkshire and opener Ken Taylor went on to 104, so the declaration left Surrey to score 368 to win. Trueman (5–19) then despatched the top order and helped by Illingworth and Wardle, took Yorkshire to a massive victory by 248 runs. Despite that mid-June reverse, Surrey went on to win their seventh consecutive title and 15th in total, but it was a sign of changing times. Throughout the

1950s Yorkshire had frustrated their supporters by winning nothing. In **1959** that situation would change but in other respects the first-class season was much as it had been since cricket resumed after the war.

There was no English County Championship or Test Match cricket in the seasons from 1940–1945. When first-class cricket resumed in 1946, the Indians were the first tourists as they would be again in **1959**, and they started their tour as most visitors used to with a three-day match at Worcester in the first week of May – one week after Derby County beat Charlton 4–1 in the first post-war FA Cup Final. The Indian's opening match at Worcester in 1946 was also John Arlott's debut as a live cricket radio broadcaster. On the first day *Wisden* tells us that 8,000 people braved "intense cold" to celebrate the return of cricket and the 1946 tourists represented All India just a couple of years before independence and partition separated India from the newly created state of Pakistan. The latter would tour England for the first time, eight years later, by which time all Test Matches lasted five days, but in 1946 England and India played just three, three-day matches.

After the brief Test Match series of 1946, the Indians played a couple more games against counties and then went down to Hastings in early September to play against the South of England in one of the traditional festival matches. We don't have these friendly 'festival' matches today, although Yorkshire's competitive fixtures there are still called the Scarborough Festival. Other festivals were played after the County Championship season ended, at seaside locations like Hastings, Scarborough, Blackpool and Torquay hoping to attract holiday makers, and while they were generally less competitive than County Championship games, they were first-class and counted in the season's averages.

The Indian tourists returned in 1952 but could not win a Test Match. In the first at Headingley, they batted a second time only narrowly behind England, but lost their first four wickets without a run scored – three of them to the young fast bowler Fred Trueman on his home ground. In **1959**, the Indians came again for their third post-war tour but this was their least successful visit and they became the first touring side to lose all five Test Matches in an English season. The England side had returned from a winter tour of Australia in which they lost the series 4–1 and with that the Ashes, held through the three previous series. Their side was in a period of change. In the second-half of the 1950s they had to find replacements from major players like Hutton, Compton, Edrich, Bailey, Evans, Tyson and Laker. Despite this, England were in a very successful period at home. Beating the West Indies 3–0 in 1957, New Zealand 4–0 in 1958 and in the year following the Indians, South Africa 3–0.

By **1959** the County Championship had grown to 28 matches per side but still without every side playing every other side twice. The competition started on Wednesday 6 May but there were seven prior first-class matches from 25 April, involving the MCC, the two first-class university sides, and the Indians at Worcester.

Hampshire opened 1959 at a sunny Portsmouth on 6 May and Dennis Baldry, newly signed from Middlesex, scored a debut century (151) for his new county. The sun continued to shine through most of the season in a glorious summer, which ended for Hampshire at Bournemouth on the first day of September. In addition to their 28 County Championship matches, they met also the Indians, the MCC at Lord's and both university sides, 32 first-class games in 17 weeks which means that in all but two weeks, they played two three-day matches each week. Fifteen men played between 10 and 32 of those matches and four others between one and three games. On some 'free' Sundays they would appear in benefit matches. At the end of the season Yorkshire were Champions again, outright for the first time since 1946.

When Surrey met Hampshire at Portsmouth in mid-August the two sides were fourth and fifth and Surrey had games in hand over the top three, Warwickshire, Yorkshire and Gloucestershire. John Arlott wrote at the time:

> The old Surrey must have been odds-on favourites to win yet, but few feel inclined now to give them best chance. Tomorrow they will be down here to play Hampshire in what could well prove the decisive match of the season.

I had no idea about this situation or its historical context when I arrived to watch day two. On the first day Henry Horton had posted his highest score of 140*, including a six into the pavilion off Jim Laker. Horton's century helped Hampshire to a Saturday total of 341–4 declared and on the Monday morning, after Shackleton dismissed John Edrich lbw without scoring, Vic Cannings took 5–57 and Surrey's declaration with nine down gave Hampshire a lead of 121. It seemed that Surrey would press for a target and then chase victory on day three. In the final hour on the Monday, Loader hit Jimmy Gray on the side of the head and in those pre-helmet days seriously damaged his ear. Gray went to hospital for stitches and took no further part in the match.

The Tuesday opened with Hampshire 146 ahead and – Gray apart – all wickets in hand. Roy Marshall took the attack to Surrey and reached his fifth consecutive score of 50-plus before he was caught-and-bowled by Alec Bedser. On the second day Surrey's 221–9 took just more than 100 overs but on this third day Hampshire scored at almost three runs per over despite losing wickets regularly. The captain, Colin Ingleby-Mackenzie, was last out for 35, but three wickets each for Laker and Bedser kept them in check and they were dismissed for 156 at 2.50pm. In those days targets were calculated against time rather than overs, so it was 278 in exactly three hours – easily the fastest rate of the match. As it happened, Hampshire would not turn to their one spinner Peter Sainsbury, but in those three hours would bowl 55 overs – 18.3 an hour, against a side going for victory. The over-rate kept both sides in with a chance.

John Arlott noted a huge third day crowd of 6,000 that saw Cannings dismiss both openers in the first half-hour, with Surrey 33–2. In the next 30 minutes, Ken Barrington and Tom Clark added 58 without being parted and after Shackleton and Cannings, the promising 'Butch' White and all-rounder Dennis Baldry tried to stem the runs with little success until just before 5pm, Sainsbury, at cover, held a catch from Clark off Baldry and Surrey needed 108 with seven wickets left in around 65 minutes. Shackleton returned to dismiss Stewart, Lock was first dropped and then bowled; Cannings returned, and at 5.26pm Barrington completed his century and was immediately bowled by Shackleton. At 217–6, Surrey needed 61 in just over half-an-hour, then with Roy Swetman out too, 40 in 21 minutes and after Loader was caught by Horton, 18 in nine minutes with two wickets in hand. That was possible, but Bedser, scoring a run-a-minute, edged Shackleton to the wicketkeeper for 35, leaving the score at 262–9.

Hampshire had taken the four first innings points for the lead and faster scoring – there were no bonus points then – so Surrey had to choose between trying for 12 probably crucial victory points, or denying a rival county their chance to win. They chose the latter course so that after an exciting day, the final over was a little disappointing. Shackleton began it needing one wicket and Surrey 12 runs. Laker played a dot ball, then took a single; last man David Gibson defended the next and realistically three fours (or two sixes) were needed. Shackleton called for a rather costly new ball but Gibson repeated his defence and the game was over, with just four runs from the final 14 balls. John Arlott suggested that it had been "a whole afternoon of glory" adding, "it could yet prove that the stake was the Championship", while "for Hampshire this was the final extinction of their … hopes" of that title. At the same time, victories for Yorkshire, Warwickshire and Gloucestershire confirmed them as the top three sides. I am not sure I followed the final day's play or checked it in the newspapers but whether or not, my first experience of county cricket had coincided with an exciting match featuring some very fine cricketers. Sadly, it was not entirely typical of its time.

Two days later, the fifth and final Test Match began at the Oval and England won by an innings, before lunch on the fourth day (Monday), without any of their players reaching three figures or taking five wickets in an innings. For the first time, England won a home series 5–0 and it is not unreasonable to suggest that had India spent the summer playing in the County Championship, they would have been unable to challenge Yorkshire, Surrey, or any of the other leading sides. They played all the counties, beating only Northamptonshire, Middlesex, Glamorgan and Kent, while losing to Glamorgan (who they met twice), Nottinghamshire and County Championship runners-up, Gloucestershire.

While the match was being played, the counties continued to chase the title and from England's side, Warwickshire's MJK Smith and Yorkshire's Ray Illingworth and Fred Trueman were therefore unavailable, which perhaps explains partly why on the Friday at Bath, Yorkshire lost to Somerset (by just 16 runs) for the first time since 1903. The younger cricket-watcher of today might be surprised to learn that England's Test Match players generally returned from each Test Match to the next County Championship game. The three men who played in all five Test Matches were Barrington (who played also in 23 county matches), Cowdrey (20) and Trueman (22) – and why only three 'ever present' players in a successful side? This was partly because the opposition was weak, and partly because England was in a transitional period, so they used 21 players, although relatively few would enjoy a sustained Test Match career. Among those who played in 1959, but little afterwards, were Roy Swetman, Gilbert Parkhouse, Martin Horton, Alan Moss, John Mortimore, Ken Taylor, Arthur Milton, Tommy Greenhough and Harold Rhodes.

As the County Championship reached its final weeks, Surrey drew again, while Warwickshire won and went to the top. They had two to play, Yorkshire and Gloucestershire three, and as the Test Match continued, Yorkshire went from Bath to Bristol for a top-of-the-table clash in which Gloucestershire beat Yorkshire. Yorkshire had stumbled at the crucial moment and Essex beat Warwickshire, leaving Gloucestershire top with two to play, but only 12 points separating the top four. Gloucestershire, with the prospect of a first title since 'WG' and the changes of the 1890s, entertained Surrey on a 'turner' at Gloucester's Wagon Works Ground and must have been pleased to put them out for 130 (Allen 5–43) but then Laker and Lock got to work and Surrey won in two days with not a pitch inspector to be seen. Meanwhile, Yorkshire beat Worcestershire with some difficulty and went to the top-of-the-table, six points ahead of Surrey.

In 1959, the crucial games began on Saturday 29 August – the penultimate round of matches for most sides, although the final game for Yorkshire against whom Sussex recovered at Hove to post 210. That Saturday evening,

Yorkshire finished in some trouble on 89–5, Middlesex were 306–8 against Surrey at the Oval, while at Worcester, the home team scored 205 and had Gloucester 38–6. Warwickshire, by not playing, probably had the best day of the top four, and once again the scores in county cricket were generally lower than we expect today.

After the usual 'day of rest', Middlesex took first innings points and a lead of 89 and Worcestershire amassed a huge lead of 361 over Gloucestershire. With neither of their challengers well placed, Yorkshire fought back through an Illingworth century to lead by 97 and in reply, Sussex ended the day on 143–3, with all to play for. On the final day, Sussex went to lunch 183 ahead, seven down and with only just over two hours to play on a shortened final day which was not untypical in the pre-motorway days. Middlesex led Surrey by the same total but with only two down and that game would end in a draw, while Gloucestershire 139–2 at lunch, lost to Worcestershire.

A victory for Yorkshire would seal the title and having taken the final Sussex wickets quickly, they needed 215 to win in 104 minutes, or about 32 overs. They lost a couple of early wickets, but Bryan Stott and Doug Padgett added 141 in an hour and needing 34 in the final half-an-hour they got there with seven minutes to spare.

Yorkshire were Champions, and would be so again in 1960, 1962, 1963, and from 1965–1968 inclusive – they were, in that period, one of the greatest English county sides. They also comprised Yorkshire-born, home-grown players whereas the current Yorkshire side, clearly the best in the County Championship, now includes 'imports' Gary Ballance, Jack Brooks, Liam Plunkett, Andrew Hodd, even in a sense, Ryan Sidebottom, plus various overseas players and their signing for 2016, David Willey. Both Yorkshire sides contributed a number of players to the England side, but perhaps only one man from each team is indisputably of top international class – Trueman in the late 1950s and early 1960s, and Joe Root today – although from the mid-1960s side, Boycott was a third. Otherwise, Jonny Bairstow might reach that top level, Tim Bresnan was a very good bowler, Close too often frustrated in Test Match, and Illingworth had some excellent later years as England's captain, while Taylor, Phil Sharpe, Padgett, Don Wilson and Vic Wilson, John Hampshire, Richard Hutton, Gary Ballance, Adam Lyth, Plunkett and Adil Rashid might rather be thought of as the very best county players who enjoyed occasional or limited international success.

The glorious summer of 1959 meant lots of runs for the batsmen on firm pitches baked by the sun and a pretty long hard summer for the bowlers. Shackleton bowled 1,373 overs in Hampshire's season, a new record for the county. There were a number of other county bowlers who also bowled at least 1,000 overs including Les Jackson (Derbyshire), Don Shepherd (Glamorgan), David Smith (Gloucestershire), David Halfyard (Kent), Ken Higgs (Lancashire), Fred Titmus (Middlesex), Jim Manning and George Tribe (Northamptonshire), Ian Thomson (Sussex) and plenty of others who were over 900. Fred Trueman 'only' bowled 803 for Yorkshire but he managed another 177 for England and his other first-class matches took him into four figures. In total, 16 bowlers passed 1,000 overs in the 1959 first-class season.

That is a dramatic contrast with today, in what is a much longer season than 1959. Modern bowlers also appear in 50 and 20 overs matches but from the County Championship in 2015 the significant measure is 500 overs – no one reached 600, and very few got to 500. In Division One those who did were the leading wicket-taker Chris Rushworth (Durham) with the highest total of 585 overs, Steve Magoffin (Sussex) and Jack Shantry (Worcestershire). In Division Two were Tom Curran (Surrey), Mark Footit (Derbyshire), Ben Raine and Charlie Shreck (Leicestershire).

In 1959 one Yorkshire cricketer who never played for the first team, none-theless enjoyed a successful summer; T Copley who in eight innings for Yorkshire's 2nd XI averaged 122 per innings and topped the Minor Counties batting averages. Yorkshire were one of nine counties to compete in the Minor Counties Championship, alongside 19 second-class counties. Despite Copley, Warwickshire 2nd XI won the title that year ahead of Lancashire 2nd XI with Dorset third, the best of the non first-class sides. Dorset's star was Ray Dovey, formerly of Kent, with 62 wickets at fewer than 12 a piece. Among the players who enjoyed successful seasons in that competition were Phil Sharpe, Vic Wilson and Brian Bolus (Yorkshire), Roy Collins, Brian Booth and Roy Tattersall (Lancashire), Jack Bannister and Ray Hitchcock (Warwickshire), Johnny Lawrence (Somerset), 'Bomber' Wells (Gloucestershire) and Bill Edrich (Norfolk). Post-war, the Minor Counties Championship was dominated by the county 2nd XIs, with only Suffolk (1946), Buckinghamshire (1952) and Berkshire (1953) breaking that hold. Hampshire competed in it from 1949–1952 when they withdrew for financial reasons so their 2nd XI and Club & Ground sides played only friendly matches until 1959 when the first-class counties' 2nd XI Championship was formed.

The Hampshire Handbook reporting on the 1958 season, the year before they entered the new 2nd XI Championship, has scorecards for two matches against the Royal Navy and Army, plus two 2nd XI friendly games each against Somerset, Sussex, Kent and Wiltshire and one match v Dorset. All these games were over two-days and with minimal travel costs. Coach Arthur Holt, their *only* coach in those days, spent relatively little time with the first team; his responsibility was to bring through younger cricketers in which respect he had a fine record. In addition to those 2nd XI games, he ran the Club & Ground team with a mixture of the promising 2nd XI and local players. They travelled the region playing all the best club sides in one-day matches and in addition to their ambassadorial function, Arthur would take the opportunity to look through the opposition's scorebook for signs of promising youngsters. In 1959, Hampshire's Club & Ground opened their fixtures at Swanage on 30 April and there were a further 30 matches during the season including games against Andover, Basingstoke, Bournemouth, Deanery (Southampton), Fareham, Fleet, Hampshire Hogs, Havant, Isle of Wight, Lymington, Poole, Portsmouth & Southsea, Southampton University, Trojans (Southampton), and United Services (Portsmouth).

Matches between county cricketers and local clubs are a rarity these days. In 1959, however, Cannings took his benefit and in those days local clubs regularly fielded sides against county XIs. In addition to the Club & Ground matches in 1959, a Vic Cannings XI played 17 benefit games against teams from the region, including Beaulieu, Brockenhurst, Burley, Frimley Green, Hartley Wintney, Isle of Wight, Little Durnford, Lyndhurst, New Milton, Portsmouth Football Club, Sarisbury Green, Southampton Parks, Throop and Winchester. These matches, plus first team games at Bournemouth, Southampton, Portsmouth and Cowes (IOW), meant that the county players could be seen throughout the region in some form of cricket. They were a *county* side, ambassadors who travelled around the county. Now there is very little away from the Ageas Bowl in West End, even for the 2nd XI.

In 1959 and the early 1960s I found it easy to love cricket. I played it at school, followed it through broadcasts, magazines and the press, and watched it on Hampshire's county grounds. In the summer, cricketers were my heroes and in winter it was the footballers. But there was competition for my affections and those of my peers. Summers in Portsmouth centred principally on its seaside resort of Southsea where the pier, the funfair and the circus all enhanced my growing awareness of popular culture beyond television, cinema and, of course, radio and there was a thriving live music scene which would soon attract my attention. In the summer of 1963 the future feature-film director John Boorman produced a 30-minute documentary for BBC television about a group of Southsea teenagers, entitled *Citizen 63*. The main subject, Marion Knight, lived a couple of streets from me and had been brought up in a strict Salvation Army family whose church headquarters were next door to the Sunday School which my parents helped to run in the 1950s. In that sense we both had conventional upbringings of that time and yet Marion, some three years older than me, was already finding modes of expression, which were contrary to most of the expectations of church, school and the older generation. Marion and her pals were members of CND. They argued over

different left-wing views of contemporary society, and were fairly contemptu-
ous of contemporary 'pop' music but only in favour of the rather more hip
options of jazz, folk and rhythm & blues. They danced at youth clubs, wrote
poetry and wore predominantly black fashions, which were simultaneously
post-beatnik and pre-mod. There was no mention of cricket (or indeed of
sport) in the film. For younger people it was just another option in a world
that offered more choices by the month – perhaps even the day.

Chapter Three: the 1960s

Most sports fans are nostalgic for the matches and heroes of their early years, and the glorious summer of 1959 was a good time to fall in love with English cricket. The benefit of hindsight however reveals that not all was well in the game in the late-1950s, while 1960 was a particularly troubled year for the sport, precipitating a series of significant changes through the following years.

Despite these problems, cricket was still sufficiently attractive in **1960** for the appearance of a new monthly magazine called the *Playfair Cricket Monthly*, alongside the well established, *Cricketer* magazine. The new magazine complemented the *Playfair Cricket Annual,* which first appeared in 1948 and is still being published. Appropriately, for the focus of this book, the first edition of the *Playfair Cricket Monthly* appeared in May 1960, and while its inaugural editorial concluded with some pleasant words about its launch, the first edition brought even its youngest readers face-to-face with the complexities of modern sport. The cover carried a photograph of the recent tour of the West Indies by the MCC, as all touring sides were then known, until they became England in the Test Matches. If it now seems odd that a national touring side should travel under the auspices of a private, privileged club, that's simply how it was, and had been. The photograph showed the two captains, FCM Alexander and PBH May, tossing before the second Test Match in Trinidad and it is interesting partly because Alexander was the last white West Indian captain. This was already an issue in that fragmented 'nation' – or collection of nations – and by the following winter the great Frank Worrell would become the first black cricketer to lead his side in Australia in what would be one of the most remarkable Test Match series.

Inside the new magazine, after adverts for cricket balls and Guinness, the editorial was headed, "Welcome to the South Africans" but this was no innocently polite greeting. It opened

> A considerable amount has been written and said in high places on the question of Apartheid. As cricketers with hosts of happy memories of such delightful fellows as Learie Constantine, Clyde Walcott, the late 'Collie' Smith and Hanif Mahommed … we must inevitably regard Apartheid as repugnant but in the same breath

we welcome, unconditionally, the tourists and our guests from South Africa.

The editorial went on to state the principal view of the majority of cricket supporters and the cricket establishment that the tourists were "welcome … not as politicians, but as cricketers, clearly anxious to divorce themselves from matters of State". That claim may be generally true of professional cricketers who are not obviously 'political' animals, but to divorce oneself from matters of state is not easy when performing under the flag of that state, and is not the same thing as opposing matters of legislative policy. One irony in that first edition which seemed to bypass the editor, came on page 28 with a full page article by John Kay about "League Cricket in Lancashire" which paid particular attention to a list of impressive professionals due in the Lancashire and Central Lancashire Leagues in 1960. Alongside Wes Hall, Conrad Hunte, Johnny Wardle, Garry Sobers, Cec Pepper, and others, the Middleton club had a new recruit, "South Africa's leading non-European player", Basil D'Oliveira whose portrait was also selected to accompany the article.

Kay reported D'Oliveira's "remarkable" record in South Africa "with centuries galore in good time and bowling performances bordering on the extraordinary", adding "he has not had the opportunity of playing with or against the leading South African cricketers" – a problem ignored apparently by those who welcomed the South Africans "unconditionally". On 21 March 1960, as the new monthly magazine was in preparation, South African police murdered 69 protesting black South Africans in what came to be known as the Sharpeville Massacre. Some of these protesters, including women and children, were shot in the back as they fled the scene and the South African Government then detained 18,000 people considered to constitute a threat to the State. South Africa found itself condemned and isolated and it left the Commonwealth shortly afterwards, which placed its Test Match status in jeopardy. The Imperial Cricket Conference (ICC), which then ruled international cricket, involved only Commonwealth countries and there was much discussion about whether South Africa could continue to play Test Matches, having departed. They did continue through the 1960s, albeit no further.

While most of the English cricket world welcomed the South Africans and argued for the separation of cricket and politics, there were a few 'insiders' who took a different view. John Arlott had witnessed Apartheid while accompanying the MCC tour of South Africa in 1948–1949 and was prepared to say how repulsive he found it. Indeed David Kynaston, in his social history of Britain 1945–1951, reports how in 1950, Arlott, a regular panellist on the BBC's radio show *Any Questions?* was dropped from the show after describing the South African Government as "predominantly a Nazi one". In the summer after Arlott's influential visit, the 21-year-old Cambridge University and Sussex batsman, David Sheppard, made his England debut. He would score three Test Match centuries and captain a successful Sussex side in 1953, but he left full-time cricket to pursue a career in the church and became Bishop of Liverpool. By 1960, while still playing occasionally, he stated his revulsion at Apartheid and his refusal to play against the South Africans.

The *Playfair Cricket Monthly* commented that it "respects profoundly the ideals which prompted" Sheppard to making this statement but asked, "Did he not exceed his licence?" In particular, the editorial suggested that boycotts appeared "nowhere in the Christian doctrine", while omitting to observe that neither did Apartheid as a desirable policy. They urged the British public to preserve their "high reputation for fair-mindedness" and "flock" to the matches.

The tour went ahead with no major disruption but in the *Playfair Cricket Annual* of the following year, Arlott described it as "the unhappiest ever made by a party of overseas cricketers in England". He added that this was not merely because of political problems, but had to do also with a side that was not selected properly or adequately for the tour. Anti-Apartheid campaigners did their best to confront the tourists around the country and for whatever reasons attendances were so poor that they were the first tourists to make a loss on an English visit for nearly 50 years. They lost the first three Test Matches and therefore the series with two matches still to play, and the throwing crisis of this period focused relentlessly on their young pace bowler Geoff Griffin who came with natural cricketing ambitions and left with his career effectively over.

This was a time when English cricket was struggling to retain and develop its audience, but the five Test Matches were hardly thrilling. There were no centurions in any of the first three decisive games; then at Old Trafford, the fourth Test Match had no play for the first two days, and only on day four did South Africa's Roy McLean reach 109 (out of 229). Not until the penultimate day of the series did any England batsmen finally reach three figures. If we move on from the broader issue of Apartheid, the series brought a focus on two difficult issues specific to cricket. One of these was an English problem of falling attendances and financial problems, and the other was an international problem, which still bedevils cricket today: bowlers with illegal actions.

Concerns about attendances were generally blamed on the quality of the cricket on offer or what modern marketing people might call the 'brand'. The *Playfair Cricket Monthly* editorial for August 1960 suggested "the tempo of modern Test Match cricket has slowed down almost to walking pace. It has, without question, lessened public interest in watching Tests", although adding, "except of course, on television screens", revealing that the "large fees paid by the BBC" were "ploughed back into the game". The irony was that television, alongside the family motorcar and improved wages, was often blamed for falling attendances. There were too many competing options, but cricket had to make itself as attractive as possible and it was not doing this. For example, throughout the 1960 Test Match series, England's batsmen scored at about 2.4 runs per over which in today's games of 90 overs per day would give a total of perhaps 220 runs. The defeated South Africans were slightly quicker at around 2.5 per over – just a few runs more per day.

Another problem was that in the decade since five-day Test Matches became the norm, too many games were finishing too soon leading the magazine to call for four-day Test Matches against most countries (perhaps not Australia). In 2015, the Ashes series equalled the shortest five-Test series in England's history but it was a series that offered much quicker run-scoring than in 1960. Another slightly odd 'problem' was that in the 1950s England won most home series with some ease. They lost to the West Indies in 1950 but over the next 10 home series, won nine of them, and drew one, which was a four-match series with the newly formed Pakistan in 1954. Over the four home seasons between 1957–1960, England won 15 Test Matches and lost none, but in the end it wasn't very interesting. Indeed, on the whole, the County Championship offered rather more excitement and, often, more quality.

In the early 1960s, after the Test Matches and County Championship, each cricket season ended with seaside Festivals. There were also a number of other games throughout the season, which in those days were a significant part of the English first-class season, and a couple were played at Lord's in the early July – the University match and the Gentlemen v Players. In 1960, any mention of the University match meant, of course, Oxford v Cambridge, which in 1960 was a rain-affected draw. Among those playing, Roger Prideaux, 'Tony' Lewis, David Kirby, Alan Hurd, Alan (AC) Smith, David Green, AA Baig, Javed Burki Nawab of Pataudi, Colin Dryborough, David Sayer, Andrew Corran and Dan Piachaud, all played county and/or Test Match cricket. In addition, there was Charles Fry who, in a few games for Hampshire, became the third generation of the Fry family to appear for Hampshire after his father, Stephen Fry, and grandfather, the great CB Fry – the only instance of this happening in Hampshire's history although more recently there have been the D'Oliveiras at Worcestershire and the Cowdreys at Kent. While graduates from 'Oxbridge' were the main contributors to the first-class game, a few post-war players from provincial universities came through into the first-class game – notably Frank Tyson, Ken Cranston and Charles Palmer. While the current Hampshire side includes graduates James Adams and James Tomlinson, their studies were a decade ago. Promising youngsters these days tend to delay their higher studies in favour of a cricket career, although Adam Riley at Kent came through Loughborough University and was in the England Performance Squad in 2014–2015.

In the **1960** match between Gentlemen v Players, five of the University players appeared for the Gentlemen. At the same time, seven County Championship matches took place but perhaps surprisingly the selection of these 22 players took precedence over the Championship – Henry Horton for example was lost to Hampshire, although it did not matter since their match at Worcester was abandoned with no toss made. The Gentlemen v Players series of matches started in 1806 but was now in its final years. There was almost always the main match at Lord's, and sometimes others were played elsewhere, including the Oval, and at the Festival grounds like Scarborough, Hastings, Hove, Folkestone and Blackpool. The matches selected 'Gentlemen' from the amateurs who played first-class cricket while generally having an independent income, and 'Players' who were professional cricketers. By 1960 there had been discussions about abolishing the distinction but there was some resistance and a desire to maintain the 'amateur spirit' in county cricket. The story of this distinction and the debate around its abolition has been told very well by the former Essex amateur, Charles Williams, whose book is subtitled, "The death of amateurism in cricket."

Williams reveals any number of inconsistencies and anomalies around the distinction between amateurs and professionals and the tradition of the Gentlemen v Players matches, which occasionally served as an unofficial 'Test Trial'. Even in the early 1800s, the Gentlemen sometimes bolstered their team with a professional or two. In the mid-19th century, the Gentlemen had to fund the fixture because the public were tired of the dominance of the professionals, and it was only the arrival of the Grace brothers – never averse to accepting considerable sums in 'expenses' – that the fixture thrived again. The final Lord's and Scarborough fixtures in 1962 both ended in downpours and only cricket lovers approaching 70 can now have any clear recollections of the fixture.

At the start of July 1960, just before the University and Gentlemen v Players matches, another Lord's tradition was the meeting of Eton and Harrow at which male spectators sported morning dress, women were in their finery with some watching from carriages and most 'parading' during the intervals. Harrow beat Eton in 1960 for the first time since 1954, but these players did not move into first-class cricket – perhaps careers other than cricket were more attractive to the well-educated young gentlemen of the early 1960s. In 1960, Eton v Harrow was a two-day, two-innings match, and while it is still graced by being staged at Lord's, today it is a 55-over contest.

English first-class Test Match and county cricket had been played for around a century before the amateur/professional distinction was abolished prior to the 1963 season. In this 'mixture' it differed from most other sports and in some respects can be seen as a strength. Wimbledon's famous tennis tournament was still resolutely amateur; league football was almost wholly professional, with a separate amateur league cup and international set-up; the Olympic Games were amateur, even to the extent of a professional in one sport being barred from competing in any other as an amateur; top-level boxing was professional, and rugby had created two codes to distinguish between amateurs (rugby union) and professionals (rugby league). Williams noted that despite some tensions in cricket between amateurs and professionals, relationships were generally satisfactory, although there remained the question of captaincy, which with England (despite Hutton's successes) and many counties, was generally still the preserve of the amateurs.

An obvious indicator of the popularity of any professional sport comes from attendance figures. In 1960, the daily *News Chronicle* compared attendances for County Championship matches from the glorious summer of 1947 to the even better summer of 1959. The aggregate figure in that first summer of Compton and Edrich was 2,200,910 but it had fallen to 1,369,673 in 1959. That was a decline of 38%, yet the previous and horribly wet summer of 1958 was even more worrying, when for the first time the figure fell below one million.

It was not all gloom, however. SG 'Billy' Griffiths, the secretary-elect of the MCC, reminded everyone that these figures did not include members, and membership had risen significantly post-war. He cited his county Sussex where membership was 638 in 1946 and 7,000 by 1960. Overall, the MCC believed that by the late-1950s, county memberships had risen by something like 75,000. The *Playfair Cricket Monthly* suggested "it is now sometimes more difficult to find a seat in the pavilion than it is in the seats round the ring". We have seen, however, that the Test Matches did not create great excitement, and the first Test Match at Edgbaston in 1960 saw a fall of almost 50% from the same West Indies attendance of 1957 while income fell from £31,000 to £15,000. The Lord's Test Match of 1960 ended early on day four with just 45,000 paying customers then at Nottingham the aggregate was just 12,000 including 7,300 on the first two days, while at Manchester there were 33,000. These gates now seem extraordinarily low against the attendances of the 21st century but with Test Match gates falling around the world they surely warn against any complacency.

By contrast, the 'Roses' County Championship match at Old Trafford attracted almost 45,000 paying customers, in addition to members, over its three days.

Eventual, runners-up Lancashire reached just 81–8 from the last ball to win the match, but they won only one of their remaining four home games, while Yorkshire won their last four home matches and clinched the title for the second year running. Nonetheless, it was a good effort by Lancashire, sadly spoiled in the final weeks by dissension, departures, the sacking of the professional, John Dyson, for "insubordination", while the amateur captain, Bob Barber fairly soon left for Warwickshire. Yorkshire announced an improvement in attendances and gate receipt, and almost 27,000 paid to watch the Headingley 'Roses' match but as the largest, and in that season, most successful county, Yorkshire were unusual.

Surrey declared 1960 their "worst-ever" season financially with an average aggregate home attendance of 4,725 per match, a fall in excess of 5,000 each game. Elsewhere, Hampshire, in a damp and unsuccessful season, announced attendances "have been disappointing even when the weather has been fine"; Somerset had a loss of £5,000 adding, "we cannot afford to go on like that" and trimmed their professional staff by five men; Sussex predicted an increase of £1 in subscriptions; Middlesex suffered a fall of 38,000 in gates and released four players; Worcestershire's attendances dropped by about 15,000, and so it continued. Only Yorkshire (first), Lancashire (second) and Sussex (fourth) had improved gates.

In January 1961, the *Playfair Cricket Monthly* summed up the situation:

> Only once in the seasons since the war has the first-class programme been watched by fewer people than last summer … at the same time it must be added that most counties had considerably increased memberships.

In the same edition, Roy Webber produced the figures available from 10 of the counties showing aggregate memberships immediately before the war as around 25,000, and between 1955–1960 nearly twice as many (*circa* 48,000). Added to gate money from those periods it showed that attendances had actually risen and the comparison was only negative against the immediate post-war figures. As Webber pointed out, these were artificially high because, as in 1919 and the early 1920s, people flocked to traditional forms of entertainment as if to confirm that their sacrifices were of value to preserve English traditions. Nonetheless, he observed, "when a day's play can bring less than 150 runs, then one cannot blame would-be spectators for staying away". He suggested also that, if taking the long-term view attendances were not significantly down but finances were, then "county cricket is far too cheap" – not least given a significant increase in the number of professionals at each county.

In its "Notes by the Editor", *Wisden 1961* reported that despite falling attendances, "exclusive of members", Sussex had a membership increase of 1,200 and gate income of £2,000 and attributed this to "the presence of only one personality", their new captain and flamboyant batsman ER 'Lord Ted' Dexter. By contrast, the editor added, "the decline in professional batsmanship since the War is one of the main reasons for an alarming fall in public support. Another is the counter-attraction of TV and sound radio".

The counties, concerned about their financial positions, asked the MCC to form a new committee of inquiry, which would be chaired by Colonel RS Rait Kerr (1961). It would be the fourth enquiry since the Findlay Commission of 1937; just four years earlier there had been one chaired by HS Altham. A number of commentators noted however, that in addition to the increase in membership subscriptions, the televising of Test Matches would realise significant fees, while perhaps affecting county gates. In Lancashire, the League clubs reported similar concerns about falling gates. Since they played one-day weekend matches with overseas star professionals, the reasons were probably not those of the dull cricket found too often midweek in the county and Test game.

The *Playfair Cricket Monthly* (September 1960) reported that county cricketers' "average earnings" were "in the region of £750" each year with "a little more" for top players. England's Test players were paid £100 per appearance for England at home. It is worth pointing out that the figure of £750 *per annum* covered less than six months, including pre-season practice, and during the winter the vast majority of cricketers found other employment, sometimes coaching abroad, or at home often employed in the businesses run by senior committee members. By way of comparison, the Minister of Labour, in a written reply to the House of Commons in November 1960, reported that manual workers would earn about £730 *per annum,* a Clerical Officer in the Civil Service would earn £789 and an Executive Officer £1,140. A professional footballer would be on a maximum wage of £20 per week *in the season,* and £17 per week out of season (circa three months) amounting to almost £1,000 pa. The men who played both sports would earn a reasonable figure and while the prominent names included the Compton brothers, Arthur Milton and Willie Watson, there were many of them. At Hampshire during the 1950s, for example, they included Henry Horton, Mike Barnard, Bernard Harrison, Ralph Prouton, Reg Dare and (briefly) Jimmy Gray.

One crucial difference with current county cricket was the movement of players. At the end of the 2015 season, David Willey agreed to move to Yorkshire who, in turn, agreed to pay £50,000 'compensation', which in any other terms is a transfer fee. By comparison, in the winter of 1960, one of

England's leading professional batsmen, Tom Graveney, lost the captaincy of Gloucestershire to the Old Etonian and amateur, CTM Pugh. Graveney was not merely unhappy about the action but also the way in which it was done, and when his contract finished in December 1960 he agreed to join Worcestershire. However, the authorities seeking to discourage repetition blocked the move preventing Graveney's appearance in the following season's County Championship. He was, instead, required to serve a period of residential qualification and one of the finest and most entertaining of English talents was temporarily lost to the county game. Eventually, he returned and helped Worcestershire to win its first two County Championships and even came back into the England side, until another quarrel finished his Test Match career. What happened to him on leaving Gloucestershire was clearly what would now constitute restraint of trade, but in 1960 counties operated a somewhat feudal system.

The issue appeared to centre on Gloucestershire's determination to appoint an amateur captain and Arlott, in his *Playfair Cricket Monthly* column, suggested

> The appointment of a professional captain should be approached far more seriously than some county committees, and even some players, seem to think. The whole concept of a professional captain was revolutionary when the wartime gap virtually forced it on some counties.

The first significant achievement by a professional county captain had been when Tom Dollery led Warwickshire to the County Championship in 1951, and two years later England's first professional captain, Len Hutton, won back the Ashes for the first time since the war – and held them on the next tour. But Hutton would never be appointed captain of his county, Yorkshire. Elsewhere, TE Bailey at Essex and EDR Eagar at Hampshire, were examples of full-time secretaries at counties who also played first-class cricket, thereby claiming that their duties as playing captain were unpaid or 'amateur'. It was also a pretty open secret that some amateurs claimed permitted playing expenses, which exceeded the professional wage. The question of the amateur/professional distinction was reviewed on occasions through the 1950s but there was always a resistance to losing what was felt to be the relatively 'disinterested' amateur spirit.

The other controversy of the time was bowlers' actions – not as is predominantly the case today by spin bowlers, but by the faster men. Throwing at any pace threatens a batsman's innings but throwing at high pace is also likely to endanger him physically and in those days no batsmen (or fielders) wore helmets.

During the 1950s a number of English bowlers had been called for throwing, notably Tony Lock who remodelled his action. Two Worcestershire pace bowlers, Derek Pearson and John Aldridge, were 'called' in county cricket and these three were among a group of bowlers called again in 1960 when the issue really blew up. It had arisen partly on the MCC's Australian tour of 1958–1959 when the home-side's pace bowlers were suspected of, but not called for, throwing. Pearson, Lock and Aldridge were all called in England in the following summer, while Harold Rhodes who bowled for England, also came under scrutiny.

In 1960 English umpires no-balled all four of those men as well as others like 'Butch' White of Hampshire who was called just once at Hove by PA Gibb, which was generally agreed to be the result of a growing hysteria. But the most public case in 1960 was South Africa's Geoff Griffin. He came with a suspect action, having been called twice in South Africa in 1958–1959, but played for the tourists v MCC at Lord's before the first Test Match and was called by both umpires, Sid Buller and Frank Lee. Two matches later, he was called again against Nottinghamshire at Trent Bridge but was selected for the Test Match team and nothing happened in the first Test Match at Edgbaston when he took 1–61 and 3–44 in his side's defeat by 100 runs. In the second Test Match at Lord's he took 4–87 including a hat-trick in England's 362–8 declared, but it became his final appearance in Test Match cricket because umpires Sid Buller and Frank Lee called him for throwing yet again. The match finished in victory for England, early on the fourth day, a Monday. Her Majesty the Queen was making her annual visit to meet the two sides and, as was traditional in those days, because of the early finish, the two teams played an exhibition, single-innings match. Griffin began a new over and was no-balled for throwing four times in five balls. In an attempt to finish the over he then bowled underarm and was no-balled by Lee at square leg for not announcing the change!

The issue was not straightforward. The umpires felt they were vulnerable to scrutiny in a cricket world that, as with Apartheid, shied away from major controversies. There were 'high level' international conferences preparing the way for the Australian tour of 1961 although in the event, a re-shaped Australian pace attack avoided controversy, since Ian Meckiff, Gordon Rorke and Keith Slater did not tour. Nonetheless, Leslie Smith reported in *Wisden* (1961) that in the previous November a "momentous" agreement had emerged between England and Australia, which would in various ways deal with throwing, behind the scenes rather than on the pitch. Smith suggested that the agreement "reflected no credit on the authorities of the two senior cricketing countries". The controversy next surfaced in England in 1963, with the action of the West Indian, Charlie Griffith, but he was not called for throwing – rather, he was cited and accused by English batsmen and journalists in various publications.

As a response to these various issues and crises, mid-summer 1960 saw the Imperial Cricket Conference, then the ruling authority in world cricket, assembled at Lord's – and for the first time it was the cricketing "heads of each country" who attended, rather than locally-based representatives. The original ICC arranged international tours, changed regulations about short-pitched bowling (another growing concern), and time wasting. The *Playfair Cricket Monthly* commented that in an average day's play, pre-war, "at least 22 overs" would be bowled per hour, whereas it had sometimes dropped as low as 15 or 16 in Test Matches – today 15 is, of course the requirement and frequently takes more than six hours to complete. County Championship matches in 1960 were generally fixed at six hours of play with no 'overtime'. In 2015, the same six hours are allocated to bowl 96 overs, therefore at 16 overs per hour, but overtime is a regular occurrence, allowances for slow rates frequently enacted by the umpires, and points deductions rare.

The ICC Conference also considered the problem of "drag" which related to the old no ball law, when an illegal delivery was judged on the back crease. The change of regulation effectively eliminated that, although in 2015 there is a problem in Test cricket because umpires often miss front-foot no balls, relying on television replays only if a wicket falls. Interestingly, the conference looked at issues of negative bowling and sought to find ways of "bringing spin bowlers back into the game". In that ambition they demonstrably failed – except perhaps (and ironically) in the shorter forms of the game. The leading statistician Roy Webber wrote the magazine report and suggested that the conference "did not appear to discuss the major problem, and that is slow-scoring and the declining appeal of cricket".

But as he noted, "the big point at the meeting was throwing" and the ICC clarified the definition of a throw, specifying a straightening of the elbow at the point of delivery, but not the wrist. The conference noted the problems with "publicity", thereby identifying the growing role of the mass media in many cricketing issues. Leslie Smith, described the "many and varied" problems of cricket at this time but added they were "not beyond solution" and he suggested that, while "to some extent, the Press has been blamed for sensationalising the difficulties", which "may be true in a few cases … the Press did not originate the troubles". He suggested the cricketers and legislators "have done (this) themselves".

Webber recalled that while the problem was dealt with effectively 60 years previously by excluding players who were judged to throw, in 1960 these players often returned to the side quickly, which he suggested "can only be regarded as a snub to the umpires". There was some disquiet when Sid Buller, the umpire who called Geoff Griffin in the exhibition match, was suddenly 'replaced' on his turn to officiate in the fourth Test Match. Webber also observed that after the calling of Griffin in the exhibition match, umpires appeared to have ceased to call no balls for throwing.

The official responses to these various issues suggested a preference for a quiet life and the *status quo* but we should not be surprised that the cricket establishment felt this way. After all, it is generally in the nature of ruling elites that they prefer things as they are since 'things as they are' got them there in the first place. Further, England in 1960 was still a country divided by class and old assumptions, and governed by a Conservative Party that had been in place for nine years even though it was beginning to show signs of wear. More specifically, there was the matter of cricket as a form of mass entertainment seeking live and broadcast audiences against competing attractions.

One of cricket's problems was being, to a very large extent, a male-dominated sport. There is often talk in the contemporary world of sports like cricket and football winning back their family supporters but there is relatively little *evidence* that crowds had ever been other than mostly men and a smaller percentage of boys. Admittedly, some photographs of cricket crowds from the early years of the century showed ladies in their finery at the great society occasions – notably at Lord's – but 'out there' among the 'ordinary' spectators it was mostly a man's world.

Away from professional sport, public houses excepted, this was not generally the case. On evenings out, the cinemas, dance halls, summer season shows, theatres and, at home, radio and television competed generally for mass audiences, male and female and sometimes young and old. But where age came into the equation, there was another issue for cricket to address, which had not been so prevalent before. The 1950s were a *relatively* affluent decade. In 1957, the prime minister, Harold Macmillan, made a speech in Bedford in which he told his audience, "Most of our people have never had it so good." In 1960, young people could leave school at 15 and the majority of those who did – like the Lambeth boys and girls – found work immediately with only a small percentage staying at school and going on towards the professions or university. The school-leaving age was not raised to 16 until 1972, so in the 1960s many 15- and 16-year-olds had some money to spend, and while up to 1960 most boys had to devote 18 months to National Service, that was coming to an end. Teenagers with disposable incomes provided a potential, and potentially life-long, audience for professional sports organisations but the sports themselves had to be attractive in competition with an increasing range of alternatives.

In the early 1960s, many boys played cricket and football among other sports at school, as well as informally in their spare time and perhaps even for boys' clubs like the boys in Lambeth, although generally girls did not. It seemed 'natural' that many boys who liked sport and participated in it also followed the professional game through the mass media, special publications and watching it live. They became *supporters* usually of their home sides, and some still are. Support is defined as bearing "all or part of the weight" of something, or providing "assistance", particularly "financial" and that is what supporters do – even more so supporters who are members or season ticket holders, although this is sometimes ignored.

Everything was not straightforward however in the search for spectators. Roy Webber's conclusion of his report on the ICC Conference suggested "bad play and bad publicity, added to unnecessary unhappy incidents, are not a good advertisement for our greatest game". It was a rather gloomy time for professional cricket in England while 'potential' cricket supporters were offered a variety of alternative attractions to compete with a whole day spent watching cricket – particularly with the 1960s suffering the worst decade of English summer weather in the 20th century.

There were two particular attractions on offer that had not really been around a decade earlier. Television attracted a mass audience after the Coronation in June 1953, and in 1960 was still for the most part an evening entertainment on just two channels. Since it also offered live broadcasts of Test Matches and occasionally other games, it played a part in keeping cricket on the public agenda. But the other temptation for young people, particularly teenagers, did no such thing.

Jon Savage has written a lengthy account of the commercial importance of the 'teenager' throughout the 20th century – indeed his book, *Teenage: the Creation of Youth 1875–1945*, takes us back into the Victorian era when it is often assumed young people were to be seen and not heard. He opens the book by telling us

> During 1944, Americans began to use the word 'teenager' to describe the category of young people from 14 to 18. From the very start it was a marketing term used by advertisers and manufacturers that reflected the newly visible spending power of adolescents … For the first time, youth had become its own target market (and) … a discrete age group with its own rituals, rights and demands.

In his extended title Savage describes his work as "a prehistory of the Teenager", and a very full and intriguing prehistory it is. But for the purposes of this book, it is what happened post-1945 that is of interest. Savage observes that this first commercially-driven identification of 'teenagers' was in the United States of America and it began to manifest itself in fashions, films, television and radio shows, and music that often appealed specifically to that age group. In 2015 we are familiar with the idea that the post-war 'baby boomer' generation is still consuming what we call 'popular culture' and that the specific teenage market is at best only a segment of that world – in the 1950s and 1960s that market was very specific as the 'generation gap' was huge.

By the time the teenage market appeared in the UK through the early and mid-1950s, there were specific products and cultural artefacts that, whether designed to or not, appealed specifically to young people who would soon be hoping to die "before" they got old. Some threw themselves wholeheartedly into popular culture in a way that was lamented by commentators like Richard Hoggart who regretted the decline of the traditional working-class culture – although a northerner, Hoggart focused rather more on rugby league than cricket in his influential book *the Uses of Literacy* (1957). In the 1950s and 1960s, some of those teenagers who did immerse themselves in popular culture did so as participants in various subcultural groups, Teddy Boys, Rockers, Mods, Skinheads, and the like. They were never the majority but increasingly 'ordinary' younger people also engaged with the new fashions, records, films and activities.

Those that attached themselves to one 'sub-group' or another, tended to do so in a somewhat tribal manner, such as the opposing fans of traditional and modern jazz, who came to blows briefly at the Beaulieu Jazz Festival (televised by the BBC) at the late-summer Bank Holiday in 1960. On that same Bank Holiday, following a well-established tradition, Hampshire met Kent at Canterbury. Kent's Oxford University pace bowler David Sayer (4–30) helped dismiss the visitors for 134 (Sainsbury 45), which took no fewer than 84 overs. By the close, White had three wickets and Kent finished on 43–4. On Monday, 110–6 became 251 all out after the Kent tailenders mauled the young off-spinner Piachaud – from Ceylon (Sri Lanka) via Oxford University. Hampshire replied with 292–9 declared (Sainsbury 73) in 128 overs. Overall Hampshire had 'entertained' the Bank Holiday crowds with 426 runs in 212 overs, effectively two runs per over. Their declaration set Kent 176 to win but it was a token gesture as Hampshire bowled 18 overs and Kent scored 50–1. It's improbable that many of the young jazz fans in the New Forest that weekend paid much attention to such a dull event. To be fair to Kent that season, they did win the last County Championship match to be decided 'properly' in a single day, when in June at Tunbridge Wells, their 187 all out was too much for

Worcestershire's 25 – the follow-on target being 37 – and 61 with nine match wickets each for Alan Brown and David Halfyard.

While Britain's popular entertainments were centred as ever on London, some new examples surfaced in the regions – initially in Liverpool in the early 1960s where the popularity of the Beatles and other 'Merseybeat' acts was paralleled by a more general fondness for 'Scouse' culture through television's *Z Cars,* the Mersey poets, comedians like Ken Dodd and Jimmy Tarbuck and Bill Shankly's football team. After "She Loves You" swept the country in late 1963, the Anfield Kop was soon singing out "Yeah! Yeah! Yeah!" after which they took Gerry & the Pacemakers' version of "You'll Never Walk Alone" as their signature tune – it would be another decade before some of them spent the summers chanting "Lancashire-la-la-la". Not many miles away, Manchester United revealed their brilliant forward, George Best, who mixed with other stars of the 'swinging sixties' and wore clothes typical of the new boutiques. Cricket did not, and largely did not wish to, keep up. Years later the cricket world discovered that some of the 1960s hippest stars were great cricket fans, including Mick Jagger and Charlie Watts of the Rolling Stones and guitar hero Eric Clapton, while Ray Davies of the Kinks wrote a song about cricket for the band's concept album, *the Village Green Preservation Society*, and the Oval in the early 1970s hosted early experiments with rock & pop concerts. But for the most part, this has been a 21st century initiative at grounds like Old Trafford which enjoyed notable successes with Take That, and at Hove with Elton John, and at Hampshire where Oasis, the Who and Neil Diamond are to be succeeded in 2016 by Rod Stewart.

It seemed that in addition to on-the-field difficulties, cricket was in decline as a cultural force in England in the early 1960s, but there was perhaps one particular group where cricket was central to matters of identity and pride and it is reflected in another British movie about the period, albeit one which did not appear until 40 years later. In 2004, Paul Morrison directed *Wondrous Oblivion*, a British tale of the early 1960s about a young Jewish boy, David, who loves cricket but does not play it very well. He lives with his family in a modest London street of terraced houses and his father is a hard-working businessman. David collects picture cards of top cricketers, which move and even talk for him but the narrative centres on the arrival of a West Indian family moving in next door. This causes negative and even aggressive reactions in the white neighbourhood but David's parents, having fled the Nazis in Europe to settle in England, are clearly uneasy with the hostile way other neighbours treat the newcomers. David by contrast is thrilled when the first action of Dennis, the father, is to set up a cricket net in the garden, which he uses with his daughter Judy. David is invited to join in, and with patience and careful coaching, learns to play well enough to win a place in the school side.

This drama of the early 1960s uses cricket to focus on the racial relationships of a Jewish and West Indian family living in a street of predominantly white British people. David, having befriended Judy, unkindly turns her away from his birthday party, his mother Ruth is attracted to Dennis, and the West Indian house is firebombed in an echo of the late 1950s racial unrest that bedevilled London and Nottingham. Despite these developments, it is an essentially gentle English drama, which predictably resolves itself in entirely positive ways. While we are not told the precise date in which the events occur, there are certain moments in the film which place it quite clearly in 1963. In particular we discover that Dennis, presumably a first generation immigrant, is shown to be a friend of Frank Worrell and Garry Sobers who were touring England on a triumphant tour that season. We see Dennis at the Oval for the final Test Match where he meets David amongst the crowd. Dennis also persuades the two great cricketers to visit the local West Indian community and the film offers glimpses of the lives of English West Indians, dancing to the latest rhythm & blues and Jamaican ska. For them there was no contradiction between dancing to those popular forms and loving cricket, and one of the saddest aspects of English cricket over the past 50 years is how young men of Caribbean origin have maintained their love of black Afro-American music, while for the most part ceasing to care much for the game in which they once led the world.

The influence of black American and Caribbean music on British popular culture since the war has been huge. It manifested itself, obviously in the period in question, through the massive popularity of English acts like the Beatles and Rolling Stones but also in the clubs, where British DJs began specialising in the original recordings of that music. Another retrospective film of the period, *Quadrophenia*, depicts pretty accurately the significance of black music for white English teenagers in the 1960s. But while Dennis and his pals in *Wondrous Oblivion* see no separation between their loves of music and cricket, the same cannot be said for young white people – football perhaps, but cricket seemed to be from the old world order, and therefore less attractive. By contrast, in *Wondrous Oblivion* there is no hint that the young Jewish Londoner, David, is interested in music or fashion, despite the fact that it was precisely young Jewish teenagers in London who gave birth to the fashion-conscious black music fans soon to be known as Mods.

In terms of time, income and accessibility, there was no particular reason why cricket could not appeal to teenagers in the 1960s, but now it was simply one of the attractions on offer, rather than the main summer interest for those who enjoyed sport. The essential challenge would be increasingly a cultural one for those teenagers who were enjoying the latest 'whatever'. Jazz singer and cultural critic, George Melly, wrote at the end of the 1960s that the new pop culture, for all its commercial intentions, "presents … an exact image of our rapidly changing society, particularly in relation to its youth". Perhaps, if cricket was to 'keep up' it would need to become "rapidly changing" too? That is what happened – particularly from 1963.

Although too much English cricket was becoming increasingly dull, there were exceptions, like some parts of the Australian tour of 1961 including, for the 'objective' viewer, a sensational last day at Old Trafford when Australia twice turned probable defeat into the victory and retained the Ashes. This followed the global impact of the series between Australia and the West Indies, which concluded with half-a-million people waving the West Indies goodbye in Melbourne with a ticket-tape parade.

After nine years entirely dominated by Surrey and Yorkshire, Hampshire won the County Championship in **1961** for the first time in their history with a side that consisted by-and-large of experienced professional cricket-ers. Their top three batsmen, Marshall, Gray and Horton had all played in the 1940s, as had their great pace bowler, Shackleton, while wicketkeeper, Leo Harrison, was one of the very few pre-war players still in the county game. Of the others, Barnard, Burden, Heath, and Sainsbury – all Hampshire born – had been important members of the team that finished third in 1955 and second in 1958. The other regular contributors were Baldry who had moved from Middlesex while only Livingstone, Wassell and White were relative newcomers to the side led by Colin Ingleby-Mackenzie – old Etonian, Admiral's son, occasional wicketkeeper and swashbuckling captain. He was then a confirmed bachelor who enjoyed weekend parties in the grand homes of his grand friends, and often in the company of as many glamorous young ladies as possible. He was fond of a bet on the horses and known to receive messages on the field from his twelfth man about the day's latest results. Ingleby-Mackenzie was in every respect a great character but was also a more astute captain than for which he was sometimes given credit – a charming man for whom his players would do just about anything, even when they disagreed with him.

A classic example came in 1961 as Hampshire met Gloucestershire at Portsmouth with both sides threatening to challenge Yorkshire's supremacy at the head of the table. Hampshire had won five of their first 10 matches and on a dark, damp Saturday reduced their visitors to 86–7. Shackleton took 5–45 in two balls under 32 overs but Gloucestershire recovered somewhat to

176 all out, and Marshall and Gray replied with 12–0. The weather worsened and when play should have resumed on the Monday, it didn't. Every match in England was affected that day, but Hampshire's day was wiped out, so on the following Tuesday morning Marshall (71*) and Gray (23*) set about gaining two points for first innings lead and a further two for doing so with a faster scoring rate. There were no bonus points then, and no points for a draw.

The openers reached 96–0 in 22 overs, easily on course for the four points, when the captain appeared on the old wooden balcony, calling them in. He declared, conceding the two points for the lead and risking everything on victory. Gray was astonished, while Roy Marshall wrote, "I was furious at his apparent madness but there was nothing I could do about it." Gloucestershire batted again before lunch and lost wickets fairly regularly (Shackleton 4–27) but this was not a mad rush for declaration runs. Hampshire used only their regular bowlers and in 47 overs, Gloucestershire made 118–8 before setting Hampshire 199 to win in two-and-a-quarter hours. In the event, Hampshire faced 42 overs in that time, and while that seems a reasonable target in these days, those players had no experience of limited-overs run chases, and scores were generally lower than today.

Marshall reached a quick 38 but Gray went for seven and after Horton's 51, Hampshire slipped from 133–3 to 162–8, facing defeat. The captain led by example, matching Horton's score but when 'Butch' White arrived at number eight, 38 runs were needed in 22 minutes. 'Butch' was well named; a powerful, young fast bowler who batted left-handed in the style of the village black-smith – he was perhaps reminiscent of Ted Burgess in *The Go-Between*. In his Hampshire career he averaged around 10 runs per innings, with five half-centuries in 374 innings but on this occasion his 33* was perhaps the most important of all his County Championship innings. Wicketkeeper Bryan Timms, substituting for the injured Harrison, was quickly run out but Shackleton kept White company as in the growing darkness he hit Hampshire towards victory. Timms still relates how Marshall and Gray, when dismissed, showered, changed and still furious, disappeared to drown their dismay in a pint or two near Southampton. Eventually, Marshall was able to record it as "the most remarkable victory of the summer" while the captain considered it "one of the most crucial" games of 1961.

The world of county cricket was rather different in 1961. In his autobiography, Ingleby-Mackenzie told how, on the Saturday evening of that match, he had disappeared to a 'Deb Dance' at Lewes, Sussex (about 60 miles away) where, at dinner, he sat next to the daughter of Lord and Lady Willoughby de Broke (who presumably weren't) and he was pleased to note she cared more for racing than cricket. On the Sunday he travelled back to Hampshire to Highclere Castle ('Downton Abbey') to play for the Eton Ramblers against Lord Porchester's XI. Keith Miller arrived late, "rushed off to be sick" but recovered so well "after a lunch of champagne cocktails" that he scored a century. This was all followed on the Sunday evening with another party at Highclere – not too far from the similar stately home of Cliveden where, four weeks later, Lord Astor would entertain an exotic international cast of politicians, diplomats, arts people and others. On that later weekend, Ingleby-Mackenzie was again at Highclere, while at Cliveden there was a fateful meeting between John Profumo MP, the Minister of State for War, and Miss Christine Keeler. Over the next three years, the scandal that emerged from that meeting would contribute significantly to a change of Government in the UK.

Given his weekend's *extra curricular* activities, the captain might have been quietly relieved that the weather prevented any play on that Monday, and he was clearly equally relieved when his gamble paid off. In the present context, it might seem that Gloucestershire had set a generous target. However, scoring rates were much slower in those days and when they reduced Hampshire to 162–8 they were certainly the favourites and could not have anticipated White's season's best of 33* in less than 20 minutes. Although Gloucestershire lost, they finished fifth that year.

Hampshire won 19 of their 32 matches in 1961 and just two others were against challenging declarations – and like the Gloucestershire game in somewhat unusual or unpredictable circumstance. One was the annual match at Cowes on the Isle of Wight. There have been recent discussions about Hampshire playing at Newclose, the new ground on the Isle of Wight, but until that happens the single matches played at Cowes from 1956–1962 and the two games played at Newport in the 1930s remain Hampshire's only competitive matches played across the Solent. In 1961, Essex, buoyed by the knowledge that a fielding injury made it unlikely that Marshall would bat, set Hampshire a target of 241 to win in about three-and-a-half hours, or around 60 overs. Trevor Bailey and Ken Preston then reduced Hampshire to 35–4 so, as in the Gloucestershire game, the declaration seemed to be favouring the bowling side. Livingstone scored 44 as the captain embarked on a fine innings shortly after lunch. They added 86 (120–5), young Wassell helped the score to 170–6, and then Marshall appeared with a runner, and with his captain added 72 in 44 minutes. Ingleby-Mackenzie made 132*, his highest County Championship score, Marshall made 36* and Hampshire won another fine victory.

Not the least remarkable of the captain's performance on the Tuesday was that it came so soon after another lively weekend. In his autobiography he related how on the Saturday evening he joined a pal and "set about breaking the world drinking record" which meant missing the last boat back to the mainland, and after falling into the Solent at around 4am, he caught the early boat on Sunday morning! On the Sunday afternoon he appeared in one of Roy Marshall's benefit matches in Portsmouth.

He had less involvement in Hampshire's third victory against a declaration, which came in early May under odd circumstances after they were outplayed for two days by Surrey at the Oval. Their victory was the result of another significant change in the County Championship: the abolition of the follow-on. Surrey scored 356–4 declared and bowled Hampshire out for 190. In the modern game that lead of 166 might not have persuaded Surrey to bowl again but in three-day County Championship cricket it probably would have done. However, in 1961, as an experiment, the follow-on had been abolished because it was felt to be another situation that would lead to defensive play by the side following-on. The experiment was short-lived but now Surrey batted again and declared two down, setting Hampshire 308 to win in 320 minutes. Marshall scored 153 and won the match. Surrey had lost just six wickets throughout, but Hampshire won. Perhaps that result led to a rapid return to the familiar follow-on regulations.

Otherwise in 1961, Hampshire won 15 matches by dismissing their opponents twice, and one other after Warwickshire declared in the first innings with nine down, losing all 10 in the second innings. It was a pretty conclusive record. Yorkshire, who finished second, also won 15 by taking all 20 wickets although the last of those (against Hampshire) came after the title had been decided. Like Hampshire, they won one match taking 19 wickets and they also won one match v Sussex chasing down a declaration target. Some Yorkshire players subsequently suggested that Hampshire won on the back of regular declarations – Illingworth citing no fewer than 16 such victories – but it wasn't so.

Generally speaking their triumph was celebrated, not least because the English love an underdog. In October 1961 the *Playfair Cricket Monthly's* editorial was headed "Australia, Coupled with the Name of Hampshire" and they described both sides as "thoroughly deserving winners". Hampshire, we were told, were "a good and happy side and (had) a determined captain". In *the Daily Telegraph*, EW Swanton hailed Hampshire "as the welcome and popular Champions of 1961", while Arlott wrote less objectively as a true cricketing man of the county

> No one could quite believe it. It could not be truly savoured, it was too impossible: but it was on the news: it must be right. Let us celebrate.

The victory was popular because Hampshire were then one of those small counties not expected to win anything – and there was only the one 'thing', the County Championship. Derbyshire had managed it once about 25 years before and Warwickshire a couple of times but Essex, Leicestershire, Northamptonshire, Somerset, Sussex and Worcestershire never – and Gloucestershire never since the major reorganisation of the 1890s.

Hampshire were deservedly County Champions in 1961 but Yorkshire were the outstanding county side from 1959–1968. When Yorkshire finished first in 1968, it was their 30th title (one shared). Surrey won their 15th in 1958 but won just one more up until 1999, while Yorkshire would not win again until 2001. Yorkshire and Surrey won almost 65% of the titles from 1890–1970 but from the 30 years beginning with Glamorgan's title in 1969, the two major sides were no longer dominant as the County Championship became a far more open competition than it had ever been – and probably more open than it is likely to be in the near future. In the last third of the 20th century, there were titles for Essex, Glamorgan, Hampshire, Kent, Leicestershire, Middlesex, Nottinghamshire, Worcestershire and Warwickshire as county cricket became a more level playing field – and to those titles, of course, could be added opportunities to win the first knock-out cup from 1963, the Sunday League from 1969 and the Benson and Hedges (B&H) Cup league/knock-out from 1972. Even the sides who were not winning the County Championship in this period, won these other limited-overs competitions, including Derbyshire (first in 1981), Gloucestershire (1973), Lancashire (1969), Northamptonshire (1976), Somerset (1979) and Sussex (1963). Suddenly, everyone could (and would) have prizes, which was great fun when it happened, although conversely it created far more pressure on players, coaches and committees to deliver success. Vic Cannings of Hampshire, who retired after the 1959 season, said "we never thought of ourselves as a great side, we were just happy to play cricket and do our best". No player is allowed to think like that today, and anyone who does will be confronted by a range of encouraging aphorisms hung around the dressing room.

In the spring of **1962**, Norman Preston, *Wisden's* editor, again looked back on the previous 12 months and reported "much satisfaction" despite the disappointment of Australia retaining the Ashes and the greater "alarm" of "small attendances" at county matches. Preston warned against "too much tampering", fearing "the game may be killed stone dead" but he also reported that following the latest Committee of Enquiry, "room has been found for a one-day knock-out competition to be inaugurated in 1963" and added somewhat naively that "it should provide some fun, if approached in the right spirit". Since he was reporting on the 1961 season, he made space to record Hampshire's achievement in winning their first title but his approval was more measured than some. He delighted in Marshall's "enterprising" approach, praised Shackleton's bowling and noted, "the eleven were bound together by an ebullient captain in Colin Ingleby-Mackenzie" but concluded

> Hampshire's success was extremely popular and rightly so but apart from Marshall and the captain, much of their cricket was of the defensive type, which is causing the authorities so much concern.

As well as the new knock-out cup, the Committee of Enquiry reported on county finances, warning "even after making some practical economies, only about half-a-dozen counties could hope to break-even in an average year *from normal cricket income*" (my emphasis). The committee then listed other fund-raising activities including Supporters Clubs, television fees, letting premises for entertainment, winter car-parking (e.g. for shopping or football) and rental of indoor nets.

Since in 2015 there were seemingly endless discussions about the structure of county cricket, it is worth perhaps noting the proposals that emerged back then from the Committee of Enquiry in addition to the new knock-out competition. The suggestion was for each county to play every other county once, either home or away, over the established three days. They would also play each other in two consecutive one-day matches at the other teams' venue and in the following year the locations would be reversed. These arrangements would require the lengthening of the 1961 season of 111 days, by about a further 17 days. By comparison, the 2015 county season lasted 166 days.

While these dramatic changes did not happen, the 1960s were a period of significant change in English cricket as they were in the wider society. In the 1963 Centenary *Wisden*, John Solan in his article "Through the Crystal Ball", observed that county cricket "is already being forced to move with the times and to reflect the changed uses of leisure".

1962 had opened with Hampshire as County Champions and the Duke of Norfolk did them the honour of inviting them along the coast to represent his XI in the one-day opening match against the Pakistan tourists at Arundel. There they raised the County Champions' flag on 28 April, and after Roy Marshall led the way with 61 of 204–6 declared (no limited-overs yet), the match was drawn with the tourists on 173–6. It was the start of a disappointing summer for both sides as Yorkshire regained the title, Hampshire slipped to 12th and England won the Test series 4–0. Overall, Pakistan won just four of their 29 first-class matches and lost to four county sides.

There is not much more to report about this season except that we might consider it a fittingly uninspiring conclusion to the old order and a very good reason for the changes that were imminent. During the season there was inevitably much speculation about the England side that it was hoped might regain the Ashes in 1962–1963, but Dexter's side and their opponents failed to recapture the spirit of Worrell's West Indians of two years earlier, and the series was drawn 1–1 with the Ashes remaining 'down-under'. *Wisden's* editor, suggested that the cricket generally failed to meet expectations, with both sides exhibiting a preoccupation in avoiding defeat. The England side lacked a good opening partnership, the best fast bowlers were ageing, and at home, the lbw law was discouraging wrist-spin on the slower wickets. That last state of affairs has never been successfully addressed, although in 2015 England's four preferred spinners for their winter tour of the UAE were all Anglo-Asians (Moeen Ali, Adil Rashid, the injured Zafar Ansari and Samit Patel), while a fifth England bowler, Monty Panesar, was released by his third county, Essex, but still hoped to revive his career.

Although **1962** was a generally dull season spoiled by poor weather, there was one modest event, which in retrospect is of huge significance. While on 28 April, Hampshire and Pakistan were playing that one-day, single innings time-match at Arundel with no restrictions on overs bowled, the enterprise of the Leicestershire secretary, Mike Turner, led a few days later to four midlands counties taking part in the first-ever limited-overs competition between first-class sides. Turner had spotted a gap in the 1962 county fixture list in which Leicestershire, Northamptonshire, Derbyshire and Nottinghamshire were all free. On Wednesday 2 May, Northamptonshire beat Nottinghamshire and Leicestershire beat Derbyshire and one week later, Northamptonshire won the 'Final' by five wickets. The matches were played with 65 overs per side, in which context the scores look modest today. In the first two matches, first innings scores of 250–5 and 168–9 were sufficient to win the games by seven and 31 runs. In the Final, Leicestershire posted 218 all out in the 57th over and Northamptonshire won by five wickets in the 60th over. Maurice Hallam was top scorer with 86 (run out) in the first match, and while bowlers generally bowled a maximum of 15 overs, in the 'Final', Larter (16) and Williamson (18.2) exceeded that. The only fielding restrictions were a maximum of six on the off-side and five on the leg-side throughout, and intervals were as normal, not between innings.

The other major event came off the field in the late autumn of 1962 while the MCC (England) side were in Australia under the leadership of the Duke of Norfolk and 'Lord' Ted (Dexter); the abolition of the distinction between amateurs and professionals. Four years earlier, a Committee of Enquiry had identified their desire to "preserve in first-class cricket the leadership and general approach to the game traditionally associated with the Amateur player". That committee comprised a number of eminent former amateur cricketers but the new committee chaired by Norfolk decided the time had come.

Wisden was merely one of the cricketing institutions to express disappoint-ment at this decision but the deed was done and while a dwindling number of amateurs remained in county cricket after 1962, they were no longer identified – now they were all cricketers. *Wisden* argued that the decision endangered "the spirit of freedom and gaiety which the best amateur players brought to the game". But whatever the case might have been previously, the most thrilling English cricketer of the post-war period, Denis Compton, was a professional. By the 1960s, Colin Ingleby-Mackenzie and Ted Dexter were perhaps the only prominent amateurs who embodied this spirit – and neither would play much beyond the mid-1960s. Many of the finest post-war amateur cricketers like May, Cowdrey and Bailey brought a thoroughly 'professional' approach to their play.

There were a number of reasons for this sudden change after years of resistance

1. With the exception of a few national 'stars', most professional sportsmen in England, particularly in team sports, had been characterised – and remunerated – as craftsmen or skilled labourers. By the 1960s, this was beginning to shift towards an identity as entertainers. The most talented individuals were represented increasingly in the mass media, and they sought rewards commensurate with that new identity. In football, the abolition of the minimum wage in January 1961 gave the best players the chance to negotiate wages. Before the abolition occurred in January 1961 they could earn up to £20 per week. Johnny Haynes of Fulham and England was then said to have increased his wages to £100 per week, and by the end of the 1960s, George Best was earning 10 times that. In 1963, George Eastham of Newcastle United went to court to argue his right for a transfer and won his case. If footballers were gaining more control over their wages and rights to move, cricketers, some of whom had been footballers also, would be taking notice. By 1967 they had organised the Professional Cricketers Association (PCA), which soon took control of protecting the rights of players in terms of contracts and wages.

2. Cricketers took up their employment in their teenage years and even in the 'rock & roll' 1950s of Teddy Boys, coffee bars and juke boxes, most had to undergo National Service which

meant a degree of obedience even deference, from all but the wildest. Since that 'fringe' element was unlikely to include many top cricketers, the world of county cricket had remained largely class-bound, hierarchical and deferential. But the last National Service recruits who went into county cricket (e.g. Roy Virgin or Barry Stead), returned in the early 1960s, after which many cricketers came straight to cricket from school and stayed there while all around them Britain began to 'swing'.

3.   There is a popular argument that the 'swinging sixties' really only occurred among a meritocratic elite in the heart of London but it is perhaps less appropriate to define it *geographically* and rather more as a matter of age. In the 1960s, cities and towns across England were filled with a burgeoning network of music clubs, coffee bars and boutiques where young people practised a degree of hitherto, unheard of independence. While most county cricketers were well behaved and generally disciplined young men, they did not grow up unaware of those attractions, nor indeed from images of them which appeared increasingly on cinema and television screens and in the newspapers. The Beatles, probably the biggest single popular cultural phenomenon this country has produced, were humorously irreverent and their irreverence alongside the new satire in magazines and on television was difficult to avoid in the mid-1960s. Whether the cricketers themselves were much a part of this dramatic social and cultural shift, the next generation of potential supporters certainly were.

4.   If each of those contextual reasons offered only a limited explanation for this change in the sometimes hermetically sealed world of county cricket, the amateurs themselves presented two further problems. Firstly, there were fewer of them for the simple reason that it was increasingly difficult for accomplished young men to support themselves for months, playing what was predominantly a professional sport. Very few were any longer of independent means, and the economic downturns of the 1960s meant that few firms were willing to support someone like Colin Ingleby-Mackenzie whose work for Slazenger's, while he captained Hampshire, seemed to consist of a few days each year at his convenience! There was also the increasing problem of so-called 'shamateurism', whereby players who claimed to be playing for 'love' were inflating expenses in a manner reminiscent of WG Grace at his worst. There were other so-called

'amateurs' who were employed by counties in other capacities (e.g. secretary) and were therefore able to claim they were not actually paid for playing. But for them in particular, the claim that their status gave them the disinterested approach commensurate with 'brighter cricket' was very doubtful.

In a comprehensive two-volume history of the 1960s, Dominic Sandbrook observed that the three national team sports of cricket, football and rugby union, plus horse racing, were given more media and public attention at that time than all the other sports together, and were often seen as "reflections of national identity". He suggested that up to the 1950s, cricket had been *the* English national sport, although football, rugby and racing were more widespread across Britain. He added, however, that by the mid-1960s, cricket "seemed to be in deep decline" principally because it appeared old-fashioned in the light of its association with the Empire and the upper classes and the "counter factors of social mobility, classlessness and technological change". While those may have been key elements in the decline of cricket's popularity, they are in themselves somewhat abstract. County and Test Match cricket had become boring, while other things, for example, shopping, fashion, music, travel, or television, were increasingly exciting, accessible and affordable. Football might have suffered the same fate as cricket and the gates had declined from the huge figures of the late 1940s, but the European adventures of Tottenham Hotspur, West Ham United, Celtic and Manchester United, the popularity of players like Jimmy Greaves, Bobby Charlton, Bobby Moore and especially George Best, plus England's World Cup triumph of 1966, all provided a sport better suited to the 'swinging sixties'.

Sandbrook also suggested that in the 1960s the England cricket team, being on a "losing streak", did not help England cricket's cause. This was not wholly accurate. They won seven home series in the 1960s against South Africa (1960), Pakistan (1962), New Zealand (1965), India (1967), Pakistan (1967), West Indies (1969) and New Zealand (1969), losing five to Australia (1961 and1964), West Indies (1963) South Africa (1965) and West Indies (1966). In 1968 they drew the Ashes series making an unprecedented 13 series in 10 years with the advent of shorter shared series in one season. In 1970, with the South African 'crisis', there would be no touring nation. Sandbrook's other argument was that English cricket struggled because of the "conservatism of the game's authorities" and their dislike of having to 'sell' the game. But the evidence from so many changes to English professional cricket in the 1960s and beyond does not support that view – whether it was inherently true of the men themselves (and they were all men), or not.

With the benefit of hindsight, cricket's problem was clear: as 1960s British leisure time became more thrilling, the cricket became less so. We have seen that Arlott described the 1960 season as a pretty desperate one, and even though an unexpected Hampshire title and an Ashes summer enlivened interest, 1961 was ultimately disappointing, as was 1962 with relatively little to recommend it outside Yorkshire. But then we come to 1963 and suddenly cricket came alive again, thanks in part to the exploits of the West Indian tourists and partly the introduction of a brand new county competition.

The West Indies tour of **1963** began on 24 April and ran through to 14 September. During that time they played every county side including two matches each against Surrey, Glamorgan and Yorkshire. They played a number of other first-class matches against the MCC and Oxford and Cambridge Universities, as well as various friendlies – some one day – against Ireland, the Minor Counties, Col. LC Stevens' XI, the Duke of Norfolk's XI, the Club Cricket Conference, Learie Constantine's XI, AER Gilligan's XI, TN Pearce's XI, and in late September a 65-overs challenge match against the first county knock-out cup winners, Sussex, at Hove. In terms of what happens today, the tour was a feat of endurance although there were no ODIs or T20s to follow the five Test Matches. Nonetheless, they covered the country, enabling most cricket fans to watch them at a convenient ground – I was lucky enough to see them while on holiday against Yorkshire at Bramall Lane, and on my first visit to a Test Match, at the Oval, when they clinched the series 3–1. To fulfil their obligations, the tourists brought 18 players for a total of 30 first-class games.

The West Indies were a huge attraction, which dated back at least to their 1950 tour when playing "cricket, lovely cricket" at Lord's, they beat England for the first time. They were less successful through the 1950s however, losing at home to England twice and in England in 1957. Then, as we have noted, they appointed Frank Worrell as the first black player to captain the side in its history. Worrell, born in 1924, played first-class cricket during the war and made his Test Match debut in the 1947–1948 season. With Clyde Walcott and Everton Weekes he formed the famous "three Ws" batting triumvirate from Barbados. His first tour, in charge, was to Australia in 1960–1961, by which time the other two 'Ws' had departed. The first Test Match was played at Brisbane in early December and centuries for Sobers (132) and Norman O'Neill (181) left Australia 52 ahead with two days to play. During the fourth day wickets fell regularly although Worrell repeated his first innings of 65, and the West Indies closed on 259–9 and needing to stretch that lead in the morning. They managed that with a further 25 runs until Alan Davidson took his 10th wicket of the match to add to an innings of 44 in the first innings. He would make 80 in the second to become the first man in Test Match cricket to record an aggregate of 100+ runs and 10 wickets in one game.

If that was personally satisfying, there was greater excitement to follow. Australia set off in pursuit of 233 to win in 310 minutes but Wes Hall dismissed Bobby Simpson and Neil Harvey with just seven scored. Two wickets fell at 49, another at 57 and by 92–6 Australia faced defeat, before captain Richie Benaud joined Davidson and added 134 for the seventh wicket. Australia reached 226–6 and seemed almost certain to win, needing seven runs in about 10 minutes when Davidson was run out. Hall bowled the vital final over – in Australia, eight balls – with Australia needing six to win. Wally Grout ran a leg-bye, then Benaud was caught behind. Meckiff defended one then ran a single, so four needed from four balls. Hall then dropped Grout as they ran a single (three from three), Meckiff pulled for two, but Grout was run out trying to win it with the third. Last man, Lindsay Kline, came out with one needed from two balls, played the ball to midwicket and Meckiff charged down the pitch, but Joe Solomon fielded, threw and hit directly, and for the first time in Test Match history, the match was tied.

Afterwards, Benaud observed, "I felt it was a pity that either side should lose this match; and the result is good for cricket." It certainly was. Australia won the second match by seven wickets, West Indies won the third by 222 runs and the fourth was drawn after Australia set out in search of 406 to win. They lost early wickets, recovered, fell away to 144–6, recovered again with a stand of 59, then lost three for four and at 207–9 were losing the match when Kline joined Ken Mackay. The two batted together for one-hour-and-forty minutes and saved the match with an unbeaten partnership of 66. So, the sides agreed to add an extra day to the final Test Match to ensure a result and a series winner and it was Australia who came out on top. On the second day, that game at Melbourne attracted a record crowd of 90,800, beating the previous highest Test Match attendance (in 1937). The final series attendances were not published but were almost certainly in excess of 750,000. *Wisden* invited the former Australian batsman Jack Fingleton to report on the tied match and gave his piece the heading "Cricket Alive Again".

So we came to **1963**. Just before the season started, the Beatles celebrated their first number-one hit record and by the close of that year they had followed it with three more, accompanied by many other Merseybeat groups, and before Christmas the first record releases by the Rolling Stones. The establishment took punishment from television (*That Was The Week That Was*) and in print (*Private Eye*). A fine, but sometimes rather dour run of British 'realist' films came to an end with *This Sporting Life* – based around the exploitation of professional sportsmen by those with the money. In their place came the added colour of the first Bond movies *Dr No* and *From Russia With Love,* plus 1960s stars Michael Caine as *Alfie* and Julie Christie as *Darling.* Television moved dear old Dixon's colleagues from Dock Green to newly hip

Liverpool with *Z Cars,* while David Jacobs' static *Juke Box Jury* made way for dancing and the "5–4–3–2–1" countdown of *Ready Steady Go!* In February 1964 the Beatles conquered the USA and other groups followed, while English 'Pop' and 'Op' artists thrilled the world. Mary Quant and Twiggy led the boutique revolution and increasing numbers of young men dedicated themselves to following fashion alongside their girlfriends. While not everyone joined in and not everyone 'swung', even those not interested or too old to participate in this brief, hedonistic indulgence were often touched by their teenage children or those of their neighbours' and friends.

This excitement was not always wholly innocent. On Tuesday, 19 May 1964, *the Daily Sketch* front page carried the headline "Wildest Ones Yet" as "Holidaymakers cower on the beach", while *the Daily Mirror* front page offered a large photograph of a neatly dressed, short-haired Mod on Brighton's stony beach, kicking a prostrate Rocker with the sub heading "The boot goes in". On the sports pages that day were reports of Hampshire's cricketers who, as tradition required, met Kent at Southampton every Whitsun, but on that Bank Holiday Monday a good crowd were frustrated first by rain and then by Kent's captain, Colin Cowdrey. On the Monday he scored a fine century but on day three his declaration left Hampshire to chase 227 at 91 runs per hour, a formidable target in those days. Hampshire fell to 62–4, the chase was off and Hampshire closed at 181–7. It was dull stuff, particularly if intended to attract the next generation of cricket supporters.

Unsurprisingly, the 'Establishment' did not much like the young hooligans, any more than in the previous decade had they liked the Teddy Boys who caused similar 'riots' in the cinemas during showings of the Bill Haley feature *Rock Around the Clock.* The Mods and Rockers, terrorising seaside towns, constituted a minority of young people, albeit an alarming and alarmingly visible minority, but increasing numbers of teenagers were having fun in the 1960s, after some years of austerity. They had the hula-hoop, the Twist, Vidal Sassoon to style their hair, Mary Quant or John Stephen to design their clothes, and the Beatles, Rolling Stones or Tamla Motown to dance to. The more earnest ones might enjoy the new British theatre, jazz or Bob Dylan and the folk revival, while marching to and from Aldermaston with the CND. Where did cricket fit, in this increasingly rich menu?

And what of their parents? Billy Butlin had launched a post-war holiday revolution but if that was too parochial, cheap-flight Mediterranean holidays began to replace two weeks by the English seaside. Elsewhere, some cinemas became bingo halls and by 1964 we had no fewer than three television channels to entertain us – although not yet any colour. For the 1963 FA Cup Final the BBC persuaded the FA that either Manchester United (red shirts) or Leicester City (blue shirts) must change since both would look the same in monochrome. Leicester lost the toss, wore white shirts and lost the game. Their side included Graham Cross who played in the summer for Leicestershire CCC and in a lengthy career played his final match in the B&H Cup v Hampshire in 1977. When he appeared in the 1963 FA Cup Final there was no equivalent to the B&H Cup, but change was on its way.

There was also change on its way for the 'Establishment'. In 1960, its legal representatives had lost the case against the perceived obscenity of DH Lawrence's novel *Lady Chatterley's Lover,* probably from the famous moment when the prosecutor asked the jury whether they would wish their wives or servants to read it. The result was, of course, an immediate surge in sales. Sex was a problem in the following year when the relationship between Minister for War John Profumo and prostitute Christine Keeler, who was also embroiled with a Russian diplomat, led to questions being asked in the House of Commons. Initially, Profumo issued a denial but by 1963 was forced to admit he had lied to the House. He resigned, and a few months later his ageing prime minister, Harold Macmillan, departed also. Macmillan's replacement was Alec Douglas-Home, really Alexander Frederick Douglas-Home, Baron Home of the Hirsel, who since 1951 had sat in the House of Lords. He had been a useful cricketer at Eton, Oxford University and briefly as an amateur for Middlesex but as a politician he renounced his title to become leader of the Conservatives and prime minister. Unfortunately, his party was in decline and his Premiership lasted just under 12 months, at which point the forward-looking vision of Harold Wilson's Labour Party ("the White Heat of Technology") won them a narrow majority, which they increased two years later in the Election of 1966. Wilson was a Yorkshireman but unlike his predecessor shown no obvious interest in cricket. Early in that first period of his Labour Government, the Conservatives, and the country, lost its great wartime leader, Winston Churchill, who was afforded a state funeral in January 1965. The old ways seemed spent.

Cricket 1950s-style seemed spent too in this modern, rapidly changing world – it was perceived by a great mass of the general public as dull and, as we have seen, too often it was. The West Indies Test series would prove a huge success but two of the contemporary publications about the tour leave one in no doubt about the context in which it was played. JS Barker, praising the West Indians, suggested they were the only cricketers "to survive the Thirty Years of Negativity relatively undisillusioned (*sic*)". He sympathised with the England selectors who were required to select a side when "English cricket had the highest level of mediocrity in the cricketing world" and suggested that in England there was a sense that Test Match cricket was "on trial", indeed he felt it was being given "its last chance". For Barker, the series succeeded largely because of the West Indies and he suggested there wasn't much of a secret as to why – "West Indians *enjoy* playing cricket … their enjoyment is communicated … and Test cricket is not something apart … it is still something to enjoy, not suffer". As for England, he concluded that at that point in 1963 "it is the near certainty of being bored which is killing cricket".

Alan Ross meanwhile noted that while England had fought out a draw in Australia in the previous winter, they had returned "with the image of Test cricket sadly tarnished". Ross described making his way through a traffic jam on the Edgware Road on a damp Thursday of the second Test Match at Lord's as "Christine Keeler was the most famous person in England, the headlines on posters dripping her evidence". But by Tuesday evening of that fabulous match, the BBC's teatime news – Keeler *et al* – was delayed to enable the nation to follow the thrilling conclusion as Wes Hall bowled ferociously in the gloom to David Allen, Derek Shackleton was run out in a race to the bowler's end and Colin Cowdrey surveyed the final balls from that end with one arm in a sling. It was a stunning game with the two sides just four runs apart on first innings, and England, needing 231 to win, closing on 228–9. There were heroes on both sides with fine innings by Rohan Kanhai and Basil Butcher, Dexter, Barrington and on that last day Brian Close, plus six wickets for Trueman, five for Griffith and three in four balls for 'Shack', recalled to colours, close to his 39th birthday.

At the conclusion of that tour, Ross recorded that the West Indies' players *and* supporters had "transformed the cricket grounds of England, making of a damp ignoble summer something romantic and glorious". He described the Lord's game as one of the "great Test Matches of modern times" and suggested, somewhat like Barker that there was little to compare with the series over the past 30 years in this country. He concluded of the visitors that "enriching the common idiom of the game, they restored to it not only spontaneity but style".

One of the few weaknesses in the side of Kanhai, Sobers, Hall, Griffith, Lance Gibbs and the others, was an opening partner for Hunte. Ironically, the best candidate batted through the 1963 English county season scoring 1,800 runs with five centuries and seven more 50s – but he was Roy Marshall of Hampshire, the young West Indian Test batsmen who had to turn his back on international cricket to satisfy the residential qualifications of a secure, 20-year career in English county cricket. Had he played for the West Indies in 1963, he would have turned his back on that security – not for nothing was his autobiography titled *Test Outcast* – and in that publication he revealed that Worrell had approached him on that very topic, but Marshall had a young family and he stayed at Hampshire. In the not too distant future a number of the fine 1963 West Indian side would appear in county cricket without jeopardising their Test Match places.

In the following spring, *Wisden's* editor confirmed the sense of optimism generated with his headline "An outstanding season" and suggested that the West Indians "enriched the game with their exuberant cricket". But his second paragraph noted another change in that remarkable year in English cultural history, as 1963 was "also notable for the introduction of the knock-out Competition, which in future will be called the Gillette Cup". The Final at Lord's, watched by 23,000 spectators, was "the first all-ticket cricket match with a sell-out before the first ball was bowled".

With the benefit of 50-plus years of hindsight we can see that the Test series of 1963 did not immediately or wholly transform the highest form of the game – indeed the following season carried some stark reminders of the possibility for boredom, but it is doubtful today whether matches will ever return wholesale to the tedium of a run-rate of 2.5 or less per over, although it would be a delight to return to the over-rates bowled in those days. Without doubt, however, the introduction of the Gillette Cup has had an impact beyond that which anyone anticipated in 1963.

Firstly, of course, it brought advertising and sponsorship to the cricket field. The various action, team and portrait photographs of 1963 that appeared in the following spring carry not a sign of a logo, an advertising hoarding, or indeed, any coloured clothing among the players. The Hampshire Handbook carried around 60 advertisements that year and that was how local business-men could demonstrate their support for the club, but their presence on match days was confined to their attendance on the ground, in some cases as members of the club's committee. In 1963, that body comprised around 30 men including Arlott and former (amateur) players CGA Paris, GR Taylor and JP Parker. The Patron was the Earl Mountbatten of Burma, the president was HS Altham and the chairman, WJ Arnold. As befits a naval and military county, there were three Captains, one Commander and one Lt-Colonel from Christchurch. Incidentally it would be the 21st century before any women were elected to the committee, by which time it was just a Members' Committee.

But while advertising and business support would play an increasingly important role in the future survival, and occasional prosperity, of county cricket clubs, the greatest change, perhaps the greatest single change in all the history of first-class cricket, was the introduction of limited-overs cricket. It is not, of course, strictly 'first-class' itself, but the various competitions, which over the years have been designated as 65, 60, 55, 50, 45, 40 and 20 overs (with variations for the weather), are played by first-class cricketers and first-class sides and are now common in most lower and junior forms of competitive cricket as well. Indeed, the 'timed' game in which it is possible to play for an honourable draw, and common in my schooldays, is now the rarity.

The new competition began on 1 May 1963 with the preliminary round eliminator between the two bottom sides in 1962's County Championship, as Lancashire beat Leicestershire by 101 runs, which seemed scant reward for Mike Turner. He had spearheaded the revolution with the midlands competition the previous year but his side were out after a game in which Marner and Hallam both scored centuries. Three weeks later in a first round of eight matches, there were victories for Derbyshire, Glamorgan, Lancashire, Middlesex, Northamptonshire, Sussex, Worcestershire and Yorkshire. And after Sussex beat Northamptonshire and Worcestershire beat Lancashire in the semi-finals on 10 July, there was a wait of two months before the season concluded with Sussex beating Worcestershire at Lord's.

Scores were not generally high in the early years. In 1963 both innings lasted 65 overs, yet in the 16 matches, 13 of the completed innings failed to reach 200 and only two passed 300. In one semi-final Worcestershire dismissed Lancashire for 59 (Jack Flavell 6–14) winning by nine wickets and in most cases the margins of victory were quite large. Nonetheless, it was probably of little consolation to Hampshire that they lost their only match that year to Derbyshire at Bournemouth by the closest margin, just six runs. Mike Barnard was last out for 98 with three balls left as Les Jackson bowled his 15 overs taking 1–24. Shackleton missed the game and although Hampshire's makeshift attack had the visitors 1–1 after five overs, Derek Morgan 59*, 2–49 and good fielding won the gold match award with a special consolation silver medal for Barnard.

In itself, a midweek defeat in the first round of the new competition in 1963 seemed of little significance in the overall season, but the competition as a whole did have an impact – not least with the televising of the Final. The whole morning was shown on BBC, after which it shared broadcasts with other events on the afternoon's *Grandstand,* the BBC's flagship sports magazine show. There was a 15-minute highlights summary presented by Brian Johnston in late evening following a varied programme including *Deputy Dawg,* a Francis Durbridge thriller, *Juke Box Jury,* Sid James in *Taxi, Wells Fargo,* the Saturday film, Eric Sykes in *Wish You Were Here* and *Maigret.* Everything was over before midnight with Sussex celebrating, after posting 168 and holding Worcestershire to 154 – just 322 runs in a whole day, maximum 130 overs, of this new excitement.

Nonetheless, here was television exposure for county cricket. It's not unreasonable to argue that the County Championship is the best supported of all major professional sports that is hardly ever shown on British television. Any Championship broadcasts are rare events whereas throughout the 1960s the BBC began to show more county teams playing limited-overs games – particularly on Sunday afternoons.

One of the essential features of the T20 format, of course, is that it suits television very nicely, not merely in England but with the IPL and the Australian Big Bash, which these days are screened globally on one of the multitude of channels that would have seemed unimaginable in 1963. The other element that would have seemed strange back then, once a television set and a licence had been purchased, was the additional requirement to pay monthly fees for the privilege of watching most of those channels, including virtually all the specialist sports channels.

The introduction of the knock-out cup was a success and a pointer to ways forward. Despite the recent experiments with the follow-on and pitch covering, it was really 1963 that began the period of extraordinary change in professional cricket, which continues to this day. Indeed, given the extent to which the modern cricket follower expects significant changes on an annual basis, it seems odd today to read in 1963's *Wisden's* "Notes by the Editor" that over the previous 30 years, first-class cricket had been "subjected to a number of changes", although these were to the Laws rather than the formats. Neither, apparently, had these changes led to "any noticeable improvement" to the game for the players or spectators. They included first-innings bonus points in the County Championship, suspension of the follow-on, pitch covering, the 75-yard boundary and the pre-war change to the lbw law. None however, had satisfied completely "the majority of the reformers" but if the editor wished for a period of stability and assimilation he would be disappointed. England in the 1960s was not on the whole a place of continuity, and the reformers would not be silenced. By the end of that momentous decade adult homosexuality and abortion were legalised, divorce laws were reformed, theatre censorship (by the Lord Chancellor) and capital punishment were abolished. There was an expansion of so-called 'comprehensive' secondary schooling and the creation of the Open University with its utilisation of radio and television after BBC-2 became the third channel, just days before the start of the 1964 cricket season. Three years later, colour broadcasting began and also in 1967 the BBC reorganised its radio channels to include the creation of the new 'pop' oriented Radio One.

Not everyone liked all of these changes, indeed, some opposed a great many, but the key point is that change was rapid and seemed almost inevitable. The other characteristic of Wilson's Labour Government of the 1960s was that it wrestled constantly with the economy before losing unexpectedly to Ted Heath's Conservatives in 1970. That following decade is often characterised as one of economic difficulties and industrial disputes, and in the context of major financial challenges, the worlds of entertainment and sport, including cricket, had to find their own solutions.

This is what cricket did, and the remainder of this book will be an attempt to demonstrate that in many key respects, what it did from the early 1960s, was to set out on a programme of never-ending change – sometimes in search of those elusive potential supporters; sometimes, as with the South African crisis, driven by far greater outside pressures; and sometimes, as with professionalization or the 'Packer affair', by pressures from within the game. All of this occurred while the cricket establishment was transformed slowly from the dominance of the public school elite to a more meritocratic, entrepreneurial class. As such, it both reflected *and* participated in the wider society becoming increasingly a global phenomenon no longer governed by a private club at the heart of London's St John's Wood.

While the cricket 'revolution' began in earnest in 1963 with the abolition of the amateur/professional distinction, the 'brighter cricket' approach of the West Indies and the launch of the Gillette Cup, in 1964 pretty much the same cricketers appeared in English county cricket, so that while the 'Gents' no longer met the Players at Lord's and Colin Ingleby-Mackenzie was no longer identified as an amateur, he was still captaining Hampshire and he was still an Old Etonian. In **1964,** the knock-out cup brought some joy to his side as the Minor Counties took their place in the first round and the match was reduced to 60 overs per side. Hampshire were scheduled to meet Wiltshire at Swindon on the same Saturday that an exciting West Ham United side beat Preston North End 3–2 at Wembley to win the FA Cup. West Ham included Bobby Moore, Geoff Hurst (once of Essex CCC), plus Worcestershire's seam bowler, Jim Standen, in goal. For Standen, 1964 was a wonderful summer, for he returned from the Final to Worcestershire, heading their averages with 64 wickets at 13 apiece as they won the County Championship for the first time. Like Hampshire in 1961, this was a popular, somewhat unexpected, first success although it was not a thrilling chase as they finished 41 points ahead of Warwickshire.

With the covering experiment abandoned, pitches once more helped the bowlers. At Worthing in June 1964, Ian Thomson took 10–49 as Warwickshire were dismissed for 196 and then 5–26 as they made 129 – yet the visitors won easily, with Sussex put out for 120 and 23 (Jack Bannister 6–16). Two years earlier Nottinghamshire had declared on 406–8 at Eastbourne but all out for 57 in the second innings, lost to Sussex by eight wickets. In 1965 Hampshire travelled to Middlesbrough and dismissed Yorkshire for 121 and 23 – still their record lowest score (White 6–10) as Hampshire won by 10 wickets.

While Saturday, 2 May pleased the football fans, it was less kind to cricket's new competition. Swindon was saturated and by Sunday evening it was clear that Monday was off as well, so Wiltshire switched everything last minute to Chippenham. The overs were still not distributed evenly among the bowlers so that any bowler might bowl 13 of the 60. Hampshire were all out with two balls remaining for just 201 but Wiltshire managed only 81 all out in the 43rd over, with Bob Cottam taking 4–9 in his 10 overs for which he received Hampshire's first Gold award from adjudicator FE Woolley, a man who might have enjoyed the shorter game. The next round took Hampshire to Edgbaston where the eventual finalists thumped them by 178 runs after a John Jameson century and MJK Smith's 88. At Lord's in September Warwickshire lost to Sussex, who took the trophy for the second year under the astute, but not always attacking leadership of Ted Dexter. He was not averse to setting defensive fields at a time when some captains thought that was not quite the right 'spirit', but he won two trophies with a side of strong seam bowlers. Eventually such reasoning would lead to increasing restrictions on captains' field-placings.

The cup competition seemed to bring a hope of greater security to county treasurers and more significant developments were imminent. Commensurate with a world that increasingly made celebrities and idols of young actors and musicians, sports stars, longed also for greater recognition and remuneration, leading *Wisden* to suggest of the **1964** Ashes series that "too many" of the cricketers "appeared to be governed by commercial interests and cricket suffered accordingly".

That series started with a drawn match at Nottingham when the whole of Saturday was lost to rain and almost 15 hours went in total. The two teams moved to Lord's where the first two days were washed out, and play having started, opener Ian Redpath batted nearly four hours for less than 40. Leeds was dry, but injuries during the match to Flavell and Peter Parfitt hampered England, and Australia went one-up. They retained the Ashes at Manchester as Simpson scored 311 of 656–8 declared in 762 minutes – Australia's longest ever innings. Barrington replied with 256 in 611 all out, leaving just enough time for Australia to face two overs of their second innings. The excitement at the Oval came principally when Cowdrey caught Neil Hawke to give Trueman his 300th Test Match wicket, the first man to reach that mark, and from his county colleague Geoff Boycott who scored his first Test Match century in another draw. The thrills of 1963 were in short supply during this following damp and attritional season.

In the winter of 1964–1965 England (MCC) toured South Africa. They departed on the October morning when Britain went to the polls and elected a change of government, while England, winning the first Test Match and drawing the others took an overseas series for the first time since the year of the previous General Election. Ted Dexter, England's captain in 1964, joined the tour late after he contested the Cardiff constituency as a Conservative candidate where he lost to the future Labour prime minister, James Callaghan. Warwickshire's MJK Smith took over the captaincy – like May, Cowdrey and Dexter he was an experienced county captain and all four were Oxbridge graduates. In the immediate future that role would pass to a number of senior, county 'pros' such as Close, Graveney and Illingworth. England went through the tour undefeated, but the South African Colts XI came within two wickets of victory, helped not least by a fine 63 from a promising 19-year-old Barry Richards.

Neither Trueman nor Brian Statham toured South Africa, and England's pace bowling was in the hands of John Price, Ian Thomson and, in an emergency, Ken Palmer, who was coaching in South Africa and was called up, much as Tony Pigot would be some years later. Mike Brearley, another future 'Oxbridge' Test Match captain, had enjoyed a successful county season in 1964 and was included in the touring party, but he had an unhappy time and it would be some years before his Test Match debut. On paper, the side did not look particularly strong but *Wisden* suggested that it was as fine as any "in terms of corporate effort on the playing pitch and harmony in the pavilion", whereas the South Africans "paid for their traditional ingrained caution at cricket". The report also celebrated the absence of any contentious incidents and "the only winner was the game of cricket". On the other hand, by the end of that winter series, England had participated in eight drawn games in 10 consecutive Test Matches and editor, Gordon Ross, in the *Playfair Cricket Annual* asked, "Are Drawn Test Matches Damaging Cricket?" He suggested that for most captains, the first priority was to avoid losing and some "pretty humdrum" cricket was the result. In the 1965 *Wisden*, Sir Learie Constantine identified a "stalemate policy" that was stifling too many games although he suggested optimistically that it was a "passing phase". Decades later, *Wisden's* survey of the best 100 matches of the century included England's draw with the West Indies at Lord's in 1963 but only one match worldwide over the next five years, and that was Railways' world-record victory by an innings and 851 runs in Lahore in 1966 – one for the statisticians but otherwise of little interest outside India.

The **1965** English season offered little warmth and too much wet. For the first time since 1912 there were two touring teams although not, as then, competing in a triangular tournament. New Zealand lost all three Test

Matches and given the awful early season weather actually made a loss on the tour. The closest result, at Lord's, was an England victory by seven wickets and in the next at Headingley, John Edrich scored 310*, England's first triple century since the war. The great England all-rounder, Wally Hammond, who had also achieved the feat against the same opponents in 1933, died just a week before Edrich equalled his achievement. South Africa's three Test Matches began with a tight draw at Lord's, followed by a fine victory at Trent Bridge. Tom Cartwright reduced South Africa to 43–4 and 80–5 until Graeme Pollock hit a magnificent century, after which his brother returned match figures of 10–78 and South Africa's victory was enough to clinch the series. At the Oval England made an heroic attempt to score 399 to win but after reaching 308–4 with 70 minutes to play, the rains returned as they did so often through the 1960s – indeed it is worth observing that any hopes English cricket had of participating in the 'swinging sixties' was inhibited not least by it being the coldest, darkest and wettest decade of all the 20th century seasons in England. Colin Bland scored a century in that final drawn game but he made as much of an impression with his magnificent out-fielding and the series brought some life back to English Test Match grounds. None of the South Africans would return to represent their country in England.

In **1965,** Worcestershire won the County Championship for the second year running but there was a new team name on the Gillette Cup. Sussex had won the first two but on a damp morning at Lord's, Boycott astonished the cricket world scoring 146 against Surrey in a 60-overs total of 317–4. Their 11 players were all Yorkshire-born and Surrey, who crumbled to 142, also consisted entirely of Englishmen – the last time a Lord's Cup Final was competed for between two sides entirely English-born. In 1966 as Warwickshire beat Worcestershire, there was Basil D'Oliveira, 'Billy' Ibadulla and Rudi Webster, and in 1967 when Kent beat Somerset they included West Indian John Shepherd while 'Aussie' Bill Alley was still playing for Somerset in his late-40s.

In **1965**, Hampshire beat Norfolk and in the next round, Kent at Portsmouth, their first victory against a first-class side, after which they were drawn at Edgbaston again where they lost by 74 runs. It is an interesting comment on the perceived importance of the cup in those early years that it was not until the fourth season (1966) that they played a cup match at their Southampton headquarters, when in awful weather they had to wait until the second day to beat Lincolnshire. By then, bowlers could not exceed 12 overs each.

Brian Statham was awarded the CBE in January. During the season he led Lancashire and took 137 wickets at 12.52 each, but despite this was critical of the quality of County Championship pitches around the country. The New Zealand captain John Reid suggested that over the 16 years since he had first toured England most pitches, apart from Lord's, Fenners and the Kent grounds, had deteriorated "to an astonishing degree". Too much grass on pitches and lush outfields that preserved the ball's shine had encouraged a generation of medium pacers rather than genuine fast bowlers. In the same vein, 50 years later, an interview with former England coach, Andy Flower, on the Cricinfo site in November 2015, criticised poor Championship pitches as the cause of the decline in English spin bowling:

> Spin bowlers don't develop because the medium-pacers bowl their overs … but when you get to international cricket, the pitches are completely different and the qualities that proved successful in county cricket will be of little use. 'Dibbly-dobbly' bowlers are not going to win you Test matches; their abilities are exaggerated by green county pitches.

Perhaps this is an English problem that simply cannot be solved? Perhaps the new regulation on the toss for 2016 will achieve something? Back in **1965**, Boycott and Barber opened for England but neither made a County Championship century, while David Green set a record in passing 2,000 first-class runs without a single three-figure innings. *Wisden* listed the 15 poorest pitches include a number of county 'headquarters' and Test Match grounds at Edgbaston, Headingley and Trent Bridge. Their proposed remedy was "marl, cow manure and the heaviest possible roller".

The Almanack, now into its second century, was also troubled that the phrase "it's not cricket" was losing its meaning in the light of throwing controversies, an excess of short-pitched fast bowling and the increasing unwillingness of batsmen to 'walk' on knowing they are out. The problems seemed particularly apparent at the highest level. In the County Championship the main concern was contrived finishes through declarations, which the editor blamed mainly on slow scoring over the first two days. Clive Inman of Leicestershire set a 'world record' of dubious merit when, fed declaration bowling, he reached his half-century in just eight minutes. More crucially, chasing the title, Worcestershire scored 363–9 declared at Bournemouth and with delays for rain, Hampshire declared on the final day on 217–6. There were no forfeits in 1965, so Worcestershire faced one ball before declaring and Hampshire, needing 147 to win were dismissed in just 16 overs and three balls for 31, with five wickets each for Flavell and Len Coldwell. The chasing counties were not delighted by Ingleby-Mackenzie's sporting gesture.

The right to forfeit was introduced for the following season and other significant changes included a relaxation of fielders permitted on the leg-side – although only two were allowed behind the wicket, while the compulsory 75 yard boundary rule was relaxed. Most decisions were based on economic factors, not least that the 2.2 million spectators who had paid to watch county cricket in 1947 was now down to just over 650,000. County memberships remained higher than the 1940s as people had more disposable income, but even they had fallen by 5,000 from above 140,000 in 1964. There had been an experiment with Sunday play in an Australian state game and this would be introduced in England in 1966.

In the winter of 1965–1966 England toured Australia and drew the five match series 1–1, still unable to regain the Ashes. Barrington was outstanding but the gaps left by the departures of Trueman, Statham, Bailey, Tyson and Laker had not been filled. For Australia, Bill Lawry hit three centuries and three men averaged over 80 with a fourth 68.33. In 1965 England had selected 20 players in the six Test Matches, seeking the right combination for the tour. Among them was the enterprising opening batsman and occasional leg-spinner, Bob Barber. He had a reasonable but not outstanding, summer in 1965 and began the Ashes series as Boycott's partner with scores of 5, 34, 48 and 0* in the first two drawn matches. Then came Sydney, where England beat Australia for the first time in 11 matches. Boycott and Barber posted 234 for the first wicket before the Yorkshireman was out for 84. Edrich at number three maintained the dominance, scoring 103, but the match will always be remembered for Barber's 185 from 255 balls. He even added a wicket to finish the first Australian innings and, following-on they fell short, to lose by an innings and 93 runs. Barber's batting here was astonishing but sadly it was to be his only Test Match century. He played seven Ashes Test Matches without again reaching 50, and in his 28 Test Matches he finished with an average of 35.59 to which he added 42 wickets.

In the latter respect he was slightly unusual as yet another England 'Oxbridge' cricketer, since with the notable exception of Bailey and occasionally Dexter, they tended to be specialist batsmen. Barber played at Cambridge University from 1955–1957 and from his final 'Varsity' match at Lord's in 1957 he, and team-mates Dexter and 'Ossie' Wheatley, would all go on to captain county sides. We have noted that Mike Brearley would be another who would captain England and so too Mike Atherton, while more recently Nasser Hussain and Andrew Strauss were both graduates of Durham University. As I write at the end of 2015 however, England are engaged in a Test series against South Africa without a single university graduate and this is increasingly the case in English county cricket.

When players like Bailey, Sheppard, May, Cowdrey, Dexter, Smith and Barber were studying, there were relatively few universities in England and Wales, and while the Universities Athletic Union (UAU) organised its own competition, the small percentage of university students meant that most cricketers went on to county staffs before the age of 20 – even if they were then inter-rupted by National Service during the 1950s. But by the 21st century more than 40% of young people go to the many more universities that were created principally as 'red bricks' in the 1960s and the converted Polytechnics in the 1990s, so the MCC Universities initiative encouraged young men to secure a future while preparing themselves for a career in cricket. By 2015 that trend seemed to have changed again. The regional academies and/ or England age group sides tend to identify the best young cricketers very early, so that the majority now choose to study only until 18 and then pursue their sporting goals.

Thanks to their fine performance at Sydney, England led the Ashes series 1–0 after three matches, but the Australian captain, Simpson, (another opening bat and leg-spinner) led from the front with a double century, Barber made a 'duck' and only Barrington (60 & 102) resisted as Australia won by an innings. The fifth and final Test Match was drawn and the Ashes remained with the host nation although *Wisden* praised the approach of the tourists with the headline "positive cricket pays".

By **1966** Yorkshire were back on top of the County Championship, the first of a hat-trick of titles for that fine side. By then, the Gillette Cup was a fixture capturing broader public attention although the Finals were not necessarily thrilling. Worcestershire posted 155–8 in their 60 overs and Warwickshire got there with just five wickets down in the 57th over with only Barber (66) passing 20. The West Indies had returned, hopefully to rekindle the spirit of 1963. Once again, they were too good for England who selected 24 players in five matches, although there was some cheer in the return of the elegant batting of Graveney, who became the first England batsman aged 39 or more, to score a Test Match century since 'Patsy' Hendren in 1934. In addition, there was an English batsman with something of a Caribbean attitude in Colin Milburn of Northamptonshire, plus a stunning fight back by Sobers and his cousin, David Holford, at Lord's. After the visitors had won three of the first four Test Matches, England's new captain, Close, led them to victory at the Oval where Graveney and John Murray posted centuries and Snow and Ken Higgs added 128 for the 10th wicket. There was no winter Test Match tour and Close would return as England's captain in 1967 before losing the role in controversial circumstances. He also led Yorkshire to the County Championship.

By the mid-1960s two more changes had occurred in English cricket. Firstly, the brief experiment with covering County Championship wickets that began in 1959 had been abandoned and the bowlers, led by the youthful Derek Underwood, exploited any help from rain and sun. Secondly, some of the world's great players had begun to appear on British television with the International Cavaliers side. This organisation had toured various countries post-war but from 1965–1970 Godfrey Evans and Denis Compton arranged their matches around England on Sunday afternoons where they played 40-over matches, similar to a shortened Gillette Cup, against county sides and others. The crowds were often large and the teams included Dexter, Sobers, Compton, Pollock, Bailey, Hall, Griffith and Trueman. As well as large crowds, they made popular television viewing and established the rationale for three further major changes in English cricket in the late 1960s.

The first in **1966**, was Sunday play for the first time in County Championship matches; the second, two years later, the automatic registration of overseas stars to play in that Championship and then in 1969 the creation of the Sunday League, sponsored by John Player cigarettes. That required some legal 'negotiations', which effectively signalled the end of the Cavaliers in this country and the BBC switched to showing the county Sunday League every week.

The double series in 1965 had been arranged at haste to ensure the swift return of the West Indies for a full five-match tour the following year. **1966** was, of course, a great sporting summer but the main event on Saturday, 30 July 1966 featured England's footballers winning the World Cup, beating Germany 4–2 with the only Wembley hat-trick by a county cricketer.

Some weeks before that, on Saturday 15 May 1966, at Ilford, Essex dismissed Somerset for just 102 in the 55th over. Essex replied with 156 all out in the 49th over and Somerset had time to lose an opener for nought that night. The next day was a Sunday, and for the first time in English county cricket play resumed in the afternoon, allowing spectators to attend church and eat their Sunday roast before purchasing the one-day membership, which permitted entry on the Lord's Day. The irony of the two first innings is that they were also part of a hare-brained scheme to enliven county cricket by limiting them in some matches to 65 overs. In the event neither team needed them in this match but on the Sunday, Somerset made a better fist of things, reaching 239–3 in a shortened day. They continued on the Monday and declared, setting Essex 290 to win. Many of the weekend spectators, now back at work, missed a thrilling finish as Essex fell just four runs short after 91 overs.

Sunday play, of course, would remain and prosper. The 65 overs first innings limit was dumped after one season although longer limitations were tried in subsequent years. In his 1970 autobiography *Test Outcast,* Roy Marshall described the limitation, introduced during his first year as captain in 12 County Championship matches for each side, as "ridiculous" despite

Hampshire's patent advantage in having three top seamers, Shackleton, White and Cottam, who could exploit the regulation. The consequence of this "harmful" regulation was that middle order batsmen and spin bowlers barely featured and nowhere is this better exemplified than in the season of Hampshire's promising young off-spinning all-rounder, Keith Wheatley.

He played in the first County Championship match, one of these restricted games, but neither batted nor bowled in the first innings. Hampshire scored 197 in their first innings and Somerset 109 but the key difference was that Somerset were all out whereas Hampshire's innings was closed with just four wickets down yet they were unable to force a victory. In the next match, Wheatley at number seven scored 11 but did not bat in the first innings of the next two matches. He scored 12 in an interesting game at Trent Bridge, where Nottinghamshire 185–8 trailed Hampshire 200–9 but managed to set them 238 to win (Wheatley bowling at last in a *second* innings, took 1–47). Next, at Portsmouth against Leicestershire, Wheatley came in at 161–6 and scored 10 as the innings ended on 189 with two overs remaining. Again, there was no first innings involvement at Dudley, then at Sussex he came in with Hampshire 64–6 and top-scored with 33 – but still there was no chance to bowl, and there was no employment at Old Trafford until the second innings of a defeat in what the Handbook called a "grim performance". Wheatley lost his place towards the end of the season but he did play in 23 matches overall and despite not bowling in *any* of these limited first innings, ended with 31 wickets at less than 30 apiece, as well as 441 runs at just under 20 per innings. He clearly showed some promise but this was no way to develop such a young player. Shackleton, White and Cottam took 287 wickets between them that season – each at under 19.

Wisden 1967 as usual reported mainly on the previous 12 months, but also included an article by Charles Bray headed "Counties Reject the Clark Plan" in which the author rather gloomily suggested that the rejection of the main proposal was "so emphatic" that the 17 counties "may have signed their own death warrant". That was almost 50 years ago yet all 17 (plus one) are still functioning. The chairman, DG Clark, was a former Kent captain and current chairman of his county's cricket committee and alongside him were senior figures past and present including GO 'Gubby' Allen, ER Dexter, DJ Insole, AB Sellers, WS Surridge, EH King (chairman of Warwickshire), OS Wheatley, FJ Titmus, three county secretaries: CG Howard (Surrey), KC Turner (Northamptonshire) and GM Turner (Leicestershire), plus Charles Bray who had played for Essex pre-war and then became a cricket correspondent. They met first in September 1965 and finally in January 1967 after which the report was submitted.

Bray described the rationale for the committee and its proposals entirely in terms of the dramatic fall in paying customers for county cricket and the recent slight decline in membership figures – this was, and remains, the underlying motive for all committees of enquiry, proposals and changes. He suggested that the only things keeping county cricket alive were supporters' clubs (especially through football pools) and Test Match revenue, including broadcasting fees, distributed via the Test and County Cricket Board (TCCB). The brief was very broad and the responses of the counties to the questions, intriguing. Seven favoured the existing structure, eight did not and two were not certain, whereas only three counties felt able to guarantee fast, true pitches, only four were broadly content with the attitudes of their players and just two with those of opponents.

Two observations that did receive significant support were that sub-standard pitches produced sub-standard cricket and that playing on Sundays was wholly desirable. During the summer of 1966, the committee, through *the Daily Mail* and National Opinion Polls, undertook a public survey to discover reasons for the decline in attendances. They also received survey results from county members and from over 100 county cricketers and convened a meeting of county groundsmen. The broad views confirmed that pitches and dull cricket were a problem within the game while what Bray described as "counter attractions and present national social habits" were drawing people *to* other activities as much as *away from* county cricket. One concern was to establish a clearer pyramid enabling players to graduate from club to county cricket, which had become a problem postwar and particularly since the abolition of the amateur/professional divide.

The findings were not unique to this period although perhaps the charge of negative approaches to the game was stronger then than it might need to be today. The report suggested that players, especially "leading players", were playing too much cricket and it rejected a proposal to extend the season to mid-September to accommodate a 32 match County Championship. In 2016 the final matches will conclude in the last week of September. Other ideas rejected included two-day, single-innings matches, seven three-day Test Matches per season, the complete covering of pitches, and no second new ball in any single innings.

The first report appeared in March 1966 and offered recommendations divided into short and long-term. The former included the 65-over limit in some County Championship first innings. Perhaps the clear failure of this experiment did not help in the Report's second and final version? Among other proposals came an improvement in pitches to be hard and fast; covering of pitches as in Test Matches prior to the start, each night and whenever play is abandoned for the day; an improvement in over rates to 20 per hour; no polishing of the ball by the fielding side; a slight change to points awarded; and various suggestions about umpires and discipline. Longer term, the committee suggested a minimum of just 16 three-day County Championship matches although counties might make separate arrangements to play a few more matches. This was not wholly clear as it was followed with two distinct proposals, for a 16 or 20 match County Championship plus a 16 match limited-overs league with, in either case, the Gillette Cup remaining as it was. They were, of course, anticipating the Sunday League by just three years and indeed the County Championship was cut to 20 matches to accommodate that so the structural change came, albeit slightly slower than they wished.

The second report appeared just before Christmas 1966 and began by noting that during that season attendances had declined further, as had the quality of county pitches. The over-rate had improved marginally but not to make any difference to public perception, and the covering regulations proposal had not been accepted. There was a view that "many spectators" seemed to have enjoyed the limited County Championship matches but they were discontinued because it encouraged negative play and inhibited the progress of middle order batsmen and spin bowlers. The change in points (10 for a win and two for first innings lead) had not encouraged positive cricket and overall the committee reiterated its criticisms of county cricket in the first report. The report then made three key Recommendations:

1. A County Championship of 16 three-day matches
2. A limited-overs County Championship of 16 one-day matches
3. The continuation of the Gillette Cup

The report suggested that two of the principal reasons for the poor entertainment value were the "continuous grind of six days per week cricket" and the fear among *professional* players that their livelihoods depend on their averages and figures. It is interesting to note that the players responded to a PCA survey in 2015 effectively citing the demands of the weekly "grind" despite the fact that they were now averaging fewer than four days per week and, unlike 1966, enjoying 12 months contracts.

The counties met at Lord's on 25 January 1967 and rejected the first two proposals. Bray reported varying comments from them: Hampshire rejected them all for at least three years and Glamorgan's secretary described them as "a lot of tommy rot", while Sussex went contrary to the report by suggesting more first-class cricket. Derbyshire feared the changes would lose them 10% of members, and Northamptonshire thought 50%.

Wisden suggested that England was now the only cricket-playing country where the game was not flourishing, adding, "the standard of English first-class cricket has never been so low". He too supported the view that while high quality pitches were not a simple panacea, they were essential to drive any improvement in standards and entertainment value. He made clear that the five-day working week, annual holidays, the motor car and television were all factors to be considered, although the first two might help counties to attract more support. He implied that one of the problems for the Clark Report was "for 20 years we have had one change after another" so that it was "small wonder that the ordinary follower of the game has become so utterly confused". Not for the first time he regretted the change in the lbw law in 1935, which he believed had led to "the ruination of attractive batting" and he described the limitation of 65 overs in the County Championship as "the final abomination". Sunday cricket, however, remained and over the decades, with changes in legislation, the decline in church-going and a willingness to be more flexible with eating, home or away, it is now taken for granted as just another day in the calendar. Attendances on Sundays may have been helped too by the growth of Saturday league cricket across the country accompanied by a subsequent decline in Sunday friendly matches.

Sunday county cricket might have attracted more spectators but it did not necessarily guarantee thrilling entertainment and probably the worst example occurred at Lord's in July **1967** when three days (Saturday-Monday) failed to reach a conclusion even on the first innings. Hampshire scored 421–7 declared in 145 overs, batting just over an hour into the Sunday, with centuries by Marshall and Livingstone and Middlesex were 126–4 at the close so spectators on a shorter Sunday had seen just 193 runs. On the final day, Middlesex concluded on 371–7 in 173 overs (Clive Radley 100*). The press and a number of suffering spectators wrote, condemning the match.

Marshall discussed it extensively in his autobiography and in part blamed the chase for first innings bonus points. But he added a comment about the pitch, which had offered little encouragement to the bowlers throughout. Shackleton once again took over 100 wickets in 1967 but on that Lord's pitch where he was often successful he took 1–84 in 50 overs, while England off-spinner Fred Titmus also managed just one wicket in 33 overs. While uncovered wickets had returned, in a weekend unaffected by the weather in mid-summer that would have no significance. Marshall believed that pitches in England had declined in quality throughout the 1950s and 1960s with many counties producing pitches to suit them – particularly their bowlers. As a consequence, the first of the pitch inspectors would appear before the end of the 1970s although variations remained with the number of outgrounds and the covering regulations.

India and Pakistan visited in **1967** on the next 'double' touring season. India came first and endured quite appalling weather in the wettest May since 1773. They lost all three Test Matches, after which Pakistan drew the first before losing the second and third. Suddenly, Close's England side had won six and drawn one of seven Test Matches, and at the end of the summer Boycott and Barrington averaged in the 90s, D'Oliveira 63 and Graveney 58, while Illingworth had 23 wickets at 14 each and Higgs 18 at 18. England even had a leg-spinner, with Robin Hobbs taking 10 wickets overall and while only one was in the Pakistan series, he conceded just 74 runs in his 51 overs. Despite Boycott's successes he was dropped after the first Test Match of the summer after scoring 246* in England's 550–4 declared. *Wisden* reported that "his lack of enterprise met with much disapproval" but after one match he returned. Whether the selectors would have taken the same action in an Ashes series is unclear, but they successfully sued Michael Parkinson and Times Newspapers for publishing an article critical of their decision.

Another Yorkshireman met controversy in a county match. Close had done all that might be asked of an England captain and was preparing to lead his county to the title and his country to the West Indies the following winter. In mid-August he took Yorkshire to Edgbaston. Warwickshire had no prospect of the title but gave Yorkshire a tough game, with their 242 just four runs ahead on first innings, so when they dismissed Yorkshire for 145 they need 142 to win in one-hour-and-forty-minutes. Even at current desultory over rates that might have meant 27 overs, in 1967 more like 30, yet Yorkshire's delaying tactics provided just 24, including two in the final 15 minutes when at one point they left the field during a shower while the batsmen and umpires remained. Warwickshire finished on 133–5, and Yorkshire took the two points for a draw. In the event they were not needed as Yorkshire led Kent by 10 points at the season's end, but Close was censured for his tactics, lost the England captaincy, and Cowdrey led the tourists to the West Indies. In the 1960s there were no longer any 'amateurs' but the professionals were certainly expected to know their place.

Despite a general light-heartedness in much of the country, English cricket rather more reflected the concerns of politicians and economists about the financial future. There was a change of control at the head of English cricket, following the agreement of the Labour Government to make public grants available to sports organisations. In order to proceed, English cricket could no longer be run by a private members' club, however benign, and so the MCC – apart from retaining international control for the Laws of Cricket – handed control to the TCCB, which would now manage the first-class game, with the newly-formed National Cricket Association responsible for all the levels beneath that, notably the coaching of young people.

In September **1967**, the fans of Kent and Somerset challenged Lord's formality with all kinds of agricultural decorations, and the Somerset fans offered an early example of the now increasingly ubiquitous 'fancy dress'. In those days tickets were hard to come by and it was a great occasion, yet in what some felt was the 'best' final to date, Kent's 193 all out in the 60th over beat Somerset's 161 – although they did fall away from 129–4. However thrilling the competition might be, the simple fact was that nine counties would play only two matches each season – and normally one of those would be early season against a Minor County side. In the oddest match of 1967, Yorkshire should have played Cambridgeshire on 13 May. The weather was so awful that they ended up 11 days later at Castleford, resolving a match of just 10 overs each, as Yorkshire chased down a target of 44.

Wisden was again somewhat pessimistic about county cricket, suggesting that the general low standard of batting had not improved, while too many contracted players were "indifferent" to the game's well-being. Leslie Deakin, the secretary of Warwickshire, proposed a significant shift to weekend cricket when people can watch, which would enable his county to cut playing staff costs from around £25,000 in 1966 to about £10,000, thereby bridging the gap in their current deficit. The weather did not help county cricket in the season but 161 drawn matches exceeded significantly the previous highest number since the second world war, which was 112 in 1962. There was one tie, at Portsmouth where Bob Herman of Middlesex, son of Hampshire's 'Lofty', and a future Hampshire bowler, dismissed Bob Cottam with the final ball. It rather made up for the Lord's misery of a few weeks earlier.

Over the next two seasons, English cricket made two major decisions that have transformed it in the years since. In **1968** each county was permitted to sign one overseas player on an immediate contract, and unlike Roy Marshall and others, that player was able to maintain his Test Match career, which in those days was almost entirely in the English winter unless his country was touring England. In 1969 the success of the televised International Cavaliers matches led to the creation and weekly televising of the Sunday League, adding another sponsor's name to an English trophy. Another overseas side that arrived in England in 1968 came from the USA. They had competed in the first international match against Canada, but had since grown fonder of baseball. In 2015, Shane Warne and Sachin Tendulkar were among those still trying to encourage the game to flourish in that vast country.

Most of the overseas players who arrived in 1968 were high quality players and, unlike today, they often settled for full seasons and even longer periods with their counties. In that first season they were Keith Boyce (Essex), Majid Khan (Glamorgan), Mike Procter (Gloucestershire), Barry Richards

(Hampshire), Asif Iqbal (Kent), Farokh Engineer (Lancashire), Mustaq Mohammad (Northamptonshire), Garry Sobers (Nottinghamshire), Greg Chappell (Somerset), Younis Ahmed (Surrey), Geoff Greenidge (Sussex), Rohan Kanhai and Lance Gibbs (Warwickshire) and Glenn Turner and Vanburn Holder (Worcestershire). Quite how the latter two clubs managed at that point to sign two men is unclear, but it would soon become quite common with the arrival of 'extra' recruits like Zaheer Abbas, Sadiq Mohammad, Andy Roberts, Bishen Bedi, and Viv Richards.

While the majority of these cricketers enriched the viewing experience, questions would be asked about their impact on young English cricketers. The argument 'for' their presence was part economic and part influence; the argument against, that they deprived home grown players of opportunities *and* they became familiar with English conditions, which they would encounter on Test tours. The argument was never clearly resolved and with the proliferation of European passports and the 'Kolpack' ruling, it is often unclear today exactly who might count as 'English'. As a consequence, England, over the past quarter-of-a-century, have picked men like Graeme Hick, Robin Smith, Allan Lamb, Kevin Pietersen, Matt Prior and Andrew Strauss whose birthplaces makes them eligible to have played for another country.

Garry Sobers was considered the greatest draw among the new overseas players and at the end of the 1968 season in a County Championship match at Swansea he set a world record, hitting Glamorgan's Malcolm Nash for six sixes in one over. He declared on 76* still with nine minutes to beat Jessop's fastest century record. Some sad news concerning his fellow countryman came with the premature death of Sir Frank Worrell in Jamaica at the age of just 42. He had done so much to breathe life into cricket since taking on the captaincy of the West Indies, and Sir Learie Constantine paid tribute in *Wisden*. A couple of months before that, Sydney Barnes, who was perhaps the most complicated and finest of all England bowlers, died in his native Staffordshire at the age of 94.

Of the 17 counties, only Derbyshire, Leicestershire, Middlesex and Yorkshire did not sign a new overseas player immediately. Derbyshire quickly turned to Chris Wilkins, Leicestershire to Graham McKenzie and Middlesex to Alan Connolly but Yorkshire, on principle, held out for some time. Over the 10 years from 1959 only Hampshire and Worcestershire (twice) had interrupted their County Championship successes and even with these new stars everywhere, they would win it again in **1968**.

In that season, the original limited-overs specialists Sussex reached their third of just six Cup Finals to-date, but lost to Warwickshire by four wickets and the midlands county drew level with them on two trophies each. Dennis Amiss (44*) and AC Smith (39*) took them to victory from the difficulties of 155–6 with an undefeated partnership of 60. The two major Universities continued to play first-class cricket and Cambridge fielded Mike Brearley, Roger Knight and David Acfield who would all enjoy good first-class careers. The very fine England bowler, Brian Statham retired while Fred Trueman had fewer than 50 wickets for the Champions and he, too, did not reappear in 1969 although he played occasionally for Derbyshire in limited-overs matches. Trevor Bailey who played with Trueman when England regained the Ashes in 1953 also retired after many years fine service for England, Essex and Cambridge University. Five years after the end of amateur status, the MCC admitted current and former *paid* players to membership for the first time. The senior men in the first cohort were Jack Robertson of Middlesex and Leo Harrison of Hampshire who had both played pre-war. Leo Harrison and his occasional amateur teammate, John Manners, are now the only two survivors from county cricket in the 1930s.

Colin Cowdrey became the first man to appear in 100 Test Matches. His England side returned from the West Indies for the summer of **1968** having triumphed after a generous brave, or perhaps even reckless, declaration by Sobers in Trinidad but they could not regain the Ashes, which remained out of reach throughout the 1960s. They had endured a 'riot' in Jamaica and they did win the final Ashes Test Match at the Oval, after spectators had helped to dry the ground on the final day. There is the famous photograph of Underwood taking the last wicket with the batsman surrounded by the England fielders, which brought to a close England's home Ashes Test Matches of the 1960s. England's footballers, pop singers and photographers might be World Champions, but their cricketers had won just two of 15 home Test Matches against the oldest opponents, one in July 1961 and the other more than seven years later. They lost four matches in the three series and nine were drawn. With no cricket World Cup, most English fans took the Ashes as the measure of cricketing supremacy on which basis Australia were well ahead throughout the 1960s. Derek Underwood was nominated as one of *Wisden's* Five Cricketers of the Year partly on the statistic that in six years, and at the age of 23, he had taken almost 750 first-class wickets – more than most cricketers take today in a career.

Even that late victory presented more problems than benefits. England built their victory on a substantial first innings of 494, thanks mainly to 164 by John Edrich and 158 by Basil D'Oliveira. D'Oliveira had played in the first of the five Test Matches which Australia won by 159 runs but was then dropped despite scoring 9 & 87* and taking 2–45 in the match. Recalled for the last match, he contributed a further wicket and headed the batting averages at nearly

90 per innings. Somehow this was not sufficient to warrant selection for the tour to South Africa and Tom Cartwright, who did not play against Australia, was selected instead. D'Oliveira was a batting all-rounder, Cartwright of the bowling variety, but when Cartwright withdrew through injury, D'Oliveira was called into the squad. The South African Government intervened, refusing to accept him as a member of the touring party and the tour was cancelled. Those are the bald facts of a case that is well known and does not warrant repetition here; the case is clearly covered in the relevant copies of *Wisden* and in an excellent book by Peter Oborne. The South Africans would enjoy one last glorious home series against Australia the winter after this and then would endure two decades of sporting Apartheid themselves.

Unsurprisingly, *Wisden*'s editor identified **1968** as an "exasperating year" although he felt that despite the endless rain he saw "much improvement" in the County Championship which he attributed to two innovations: the arrival of the overseas stars and the bonus points system in the first innings of the County Championship. This was the third change in three years, with the abolition of points for first innings lead, replaced by points for runs scored and wickets taken. That system is still in place albeit with many adjustments over the years. The editor identified Garry Sobers as the outstanding overseas personality, mentioning, of course, his six sixes in a Malcolm Nash over at Swansea although in the following year, it was Nash and Glamorgan who would celebrate the County Championship title, not Sobers' Nottinghamshire.

1969 saw another double tour by New Zealand and the West Indies. England won both series 2–0 with one draw in each three-match series. With Hall and Griffith gone, and another wet start to the season, the West Indies' attack was less fearsome and was out-bowled by Snow, David Brown and Barry Knight. Boycott scored two centuries but Sobers managed a top score of just 50*. Cowdrey was unfit so Ray Illingworth began a long spell as England's next captain in the first Test Match at Old Trafford. Tom Graveney celebrated his 42nd birthday on the fourth day (Monday) having scored 75 in the first innings over days one and two. The day itself was limited to about one hour's play but Graveney had little cause for rejoicing; on the previous (rest) day he had taken part in one of his benefit matches, against the regulations of the TCCB and the instructions of the selectors, and this proved to be his last appearance for England. Another professional had been dealt with and John Hampshire was called into the next match, scoring a century on debut.

In the series against New Zealand there were outstanding performances by Edrich and Underwood. Despite his centuries in the summer's first two Test

Matches, Boycott then endured a sequence of three noughts in five innings but he retained his place.

Graveney's benefit was interesting because the convention had been for some years for players to be awarded the honour after 10 years as a 'capped' professional. Graveney had played 12 years for Gloucestershire and his benefit with them in 1959 realised the considerable tax-free sum of £5,400. He joined Worcestershire in 1961 and was 'capped' the following season so after just seven years he received this second benefit. He retired from English county cricket in 1970. Ten years was no more than a 'convention' but it was generally held to although at Hampshire, Roy Marshall arrived in 1953, qualified to play in competitive matches and was 'capped' in 1955 and received his benefit in 1961. Peter Sainsbury, 'capped' the same year, waited until 1965 for his benefit. In the 21st century, the 10 years convention is frequently ignored.

On the domestic scene, *Wisden* described the new Sunday League as "an instant success" while warning that it must never be seen as a "substitute" for "genuine first-class cricket". Roy Marshall celebrated it for its "record attendances" that led to "a much-needed cash boost" and the fact that cricket became a topic of conversation again. To those "traditionalists" who argued that the 40-over game was not 'cricket', he stressed that it was "entertainment", adding, "if professional cricket is to survive it must offer the goods which the public want". He also discussed the idea of 16 four-day County Championship matches, probably played mid-week, with two limited-overs matches on Saturday and Sunday. He supported the proposal for four days and also wanted "two divisions of the one day league with promotion and relegation".

The Sunday League made its debut on 27 April **1969** as Lancashire travelled to Hove and the two Kens, Shuttleworth and Higgs dismissed both Sussex openers and Tony Greig for nought. Jim Parks made 70, but the home team and first successful limited-overs side lost by five wickets to the team that would not merely inherit their mantle but would do so in emphatic fashion over the next few seasons.

Wisden carried a tribute to Enid Bakewell who, on an England Women's tour of Australia and New Zealand in 1968–1969, had completed the 'double' of 1,000 runs and 100 wickets. The editor celebrated the recent changes in English cricket, while hoping there might now be 10 years free from tampering with the Laws and structure. He referred to the repeated calls for 16 four-day County Championship matches but expressed concern that these might be rather dull. Writing three months before the start of the **1970** season he was unsure whether South Africa would tour England. As usual, the *Playfair Cricket*

Annual offered pen-pictures and fixtures for that season's tourists but in the event, of course, the South Africans never arrived. That generation of Test players had welcomed Australia in the winter and won every match of the four-match series. The experienced Graeme Pollock scored 517 runs at 73.85 but debutant Barry Richards pushed him hard with 508 at 72.57. Mike Procter averaged nearly 35 with the bat and took 26 wickets at 13.57. They were an awesome side and might well have dominated Test cricket for some years. The thought of seeing them contest a series with the mid-1970s West Indians is intriguing but, of course, that could not have happened even before 1970 – and it was not the least of the reasons why the tour was stopped.

I use that phrase deliberately. As in 1961 and 1965 most of the cricket establishment wished to welcome the tourists 'despite' the political situation. But by 1970, a consensus of broadly left-of-centre activists had learned about political protest and united under the banner "Stop the Tour". They were able to draw on the influence of the 'events' involving a coalition of students and workers in Paris from May 1968, while the British variety had mounted significant protests against the Vietnam War in the spring and again in October 1968 leading to a confrontation with the police in Grosvenor Square. It is not the case, however, that the whole country opposed racial injustice. In that same, somewhat tempestuous, year the Conservative MP Enoch Powell made his notorious 'Rivers of Blood" speech, warning about the impact of increasing immigration and creating a furore. Edward Heath sacked him from his Shadow Cabinet, suggesting that the speech could only "exacerbate racial tensions". *The Times* called it "evil" but some London Dockers went on strike to protest against Powell's sacking and a Gallup Poll found almost 75% of British people supported what Powell had said. The question of race was wrapped up with that of immigration, often in dramatic or dangerous ways. The cricket establishment avoided any involvement in that debate and while they deplored the South African situation that did not prevent them from insisting that sport and politics, even at a national level, should be kept separate.

Despite this unhappy situation, by the end of the 1960s, cricket seemed to be offering more entertainment and excitement, as if it was at last catching up with the rest of the country. This was especially the case in the northwest where Liverpool had been at the heart of a different kind of 'cultural revolution' a few years earlier. For decades Lancashire's fans had looked back with longing on the years when they won County Championships regularly but at least in 1969 Jack Bond's side won the first John Player Sunday League title, and they won it again in 1970. Between then and 1975 they also won four Gillette Cup Lord's Finals – six limited-overs titles in seven years.

In **1969,** Glamorgan's victory against Essex with a last-ball run out enabled them, in the following match, to clinch their second County Championship title and bring to an end for many years the dominance of Yorkshire – or indeed any other one county. Through the 1960s county teams unable to knock Yorkshire from their County Championship perch could at least hope to win the Gillette Cup or, at the end, the John Player League, and by the end of that decade there had been limited-overs trophies for Sussex, Kent, Lancashire and Warwickshire as well as County Championship titles for Hampshire, Worcestershire and Glamorgan.

The 'swinging sixties' were over. English cricket had often struggled to capture the mood but by the end of that decade, with new competitions in place and a younger international generation of exciting cricketers, there might be a brighter future.

Chapter Four: the 1970s

Throughout the 1960s and early 1970s English cricket transformed a professional game that was in danger of expiring through lack of interest and excitement. Many of the changes were direct responses to economic concerns but to a large extent they were implemented alongside respect for some of the greater traditions, in particular Test Matches and the County Championship. The 1970s saw the introduction of ODIs but not excessively, and they were focused mainly on the first World Cups. The County Championship was still played on a variety of grounds on uncovered pitches and while many of the master batsmen enjoyed considerable success, they did so against some very fine and varied bowling.

It is true that the County Championship needed good pitches and appropriate weather to be at its best and this was not always the case, especially in England. It is true also that English cricket typically struggled to produce top quality bowlers of the highest pace. English cricket was not perfect – it never has been, and it never will be. It may be that the Benson & Hedges (B&H) Cup was a competition too far, but from 1969 until1971 the balance of Test Matches, the County Championship, the Sunday League and the Gillette Cup achieved something fine. They offered different versions of the game that would continue to please the traditional cricket supporters while creating new forms of the game, which appealed to a 'new' audience. Neither was it the case that these were necessarily discrete audiences. Some wished to watch only the longer or shorter forms, but many cricket lovers enjoyed both, and some who came to county cricket for the first time to watch 80 overs on a Sunday afternoon, developed a fondness for the longer games. All the matches in the various competitions were played in daylight with a red ball and white clothing, offering a balance of tradition and innovation appealing to the desire for novelty and nostalgia, which characterises entertainment in modern western societies.

If this makes English cricket at that time appear to be enlightened, progressive, and ahead of the game, perhaps it was. We are rarely inclined to credit English cricket with such attributes, partly because it seems that every decision made is driven almost wholly by economics or increasingly 'player-power' and partly because supporters tend to see those who control English cricket as drawn wholly from the 'establishment' – whether the old 'upper class' guard at Lord's or the newer meritocratic merchants who are currently tenants at Lord's. To some degree, for 15 years from 1972, English cricket offered a balance of competitions that appealed to the traditionalists and the 'fun seekers' in a way that no other professional sport did. But even in that relatively settled period, it went on tinkering and changing until we reached the battle for county cricket's future, perhaps even its soul, in 2015. It seems that on one side are the England & Wales Cricket Board (ECB) reformers, the cricketers and a few county executives and/or chairmen, and on the other, the loyal county members, many of whom feel increasingly disenfranchised but are seen too often as a 'problem' while English cricket chases a 'potential' new market.

More of that later, but let us hold for now with the idea that the diversity which professional cricket offered as a spectator sport in the 1970s both anticipated and reflected the same diversity of desire in the broader entertainment culture. Cricket was helped greatly in this by another element of popular culture – the television screen. Regular Test Match broadcasts began in the 1950s but televised county cricket was a relatively new phenomenon, and after a few experiments with County Championship matches, the companies (mostly the BBC) settled for one-day county and five-day Test Matches. In their early days, ITV's regional stations had shown some County Championship matches, but the appearance of *World of Sport* in 1965, with front-men, Eamonn Andrews, and then Dickie Davis, saw the commercial channel favouring horse-racing or TV-friendly sports like wrestling. Fred Trueman had a 'roving reporter's' role and in 1973 he landed another job as host of ITV's *Indoor League* – a mixture of northern working-class sports like bar billiards and darts, but he had to move to BBC radio and *Test Match Special (TMS)* before he was invited to offer his cricketing experience and wisdom, by which time, on his own admission, he was not always sure what was happening "out there".

The 1970s was an odd time – in certain respects both the best and the worst. While unemployment rose, credit became more freely available; while entertainment became more lavish, the rubbish piled up in the streets. On television, in particular, there was still a market for the best of the old variety acts like Ken Dodd or Morecambe & Wise. Nostalgia for an imagined past also drew large audiences for *Upstairs Downstairs, Dad's Army, Poldark* or *The Duchess of Duke Street,* while *The Good Old Days* ran for 30 years from the early 1950s. Game Shows grew in popularity in the 1970s, probably headed by *The Generation Game*, while quiz shows included *Mastermind* and the BBC's *Question of Sport,* launched in December 1968. Fans of TV 'Cop' shows like *Dixon of Dock Green* or *Z Cars* now had a tougher, more violent 1970s hit in *The Sweeney,* while the greed and acquisitiveness of the 1980s was anticipated in the American series *Dallas.*

In the 1960s many of the new wave of popular entertainers like Bob Dylan or the Rolling Stones had rejected traditional 'showbiz glamour' in favour of promoting an image of authenticity. But in the popular music of the 1970s, the excesses of many rock bands, the 'glam' images of Marc Bolan and David Bowie or the newer sounds of the synthesisers re-imposed a certain 'distance' between performers and their audiences. Authenticity was sought in the growing popularity for reggae, spearheaded by Bob Marley while black soul music became more lavish in the discos and more 'streetwise' in the early versions of rap. As ever, in the 'modern' world the younger generation found new heroes, whether in the heavier rock and pop acts or the new teenybopper attractions of David Cassidy, the Osmonds and the Bay City Rollers. There was also nostalgia for a mythical rock & roll past created in the records of the Rubettes, Showaddywaddy and Mud, or 1970s movies like *That'll Be the Day, American Graffiti, Quadrophenia* and *Grease.* Nostalgia even brought a 'pop' revival to the Christmas market that had been largely ignored by the sharpest pop stars of the 1960s. In the 1970s it returned, through the extravagant efforts of Slade, Wizzard, Greg Lake and others. For some people, even the young, the future was coming too quickly and there was comfort in the older certainties, including the relative innocence of their own parents' rock & roll rebellion.

It was not all fun of course. The United States continued its war in Vietnam under the 'leadership' of a corrupt President, and the UK was living with an escalation of the Irish 'troubles'. Alongside pop and television's nostalgia came the post-satire popularity of the Monty Python gang, while Germaine Greer's *Female Eunuch* led the popular front of Feminism's second wave. In the cinema, neither *Clockwork Orange,* nor the excesses of director Ken Russell, made for 'easy' viewing. There were economic crises and oil crises; there was escalating trouble in the Middle East; and around the corner loomed something called Punk.

The 1970s seemed to be extending many of the unanticipated develop-ments in 1960s British society, particularly involving young people, while popular entertainment explored new and increasingly lucrative projects. In 1971 Britain's currency went decimal and that 1960s dream, the Open University welcomed its first students. By the mid-1970s some young men in Britain had turned away from the shaven-headed violence of the skinheads and were sporting an androgynous look. Even cricketers began to sport longer hair although in some cases they asserted their masculinity with moustaches and 'sideburns'. Longhaired Jackie Stewart won three Formula One titles between 1969–1973 before retiring. At one point, the 'mullet' of a popular England football star developed a bubbly 'perm'.

The Conservative Government, which came to power in 1970 in a surprise victory, was fighting 'enemies within'. Heath's cabinet suffered in a bruising encounter with the Miners' Union and the return of serious sectarian violence on the streets of Northern Ireland reached the pubs and streets of mainland England – in 1971 the first British soldier was killed in the province, the IRA bombed the Post Office Tower and a policy of internment without trial was introduced. In January 1972, British soldiers shot and killed civil rights demonstrators in what was known as 'Bloody Sunday'. Mainland terrorism escalated in 1974 with bombs and deaths in Westminster, Guildford and Birmingham, and in 1979 an IRA bomb killed Earl Mountbatten of Burma.

In October 1974 the Labour party returned to power, which was effectively the end of Edward Heath's time in charge of the Conservatives. In February 1975, Margaret Thatcher became the first woman to lead a major political party. Four years later she would become Britain's first (and so far only) woman prime minister. The Labour Government held a referendum on Europe in 1975 and the British people chose to remain members. During the late 1970s Wilson's and Callaghan's Government battled inflation, which rose to 25%. Struggling with increasing wage demands, it began to battle with itself until Britain moved towards the late 1970s 'Winter of Discontent', just as world cricket faced its own serious discontents from its workforce.

During the summer of 1975, the entertainment world was terrorised by the cinematic release of Steven Spielberg's *Jaws*. It was the highest-grossing film in history until superseded by *Star Wars* a couple of years later and set a new pattern for mass advertising and mass releases leading to quick (and in this case) sustained profits. During the winter of 1975–1976 there was no England cricket tour, but at home, emerging from the Chelsea boutique SEX owned by Vivienne Westwood and Malcolm Maclaren, a group called the Sex Pistols began performing mostly around London. Their first major review appeared in the music paper the *NME (New Musical Express)* when their guitarist Steve Jones took the opportunity to confirm "Actually we're not into music; we're into chaos." On the weekend of 24 and 25 April 1976, the English cricket season opened with the first matches in the B&H Cup and then the Sunday League, and the following day the first album by New York punk rockers, The Ramones, was released. It would be some years before cricketers like James Anderson and Kevin Pietersen emulated the punks, appearing with brightly coloured hair, but cricketing chaos was just around the corner – initially for England's players and then on an international scale.

In other sports, in 1971 Arsenal were the first 20th century football team to complete the League and FA Cup 'double'. England lost to West Germany in the 1970 World Cup finals after their captain Bobby Moore had been charged with theft, while Pele's Brazil won another Final. Alf Ramsey's great mid-1960s side broke up before England failed to reach the 1974 finals, won by West Germany, and they have yet to reach another tournament Final. At the Munich Olympic Games of 1972, Arab Terrorists killed two Israeli athletes and held others hostage. In the shoot-out that resulted, the terrorists were all killed. Wimbledon Tennis accepted professionals and, through the 1970s stars like Jimmy Connors, Bjorn Bork and Chris Evert, won a number of the major trophies although there was a boost for British tennis with the women's title won by Virginia Wade in 1977. In April 1974 Michael O'Brien ran naked onto the field at Twickenham – Britain's first 'streaker' at a major sporting event. His act was emulated on a number of occasions including Test Matches, once memorably described on air by John Arlott. West End theatre land enjoyed the revival of musicals – particularly those of cricket-loving Tim Rice and his musical partner Andrew Lloyd Webber. Away from popular culture, some architects turned away from the austerity and purity of modernism towards post-modern decorative styles. Fun was fun, perhaps because the economic, social and labour situation was anything but fun: Crisis, What Crisis?

Cricket joined in, live and on television. From 1969, British television showed far more cricket than ever before and when the B&H Cup, the ODIs and the World Cup arrived, the number of broadcast matches increased, although the County Championship remained notable largely by its absence. With club and school cricket increasingly adopting the limited-overs model, playing for time and playing for a draw was rather less an element of cricket as a whole outside the professional higher levels, which probably had a significant impact on what some spectators expected – more 'glam', more decoration, more entertainment, more fun and the opportunity to watch a whole match with a positive result in a single day.

But did everyone want and need instant excitement all the time? In some respects it is too easy to characterise a period in the way it is presented above, but culture and society is always more complex. The 'new' does not necessarily destroy the old, even if it displaces it at the heart of the 'Zeitgeist', and whatever might be attracting the major audiences is not necessarily what everyone wants, or needs. One of the sophistications of modern, western societies is that they offer the broadest range of the contemporary and traditional, the superficial and the complex. Television both echoes and contributes to that state of being. When free-to-air Test Match cricket was broadcast in Britain from the 1950s to the 1980s, it competed with two or three programme alternatives, but from the 1990s it became merely one of a deluge of programme options, which these days number in the hundreds, including the options for re-watching and time shifting. Cricket is merely one of a range of alternatives but one of the attributes of English cricket is that it offers a range of forms (products, if you must) far broader than in any other major team sport. Rugby Union is generally rugby, 15-a-side over 80 minutes; football is football, 11-a-side over 90 minutes; and much the same applies to other sports. But cricket cannot be characterised in that simple way beyond 11-a-side. Does cricket last 20/20 overs, 40/40 overs, 50/50 overs, Duckworth-Lewis variations, three days, four days, five days, one innings each, two innings each? The answer is, yes, and instead of seeing these variations as a *problem*, they should be celebrated.

Cricket, unlike other sports, offers the sort of variations that are to be found elsewhere in our culture: do we prefer opera, pop, rock, old masters, modern greats or YBAs? The theatres offered *the Rocky Horror Show, Godspell* and *Jesus Christ Superstar* but among the more challenging playwrights of the period covered by this book were the cricket fanatic, Harold Pinter and Samuel Beckett. The latter is surely the only writer of his kind ever to appear in *Wisden's* list of first-class cricketers, having played two first-class matches for Dublin University against Northamptonshire in 1925 and 1926. These men wrote plays that were intellectually challenging and demanded total engagement from the audience, but there was an audience for their work just as there was for light entertainment.

The Sunday League started in England in 1969 followed by the first ODIs in the early 1970s. Since then the challenge for cricket in England and elsewhere, has been to innovate while respecting tradition and to balance the various demands on players with the diverse interests of cricket's audiences. While the Richard Wattis caricature in the 1953 film *The Final Test* may not have wished for too much excitement, he will have been interested in quality, which is sometimes elusive and yet increasingly visible. I am writing this on 5 November 2015, and while I chose to get some sleep in the early hours of the day, I could have turned on *Sky Sports* around midnight, to watch Australia smash 389–2 against New Zealand in Brisbane. I was up by 6pm to see Pakistan's spinners take them to a match and series victory against England despite tremendous pace bowling by James Anderson and another battling innings by Alistair Cook. And now, mid-morning, I am watching India take their second South African wicket, having fallen to 201 all out. In each case, the play is accompanied by varied replays, informative and illuminating commentaries and thoughtful analysis by some of the finest, recent Test cricketers. It helps those of us who 'merely' watch (and pay) to be far better informed about what we are seeing, but perhaps as a consequence the gap between that and many days of current county cricket is, too often too great, with so few of these Test cricketers participating in the English domestic season.

Decades are not always ideal ways of dividing up history although their appeal to clarity is obvious. In terms of English cricket, it might make more sense to see the first postwar period, stretching from 1946 to 1962, followed by the highly significant 10 years spell from 1963 to 1972. During that latter period we saw the first knock-out cup in 1963; the immediate signing of overseas cricketers (1968); the weekly televising of the first limited-overs league from 1969; the first ODI (1971); and in 1972 the third of those shorter competitions, the B&H Cup competition with its mix of league and cup. At the start, it lasted 55 overs, shorter than Gillette's 60, longer than the Sunday League's 40, and it would open the new season, with an early elimination through regional mini-leagues in which Hampshire found themselves a south west side.

In the early years, even winning the Gillette Cup required a team to play just four or perhaps five matches in a season, and two sides, Sussex and Warwickshire, won it twice in the 1960s. Otherwise, Hampshire were not untypical in playing just 15 limited-overs matches in the first six seasons from 1963 to1968 – the six defeats dumping them out of the competition in which they never progressed beyond the semi-final stage. Then, from 1969, the Sunday League brought 16 matches every year for all 17 teams in addition to the cup. For the first time, all the counties played limited-overs matches in most weeks and a new audience grew alongside the traditional County Championship followers.

In **1970**, one of the consequences of the cancellation of the South African tour was the substitution of a five match series between England and the Rest of the World. Despite the strength of the 'touring' side, these matches were not accorded the status of Test Matches but some of the cricket was of a high standard. The Rest of the World won the first match at Lord's by an innings as Sobers took 6–21 and then scored 183, following Eddie Barlow's 119. South Africa's Apartheid laws prevented their side's participation in Test cricket for around 30 years, yet here were Barlow, Richards, Graeme Pollock and Procter playing alongside some of the world's finest black cricketers (Sobers, Clive Lloyd, Kanhai, Engineer, Intikhab Alam and Gibbs). At Trent Bridge, Barlow and Lloyd scored centuries, but so did Brian Luckhurst in his second England appearance and his side won by eight wickets.

D'Oliveira, a key figure in the South African 'problem', was the first centurion at Edgbaston. Lloyd made another century and despite England's 409 which ended in the 206th over, the Rest of the World won to regain the lead. The tightest game at Headingley gave the Rest of the World another victory by two wickets – Barlow took 12 wickets and there was another century for Sobers. The winning target was 223, and England were hopeful at 183–8, but Richards and Procter made a decent ninth wicket pair and they took the side to victory. There were more centuries (Pollock, Boycott and Kanhai), and 7–83 for Peter Lever, as the Rest of the World won the series 4–1 at the Oval.

The **1970** Rest of the World series coincided with a good summer and an experimental lbw law, which discouraged 'pad play'. After two years the experiment was adapted, largely to satisfy the different conditions in Australia and the West Indies. There was a fear that it might still cause problems for typical English in-swing and off-spin bowlers but the four bowlers to take 100 first-class wickets in the season were all spin bowlers and two were off-spinners: Titmus, Don Shepherd, plus Norman Gifford and leg-spinner, Hobbs. Lancashire, after going years without any trophy, retained the Sunday League beating Yorkshire in front of a crowd of 33,000 on a Sunday afternoon at Old Trafford – a match also shown on BBC2. They also won the Gillette Cup for the first time and, along with Glamorgan, challenged for the County Championship that Glamorgan had won in 1969. In the end, Kent, at the bottom of the table in early July, clinched the main prize.

Despite that remarkable Sunday League attendance, *Wisden* noted that not one of the 17 counties recorded a profit in **1970** despite a rise in attendances at a few counties, notably Essex and Kent "who play their home matches at so many delightful and picturesque places". There was discussion about another reorganisation to fit a second limited-overs league on Saturdays, thereby pushing County Championship matches into mid-week with an inevitable loss of members. *Wisden*, again referred to the suggestion to play 16 four-day County Championship matches, which would be adopted finally two decades later. Even in 1970, the proliferation of limited-overs competitions led England's selectors to lament the impact on young batsmen, particularly those batting in the middle order. A good example was at Hampshire where, for years, Trevor Jesty batted at five or six in an innings opened by Richards and Greenidge. As a young man he excelled as a limited-overs all-rounder while taking some years to hit a first-class century, yet by the end of the decade he was one of the finest English batsmen in county cricket, but he never played Test cricket. He was not alone and the TCCB acted in 1972 to limit counties to two overseas players (from five), requiring players to qualify for England by residence over a 10-year period. Counties could still 'dodge' these regulations so that, for example, Greenidge who was raised for some years in Reading and initially qualified for England, played for a few seasons after his West Indian Test Match debut alongside Richards and Andy Roberts.

Following the Rest of the World series, England toured Australia under Ray Illingworth and regained the Ashes, which had been lost on the 1958–1959 tour, while Australia failed to win one match at home for the first time since

1888. That was made more surprising for there were notionally seven Test Matches, although the last one replaced the scheduled third, which was abandoned without a ball bowled. England won the fourth Test Match by 299 runs thanks mainly to Boycott (77 & 142*) and Snow who took 7–40 on the last day – perhaps this was the match that persuaded folksinger Roy Harper to write and record his song, "When an Old Cricketer Leaves the Crease", including a tribute to the two?

The fifth and sixth matches were drawn and on the second evening of the final match, after England posted just 184, Australia rallied from 66–4 to lead by 80. During the session, a ball from Snow hit Ian Redpath on the head and after Redpath retired hurt, Snow, fielding on the fence, was embroiled in an altercation with a spectator, bottles were thrown onto the field and Illingworth took the England team to the dressing room. Play resumed on day three and England set Australia 223 to win. Snow took an early wicket but then dislocated a finger trying to catch Keith Stackpole. In his absence, five other bowlers worked their way through the batting and England won by 62 runs to 'take back' the trophy. In the sixth Test Match, Dennis Lillee made his debut, while in the last Test Match his partner was Tony Dell who happens to be one of the very few Test cricketers born in Hampshire – the New Forest to be precise. In that final Test Match, Ian Chappell captained Australia for the first time and he, Lillee and the others would fairly soon take their revenge.

The abandonment of the third Test Match at Melbourne over the New Year was a highly significant moment in the history of international cricket, for in its place on 5 January **1971** the two sides contested the first ODI – albeit arranged hastily as a substitute. The match consisted of 40 eight-ball overs and, while the England players had an advantage in that they had all played limited-overs cricket for their counties, so too had Greg Chappell, McKenzie and Connolly in recent English seasons. Sadly, this did not work in England's favour as they were dismissed for 190, an innings built entirely around 82 by John Edrich. In reply, Australia had five overs and two balls to spare when they won by five wickets, Ian Chappell scoring 60. Ashley Mallett, Keith Stackpole and Illingworth each took three wickets. It would be 18 months before the next ODI (in Manchester) between the same two sides, but a start had been made.

Lancashire followed their limited-overs 'double' in 1970 with a second Lord's Cup Final triumph in 1971. In July 1969, the Americans had won the Space race with the first moon-landing, and exactly two years later on Monday 26 July **1971** the USA launched their Apollo 15 spacecraft, also heading for the moon. The latter was clearly visible two days later as Lancashire beat Gloucestershire in the most notable of their early limited-overs matches – not a title clincher, but rather a Gillette Cup semi-final from Old Trafford. The BBC showed Gloucestershire batting first with Procter (65) top-scoring in their 229–6 from 60 overs. Lancashire made a solid start but from 156–3 they fell to 163–6 as the day grew darker and the huge crowd thronged the boundary rope, most hoping for a home win. Staying with the game, BBC-2 cancelled the 7.30pm *Newsroom* and the 8pm's *Man Alive* about the alarming increase in bankruptcy. At 8.50pm, as singer Jake Holmes was due to present a brief show of his songs, the match was reaching its conclusion and the players and umpires were handling frequent crowd invasions. Bond and Jack Simmons added 40 for the seventh wicket but 27 runs were still needed when David Hughes arrived at the crease. On television, which for this broadcast was still in black and white, the lights around the ground and nearby station glowed brightly as Hughes hit John Mortimore for 24 runs in one over to win a famous victory. It became a legendary game in a competition, which over recent years has lost much of its glamour, and it was another of *Wisden's* matches of the century.

In many respects the Final matched it, as the game swung to-and-from Kent and Lancashire. Clive Lloyd's 66 took Lancashire to 224–7, with Underwood taking 1–26 in his 12 overs. Kent, like Lancashire, lost a wicket without scoring and at 105–5 were struggling, but Asif Iqbal scored a superb 89 and seemed to be winning the game until he drove at Simmons, and Lancashire's captain, Jack Bond, took a stunning catch. Kent, were 197–6, but managed just three more runs and Lancashire had won again. They would have completed another 'double' but lost at home to Glamorgan allowing Worcestershire – who were not playing – to pip Essex for the Sunday title on a superior run rate of 0.0037! Surrey won their 18th outright County Championship in **1971** when a second bowling point at sunny Southampton brought them level with Warwickshire, who they beat overall by virtue of more victories.

Despite these excitements *Wisden's* editor warned that too many unimaginative performances threatened the future of first-class cricket in England, especially against the obvious lure of the shorter competitions. He was troubled by the consequences of the experimental front-foot no ball law, by dissent shown by players on the field and proposed that there was a need for greater clarity about overseas tours, still under the banner of MCC not England. He praised the Test Match performances of India and Pakistan, but was troubled that in 1972 the County Championship would be reduced to 20 matches per side to accommodate the new B&H Cup, the early season regional group stages of which would be staged on Saturdays.

These changes in professional county cricket were mirrored in club cricket. While in the northern counties there had been major leagues throughout the 20th century, this was less so further south, although it is not true that there was no competitive club cricket in southern England. For example, the outstanding amateur bowler, Charlie Knott, came to Hampshire's attention playing evening knock-out cup matches in the Southampton Parks in the mid-1930s. Charlie met Hampshire's new captain/secretary on his appointment in late 1945, and when the former Oxford University 'Blue', Desmond Eagar, enquired where Charlie had played his early cricket, he was confused by the reply "in the parks".

In central southern England the elite Southern League and the larger Hampshire League were both running effectively by the early 1970s and the Portsmouth area was not unique in running an early version of an evening T20 League on Tuesday evenings. The Hampshire League website records the origins of the Saturday league:

> Following the formation of the Southern League in 1969, a general inquiry in 1970 … showed a widespread interest among clubs tired of the surfeit of draws in 'friendly' cricket and looking for a competitive edge with rewards, in the form of promotion, for success. The inaugural meeting of clubs was held on 19 February 1972.

The site adds that the first Hampshire Cricket League's County 1 Division fixture took place at Hayling Park on 28 April 1973 between Hayling Island CC and Portsmouth & Southsea CC. Two weeks later, 64 teams contested five divisions. League cricket in Hampshire, and indeed throughout most of the UK, is now an accepted fact and *The Cricket Paper* offers news stories, photographs, results and tables of most of the leading leagues each week.

In the Hampshire region, the Southern League is the leading competition. When it started in 1969, most of its top clubs were from the major towns and cities in the region: Basingstoke & North Hants; Bournemouth Amateurs; Bournemouth Sports; Deanery (Southampton); Gosport Borough; Havant; Old Tauntonians (Southampton); South Hants Touring Club (Portsmouth); South Wilts (Salisbury); Trojans (Southampton) and Waterlooville. They played each other once and Trojans emerged as the first winners. By 2015, barely one of those Hampshire town/city-based sides was still in the leading division and some of them no longer existed, although South Wilts and Havant remain the leading two teams, and South Hants, now called Portsmouth, are working their way back up through the divisions. But to a large extent, the leading clubs today are based in suburban and rural centres to the north of the M27 and there is barely one significant club in Southampton. In addition, many of the smaller village clubs that competed in the early years of the Hampshire League have suffered from the impact of becoming expensive commuter locations and some teams have either ceased altogether, or play only Sunday friendly matches.

Back in the world of Test Match cricket, in **1972,** England and Australia battled to a 2–2 drawn series with a number of fine moments. At Lord's, on his debut, the Australian Bob Massie swung the ball to great effect, recording match figures of 16–137, the most wickets ever by an Australian in one Test Match and, at the time, the best debut figures in Test Match history. England retained the Ashes at Headingley with Underwood's 10–82 decisive on a damp pitch during a period of some concern about the pitches in Leeds. The visitors had their revenge with victory on the sixth afternoon of the sixth Test Match. One interesting statistic in the period, and not just pre-on-line scores but pre-television teletext, is that the Post Office's phone-a-score facility took more than 15 million calls. Ceefax, the first teletext service, began in 1974 and closed in 2012.

In the same season, England and Australia also played the first ODI series, which England won 2–1. Dennis Amiss scored the first ODI century in that first match – played with 55 six-ball overs per side. By then, Leicestershire, under Illingworth, had won the first trophy in their history when they beat Yorkshire by five wickets in a one-sided Lord's Final for the brand new B&H Cup – also played over 55 overs per side. The competition was between the 17 counties, plus Minor Counties South and North and Cambridge University – four zonal leagues of five teams each. The competition should have been launched with eight scheduled matches on Saturday, 29 April 1972, but the weather was so awful that not a ball was bowled anywhere and the matches were concluded over the following days. On the next weekend, Hampshire were due to play their first game against Gloucestershire at Moreton-in-the-Marsh but that took three days to complete, Hampshire winning while Gloucestershire's 70 all out was the lowest of the season. Mike Procter was unable to prevent his pal Barry Richards, top scoring but Procter had his day against Somerset at Taunton, scoring154* and taking 5–26. Some years later he would return to haunt Hampshire in the same competition but in this first year, the one hat-trick was taken by Graham McKenzie for the eventual Champions who also posted the highest score of the first year, 327–4 against Warwickshire at Coventry.

Limited-overs cricket always offers the prospect of an exciting finish but in this first year of the B&H Cup, after the zonal preliminaries, that was not the case in any one of the seven knock-out matches, all of which were one-sided. Nonetheless, for the first time, four different counties won a trophy in **1972,** with Lancashire repeating their Gillette Cup success, Warwickshire winning the County Championship and their runners-up, Kent, winning the Sunday League. A successful summer in the Test Matches, with England retaining the Ashes after a 2–2 draw, meant that every county received £25,000 from the central share-out. Against that, the fixture list seemed to require too much travel and too many limited-overs matches for players to prepare adequately for a five-day Test Match cricket. Only Leicestershire and Hampshire reached an average of 18.5 overs per hour, while in the Test Matches the Australians averaged only around 15.5.

In the following year, Kent won two more trophies while Hampshire were County Champions and Gloucestershire won the Gillette Cup. Indeed, from 1968, the last of Yorkshire's regular triumphs until 1976, nine different sides won the County Championship with no repetitions until Kent (1970) and Middlesex (1976) shared it in 1977. In that period, three teams who were not County Champions, Gloucestershire, Lancashire and Northamptonshire won limited-overs trophies, a total of 12 winners in nine years.

From **1972**, the English domestic game settled into a more regular pattern for some time with the County Championship, the Sunday League, the Gillette Cup which became the NatWest Trophy with its September Lord's Final, and the B&H Cup with a similar Final about two months earlier. Other than that, Yorkshire hosted a number of four-team Festival tournaments at Scarborough or Harrogate, each sponsored by companies Fenner or Tilcon. It seemed they were designed to enable Yorkshire to win a trophy of sorts during the fallow 1970s, but they rarely triumphed.

For some time, the key change in domestic cricket was in the number of matches each side played in the three-day game. That was reduced to 20 in **1973** when Hampshire were the first team to win the County Championship undefeated since Lancashire in 1928. Remarkably, apart from one limited-overs appearance by John Rice, they used just 13 players all season in the four competitions. The TCCB celebrated the 100 years since regulations were enforced to prevent players appearing for more than one county during a season, and the Post Office published a booklet of 'WG' stamps. Which was the anniversary of the County Championship is a matter of continuous debate, but if such celebrations attract greater attention for the original county competition it might be wise to celebrate them all: 1863, 1873, 1890, 1895 – whatever.

1973 was a glorious summer on the whole, although it would be surpassed by 1975 and 1976. England, having struggled on occasions against New Zealand, were hammered in two of the three Test Matches by the West Indies, while England's women's team won the first World Cup. Following victory against Australia at Edgbaston, which was built upon a fine century by Enid Bakewell, England's captain, Rachel Heyhoe (later -Flint), accepted the trophy from HRH Princess Anne. In the winter, England's women drew a five-match series in the West Indies, 1–1. In 1976 women were 'permitted' to play at Lord's for the first time when England met Australia. The 1978 women's World

Cup in India was won by Australia with England runners-up. Australia won the next two in 1982 and 1988 and this has now become a regular event, as is the multi-format women's Ashes.

1974 was a wet summer. Hampshire led the County Championship through the season until the final match but suffered with the weather in the closing weeks losing the whole of the last day of their penultimate match and then all three days v Yorkshire at Bournemouth. They beat Worcestershire by an innings at Portsmouth in August but the midlands side kept going and beat Hampshire to the title over the last three days of the season. There was another change in the County Championship. While there was no prospect of returning to the very bad year of the 65 overs first innings limit, a new restriction was imposed with the first innings of every match being restricted to 100 overs per side, although the side fielding first could claim extra overs by dismissing their opponents in less than the maximum. Simon Heffer in *the Daily Telegraph's* book of the 100 best county matches to celebrate the 1990 centenary described this as "one of the most pernicious and damaging changes", although since three-day matches might last around 350 overs, why the pitches could not allow the first innings to be complete in 200 of those, is not clear. Heffer argued that it denied lower order batsmen their chance and chose to illustrate this with Warwickshire's extraordinary 465–1 against Gloucestershire when the only wicket fell in the first over without a run scored. But in this case, even Warwickshire's numbers four and five were denied a bat by Jameson (240*) and Kanhai (213*) while their opponents would have welcomed 100 overs, being bowled out for 243 in the 70th and losing by an innings. As Heffer reported, the restriction was "abandoned after eight years".

Maintaining the damp theme, the Gillette Cup Final was the first to be rained-off completely on the Saturday, and when they started on Monday, Kent beat Lancashire (all out 118 in 60 overs) even though not one of their players reached 20. In the B&H Cup, Surrey won their first limited-overs trophy, beating Leicestershire, who won the Sunday League. England beat India 3–0 including two innings victories but the three-match series v Pakistan failed to produce a result. Headingley lost the last day to the weather with both sides in sight of victory, and then there was controversy in the second Test Match with Pakistan accusing the Lord's ground staff of careless covering during rain. The final Test Match at the Oval was played on what the *Playfair Cricket Annual* called "the most placid wicket in the world", Pakistan scoring 600–7 dec (Zaheer Abbas 240) and England 545 with centuries by Amiss and Keith Fletcher (122 in eight-and-a-half hours). It was a tedious match and there was just time for 30 overs of Pakistan's second innings (94–4).

Fines for poor over rates were imposed on a number of counties – they make interesting reading in 2015 when teams were expected to bowl 16 overs per hour but often failed to do so. In 1973, four counties had achieved an overall average of 19.5 overs per hour, in 1974 only Middlesex (19.8) did so, but in the latter year only four of the 17 counties failed to reach the required average of 18.5 overs per hour – the equivalent in a six-and-a-half-hour day of 120 overs.

Given the poor weather and an unexciting Test Match summer, it was perhaps no surprise that the counties shared just £460,000 from 'Lord's', whereas in 1973 it had been almost £600,000. *Wisden* reported difficulties at a number of counties, notably Gloucestershire who lost around £30,000 in the year, while Hampshire, in the middle of the most successful spell in their history, lost £10,000. Gloucestershire considered selling the Bristol ground before launching an appeal and Middlesex asked members to donate at least £10 each to avoid bankruptcy.

If England's performances in **1974** were satisfactory, during the following winter they went to Australia, met Jeff Thomson and Lillee for the first time, lost four of the first five Test Matches and had the merest consolation in a victory in the final one. They travelled without Boycott who was selected but withdrew, citing the pressures and tensions of Test Match cricket leaving him unable to face the tour – much as he had done in 1972–1973 for the trip to India and Pakistan. During the previous summer he received a benefit in excess of £20,000 from Yorkshire, a huge tax-free sum in 1974, when the average salary was less than one-tenth of that. After Australia, England went to New Zealand where a short-pitched ball from England's Peter Lever was deflected by tail-ender, Ewan Chatfield, into his face. Chatfield only survived after receiving heart massage and mouth-to-mouth resuscitation on the pitch. Batting helmets were still a few years away.

There was now a short period of stability in the domestic game, although in 1977 the County Championship was increased to 22 matches per county. Internationally, the mid-1970s featured two ferocious pace attacks, Australia and West Indies, and they met in an epic match at Lord's to decide the destination of the first Cricket World Cup (known as the Prudential Cup) in **1975**. This was the first of three consecutive World Cups played in an English summer and it was blessed by the weather – there was not one minute of interruption for rain. The eight nations excluded South Africa but included Sri Lanka and East Africa. In the early rounds, West Indies celebrated a remarkable victory against Pakistan with a 10th wicket unbeaten partnership of 64 by Deryck Murray and Roberts. In the Final at Lord's, West Indies were struggling at 50–3 but Lloyd posted a superb century leaving Australia to chase 292 to win in their 60 overs. The match went beyond 8.30pm as Australia, 221–6, slumped to 233–9 before Thomson and Lillee took them within 18 runs of victory, when Thomson was run out. The strangest match was probably the first, as England posted 333–4 against India who replied with 132–3 from their full complement of overs. Sunil Gavaskar opened the batting and at the close was 36* from 174 balls, with one four. Farokh Engineer, with some years of experience in this form of the game with Lancashire, was not required to bat.

India soon learned a different approach and it had major consequences for world cricket that resonate today. Australia beat England in the semi-final with Gary Gilmour taking 6–14 and the two sides then played a four Test Match series, with Australia winning the first Test Match – sufficient to retain the Ashes. England found an improbable 'star' in the Northamptonshire batsman David Steele who arrived at the wicket at Lord's at 10–1, saw England fall to 49–4, and scored 50 on debut ending the season at the head of the averages. The Lord's Test Match had record receipts for any match in England of almost £120,000. The third Test Match at Headingley had a dramatic start as Phil Edmonds took 5–17 on Test Match debut. The end was, sadly, even more dramatic, with the match interestingly poised. Australia were about halfway to the target of 445 with seven wickets left and a day to play, and their opener, Rick McCosker, was 95*, but neither he nor either side reached their target after vandals climbed into the ground overnight, dug holes into the pitch and filled them with oil – the match was abandoned.

Gordon Greenidge appeared for the West Indies in the World Cup, but also played most of the 1975 season with Hampshire and he and Richards led the way as Hampshire scored 371–4 in 60 overs v Glamorgan, then a record for a 60 overs match. In the next round by contrast, Lancashire dismissed them for 98 and went on to win another Lord's Final. Hampshire's consolation was their first Sunday League title and they finished third in the County Championship, a sequence of one, two and three in three seasons. Leicestershire, under Illingworth, won the County Championship for the first time, but there were concerns about the limitation of 100 overs in the first innings and the number of bonus points available. In late-August, Greenidge struck 259 v Sussex, in Hampshire's 501–5 – the highest total in a restricted first innings – after which they forced Sussex to follow-on without taking all 10 wickets in a score after 100 overs of 259–8, which was only just beyond half Hampshire's 100 overs total; but Hampshire could not win the game.

Although England had no winter engagement in 1975–1976, Greenidge toured Australia with the West Indies but in two Test Matches scored just 0,0,3 & 8 and lost his place. He won it back the following summer in England with a vengeance. South African, Tony Greig, had replaced Scotsman, Mike

Denness, as England's captain from the second Test Match of the previous summer and in **1976**, in a BBC television interview at Hove before the series began, he announced his intention to make the West Indians "grovel". It was not perhaps the wisest observation by a white South African and it rather backfired. Viv Richards opened the series with 232 at Trent Bridge, although England avoided defeat but in the longest and hottest summer the West Indies' pace attack caused England significant difficulties. They drew the second Test Match, scoring 250 and 254 but then at Old Trafford with just 71 and 126, they lost by 425 runs. On the Saturday evening England's openers Edrich and Close, both over forty, were bruised and battered by Roberts, Michael Holding and Wayne Daniel and it was much the same in the next two matches, both won by the tourists. Richards reached 291 at the Oval and he and Greenidge scored three centuries each – all that England managed between them. Holding took 28 wickets at 12.71 and Roberts the same at just under 20 each. West Indies also won the three limited-overs matches.

While the series was lost, it generated huge interest. In 1975 the counties had shared a pot of some £661,000 from the central body's Test Match receipts, television and radio income and sponsorship, etc., but in **1976** it was up to £950,000. Among the counties, Middlesex won the County Championship for the first time since 1947, Kent won the Sunday League and B&H Cup while Northamptonshire won the Gillette Cup, the first trophy in their history; this left only Somerset and Essex waiting for success. It would come to both counties very soon.

Despite his reverse in the summer of **1976**, Greig reinvented himself as a spin bowler and led his side to Test Match victory in India that winter – England's first series win there for more than 40 years. While the success was welcome, it was not entirely smooth sailing. In the third Test Match, the Indian captain, Bishen Bedi, accused John Lever and Bob Willis of using Vaseline to change the condition of the ball. The Cricket Council spoke to the England captain and manager (Ken Barrington) and cleared the two bowlers of all charges. England had used 21 players in the five Test Match series against the West Indies and struggled to identify the best young cricketers. One initiative was to send four promising county players to Australia during the winter – the four were Ian Botham, Mike Gatting, Bill Athey and Graham Stevenson, all of whom would play for England. Meanwhile, the MCC announced plans to build their seven-lane indoor school on the Nursery Ground.

Interestingly, there were only Test Matches on the tour of India, no ODIs. This was increasingly unusual, however. On the whole, the 1970s *felt* like a turbulent decade and cricket echoed that with the South African issue at the start of the decade and the 'Packer' affair towards its conclusion. The English season of 1962 had opened with a single touring side and one County Championship, but just 15 years later there were four domestic tournaments, three of a single innings per side, while in addition to limited-overs matches between Test-playing nations, the first World Cup had taken place. Amid all the uncertainty, two events, one cricketing and one for the Nation, offered a comforting sense of history and tradition, continuity and certainty. Sadly, the cricketing case was to evaporate all too quickly.

In March **1977**, following their tour of India, England played Australia at Melbourne in the Centenary Test Match. In the first-ever Test Match in 1877, Charles Bannerman, born in Woolwich, London, opened the batting for Australia and scored 165 (retired hurt) in an all out total of just 245. It was enough. They led England by 49, scored 104 all out and bowled England out for 108. Apart from Bannerman, only the England opener, Harry Jupp, (63) reached 50, while Thomas Kendall, also born in England, took 7–55 to win the match. People today are often bewildered by the movement of cricketers around the world so it is worth noting that only five of the Australian side were born in that country although they all settled and died there. Australia won this 'timeless' match in four days by 45 runs. One hundred years later, the result was exactly the same. Australia 138 & 419–9 declared beat England 95 & 417 by 45 runs. Derek Randall scored a wonderful 174 to give England hope, but Lillee took 11–165 to lead Australia to victory. Greig took four wickets for England and in the second innings scored 41. He would never play in a Test Match again.

England's next Test Match was, again, against Australia at Lord's on 16 June 1977 and the captain was Mike Brearley. Just a month before that Greig was sacked, after it was revealed he had played a leading role in helping the Australian media tycoon Kerry Packer to sign 35 leading international cricketers to play in his own televised cricket 'circus'. Packer took this step after the Australian Cricket Board rejected his decision to reject the offer to screen Australian Test Matches and Sheffield Shield matches on his Channel 9. Packer paid his stars about £12,000 for three years, by comparison with Greig's annual salary, as England captain, of just over £1,000. The story has been told many times and does not require further detailed examination here. Packer's World Series Cricket improved the remuneration of leading players and he also introduced coloured clothing, floodlights and a white ball. The matches were contested fiercely but they have never been recognised as first-class. In 1979 the two sides resolved their differences, principally as a consequence of the legal battles taking the Australian Board into serious financial difficulties. The players returned to Test and first-class cricket, which was, however, never quite the same again.

While world cricket, and therefore English cricket, was undergoing what David Frith suggested was its "First World War", HM Queen Elizabeth II celebrated her Silver Jubilee, including a limited-overs international completed in the rain to avoid spilling into the second day in June when the Jubilee was celebrated across the country. During the series Boycott became the 18th batsman to reach 100 first-class centuries and he did so on his home ground against Australia. Meanwhile, Botham made a very promising Test Match debut in the same series and was chosen as one of Wisden's 'Five Cricketers of the Year'. On the domestic front, Ron Alsopp at Trent Bridge won the Groundsman of the Year award and Ernie Knights retired after 51 years tending the Hampshire ground at Southampton. At Swansea in mid-season, Worcestershire were dismissed for 169 as their captain Gifford was second highest scorer with seven runs – some way behind Glenn Turner's 141* which, at 83%, was the highest proportion ever of one completed innings.

The Jubilee may have offered a sense of tradition, ceremony and continuity, but it was somewhat disrupted by the Sex Pistols who released their single "God Save the Queen" in the week before the main celebrations and it reached the top of the charts despite being banned by the BBC and IBA. A couple of months later, the original rock & roll rebel, Elvis Presley, overweight and suffering from drug misuse, died at home.

Tradition was under attack in cricket too. Frith's article appeared in the Hampshire Handbook of 1978, by which time he could describe how further talks between Packer and ICC broke down in mid-summer and how in November the High Court in London ruled that any attempt to prevent World Series cricketers returning to the county game would be unlawful. When Hampshire went to Bristol for their final County Championship match in **1977** they thought it might be the last they saw of Richards, Greenidge and Roberts, although the latter was not playing.

Gloucestershire had never won the title since the changes of 1890 but victory in this game would correct that. Hampshire, beset by injuries all season, were able to field their main batting line-up and the two pals, Procter and Richards, ensured a first innings difference of just six runs. John Southern (6–81) kept Hampshire's final target to 271 and although Richards went cheaply, Greenidge (94) took Hampshire to a comfortable victory. While Gloucestershire won the Lord's Final of 2015, it is difficult to imagine they will ever come that close to a County Championship title again.

Frith suggested that what was most at threat in English cricket from Packer's intervention was "harmony" in county sides, while adding that had perhaps been the case ever since the signing of overseas stars which had introduced significant differentials in players' wages. But in 1978 this might be far worse with the return of World Series players. However, the court ruling of November meant that those players had the legal right to return and would remain available to the county clubs at least until the completion of their contracts.

So, it was on 22 April **1978** that Richards and Greenidge opened Hampshire's batting in their first B&H Cup match v Combined Universities XI which included Ian Greig, Tony's brother, Paul Parker and Vic Marks. Hampshire won easily. The following weekend, Roberts was back also, but both the B&H Cup match and the first County Championship game (at Lord's) were abandoned without a ball being bowled. It was an ominous start to a complicated season. Richards had enjoyed a benefit in 1977 and after a winter playing against the world's finest players, the treadmill of another county season frustrated him. On 30 June he arrived at Southampton for the final day of a match against Leicestershire and announced his retirement from first-class cricket. Chris Balderstone dismissed him that day as Hampshire crashed to an innings defeat.

Andy Roberts had been bowling fast fairly continuously for some years and requested a break, but with Hampshire pressing for success in the Sunday League, the other players intimated this would not be popular. In mid-July he played a Sunday League game at the Oval and then he, too, walked away, although he would return to county cricket some years later with Leicestershire. Despite the loss of those two great players, Hampshire won the Sunday League on a thrilling final day as Greenidge hit 122, aided by Jesty (47 & 5–32). They had to wait some time to see whether Somerset might win and overtake them but Somerset failed from the last ball and it would to be another year before their NatWest and Sunday League 'double' were the first trophies in their history.

1978 was generally a wet summer but there was the encouraging rise of Botham and David Gower to cheer English followers, and England won five of the season's six Test Matches against New Zealand and Pakistan. Pakistan had given England a tough series on their home soil in the winter as the England touring squad omitted all their 'Packer' players and struggled to compete. Glenn Turner, awarded a benefit by Worcestershire, chose to play county cricket over his country's Test Match tour. Kent meanwhile retained their Packer players Underwood, Woolmer and Asif Iqbal and won the County Championship, although some members resigned in protest at their decision to select them. In addition, they won the B&H Cup and secured a total of £14,000 in prize money. Sussex won the Gillette Cup under wicketkeeper Arnold Long who had replaced Greig as captain.

The TCCB established another 'Working Party' consisting of the Chairmen of

Surrey, Glamorgan and Lancashire to examine the structure of English cricket. They proposed a new governing board of control for cricket in the UK "based mainly on the first-class counties and the National Cricket Association". The intention was to abolish the Cricket Council and thereby lessen the influence of the MCC but Norman Preston pointed out the anomaly that the MCC funded the NCA and provided free offices for the TCCB and NCA. Meanwhile Cornhill Insurance agreed to sponsor English Test Match cricket to the sum of £1m over the next five years.

The second World Cup arrived in England in **1979**. The West Indies dominated and won it again, although England reached the Final. They got there beating Australia by six wickets, Canada by nine wickets – having dismissed their opponents for a record low of 45 – Pakistan by 14 runs and New Zealand by nine runs in the semi-final. The whole competition was over in just 15 matches and in the Final, Richards' 138* helped set a target of 287 in 60 overs. Brearley and Boycott, opening for England, both scored half-centuries but took so long about it that England then sacrificed wickets, falling from 183–2 to 194 all out. Joel Garner took five wickets in eleven balls to end the match.

In domestic cricket, Somerset and Essex, neither of whom had won anything before, shared the four major titles in **1979**, while Somerset's Ian Botham completed the fastest Test Match 'double' in 21 matches, at just 23 years of age. It was not all glory for the west country side however, as their captain Brian Rose exploited the B&H Cup qualification regulations to ensure a quarter-final place by declaring against Worcestershire and losing the match in around quarter-of-an-hour, thereby safeguarding their wicket-taking rate. The TCCB condemned his actions, banned Somerset from the competition, and Glamorgan took their place. In February 1981, the Chappell brothers, Greg and Trevor Chappell, were similarly condemned when New Zealand reached the last ball needing six to tie the match. The older Chappell, Greg, ordered his younger brother to bowl the ball underarm along the ground and Australia won a match that would otherwise be long forgotten. The action was subsequently outlawed. There was more controversy with Australia when Lillee arrived at the crease with a noisy aluminium bat – the laws were then amended to require bats to be made from wood, as part of the fifth rewriting in 200 years. Meanwhile, the Australian authorities reverted from eight to six ball overs, leaving just Pakistan with the longer version. There had been much excitement throughout the decade, but equally much controversy.

Chapter Five: the 1980s

The West Indies dominated international cricket in the post-Packer decade, while a significant number of cricketers, either born there or of Afro-Caribbean origin, also made their mark in English county and Test Match cricket. Some were born in the UK, often the children of the postwar immigrants, others like Gordon Greenidge travelled to this country at school age and learned to play in English conditions. Eventually he appeared in county cricket with and against many of his Test Match team-mates including Desmond Haynes, Lloyd, Kallicharan, Kanhai, Murray, Roberts, Malcolm Marshall, Holding, Colin Croft, Daniel and Gibbs.

From the registration of overseas players in 1968, black cricketers became a common sight in English county cricket and while there were one or two unpleasant incidents on county grounds, for the most part, spectators took their presence for granted and enjoyed their performances. Things were less comfortable in the wider society. Dominic Sandbrook has chronicled the period from the Suez Crisis (1956) to the election of Mrs Thatcher (1979) in great detail, in publications and television series, and in his book about the late 1970s he writes extensively about issues of race, covering right-wing attitudes to immigration (Powell, Clapton, the National Front, the British National Party) as well as organised reactions to that, varying from legislation to organisations like Rock Against Racism and the Anti Nazi League. In one section he comments on the integration of Caribbean and Asian immigrants through their contribution to the British diet and then turns his attention to the "even more striking" role of black sports people to British life. He cites boxer John Conteh, Colin Sullivan – who captained Great Britain's rugby league side – and then the three black footballers (Brendan Batson, Laurie Cunningham and Cyrille Regis) in the successful West Bromwich Albion side of 1978–1979, adding Viv Anderson as the first black footballer to represent England in that same season.

In part, Sandbrook's interest in the footballers centres on the battles they had to fight against racism on-and-off the pitch, and this perhaps warrants his focus. But it is interesting that cricket gets just one brief mention very early in his volume (an England Test Match defeat in West Indies) and then disappears from the story of Britain in the 1970s. It is similarly ignored by Arthur Marwick's account of the 1960s, which emanated from a major Open

University project. It is not that these important social historians failed to do their work – both projects cover considerable ground in great detail – but rather it reflects in part the fact that cricket was no longer seen as a key element of British social history. On the other hand, David Kynaston's series of histories of postwar Britain, covering to-date 1945–1962, have frequently referred to cricket – including many of the key issues of the period. This is perhaps because his publications are based more on the accounts of ordinary people than on official archival research although it helps, no doubt, that he is a cricket lover who has also published a book about the 'Gents' v Players in 1898.

Had it been different, Sandbrook could have chronicled many contributions by cricketers of Caribbean or Asian origin to English cricket. At Hampshire, there has always been at least one black cricketer since I first watched them in 1959 (Danny Livingstone), and in the 2015 season, Hampshire's remarkable late escape from relegation ultimately owed more to the bowling of West Indian Fidel Edwards than any other player. Further, while Sandbrook considers for obvious reasons that West Bromwich Albion's team in the late 1970s was a key moment, he ignores, as one example, the number of black players who had joined Danny Livingstone by the early 1970s. Indeed, in a County Championship match against Derbyshire at Basingstoke in 1971, Hampshire fielded Livingstone, Greenidge, John Holder (later an umpire) and Larry Worrell (cousin of Sir Frank) *plus* their white West Indian Roy Marshall – four black players in one side, seven years before Batson, Cunningham and Regis. The West Bromwich Albion trio were nicknamed 'the Three Degrees' so perhaps Hampshire's cricketers were 'the Four Tops'?

Black cricketers first appeared for England's Test Match side shortly after Viv Anderson in soccer and, given England's willingness to pick a succession of South Africans once that international ban was imposed, it is worth pointing out that when Gordon Greenidge made his Hampshire debut in 1970 he was eligible for the England side. That only changed at the point when he was selected by West Indies, and in his autobiography he revealed the difficulties he encountered on returning to the Caribbean, where some supporters were less than generous about his 'Englishness' – at least until the runs flowed!

On the tour of the West Indies in 1980–1981, Roland Butcher, born in Barbados, made his England debut at his 'home' ground in the third *scheduled* Test Match of the tour. England lost the first Test Match by an innings and the two sides should have then met in the second Test Match in Guyana. But England had called up Surrey's Robin Jackman as a tour replacement for the injured Bob Willis, and when he arrived in Guyana his entry visa was revoked because, since 1968, he had been spending his winters coaching and playing in South Africa and he had married a South African. In a diplomatic standoff, the Test Match was cancelled and the England party flew to Barbados, which they found more accommodating. Both Jackman and Butcher made their Test Match debuts but West Indies won by 298 runs. Butcher also played in the fourth and fifth drawn Test Matches but then his international career was over. One year later when England beat Australia in that remarkable Test Match at Headingley in 1981, the side comprised eleven white English-born players and in the next couple of years, South Africans Allan Lamb, Ian Greig and Chris Smith followed Ian's brother Tony into the England side.

But in November 1982 the Middlesex pace bowler Jamaican-born Norman Cowans made his Test Match debut for England in Perth, and bowled England to victory in the thrilling fourth Test Match of that series. In March 1986, Cowans' Middlesex team-mate, Wilf Slack, who was born in St Vincent came into the England side against his fellow-countrymen at Trinidad, and in August of that year Warwickshire's, Gladstone Small from Barbados, opened England's bowling against New Zealand at Trent Bridge. In the following winter, Phil De Freitas from Dominica had five wickets in his first Test Match appearance at Brisbane, although Cowans, Slack and Small had been discarded at a time when England's selectors rang the changes at the expense of stability. In the England sides of the near future came English-born David Lawrence (first Test Match 1988), Devon Malcolm (Jamaica, 1989), Chris Lewis (Guyana, 1990) and Neil Williams (St Vincent, 1990). These crick-eters lived in England and came through the county game, as did other *county* cricketers like Alan Warner (Derbyshire & Worcestershire), Martin Jean-Jacques (Derbyshire & Hampshire), Mark Alleyne (Gloucestershire), Cardigan Connor (Hampshire), Ricardo Ellcock (Worcestershire & Middlesex) and Keith Piper (Warwickshire). These county and England players were often the children of cricket-loving parents from a time when the West Indies attracted voluble 'ex-pat' support on tours of England. Alleyne and Piper were two of the notable 'graduates' of the Haringey Cricket College, London, run by West Indian Test Match cricketer, Reg Scarlett. Sadly, it ran into funding problems and closed.

While social historians like Sandbrook and Marwick have tended to pay little or no attention to cricket as a key element in British life over the past 50 years, to some extent the black British community found a sense of identity through cricket in an often-alienating social and economic context and this was reflected in their participation in cricket sides, and their support for touring West Indies teams. The degree to which they felt able, or were enabled, to participate fully in English cricket was reflected in a Channel 4 film from 1987, *Playing Away*. Superficially this was a British 'comedy' featuring a number of familiar character actors. It recounted the tale of a black cricket team from Brixton spending the weekend in an English country village to play a 'friendly' match as part of that village's multi-cultural festival. The Director, Horace Ové, is perhaps the most prominent of the first generation of black British filmmakers and photographers, and while some of his earlier films like *Baldwin's Nigger* or *Pressure Drop* are more radical in style and content, *Playing Away* explores the kinds of tensions that can permeate the cricket field as much as anywhere else in a society. In 1988, Professor Colin McCabe suggested that it participated in the question of what it means to be British, adding that this was one of a number of films that rejected any single answer but rather celebrated "a culture of differences".

It is a idea that has not gone away, but at least one aspect of those differences was depicted in another British film from the same year. John Boorman's somewhat autobiographical account of his wartime childhood on the outskirts of London, *Hope and Glory*, includes a memorable moment when the young boy is taught to bowl a particularly effective ball which he first employs in a back-garden 'match', dismissing his father. Almost inevitably, given its mythical status, that ball is the googly, yet it is interesting to reflect that this thoroughly English scene – back garden cricket, white family, banks of the Thames overhung with willow trees – centres on a type of bowling that became almost obsolete in top English cricket until the recent emergence of a British Asian, Adil Rashid, who even then had to exercise considerable patience before his opportunity in October 2015 when he became the first leg-break and googly bowler to take five wickets in an innings for England since Lancastrian, Tommy Greenhough in 1959. After Greenhough came Robin Hobbs, Ian Salisbury, Chris Schofield and Scott Borthwick, but somehow the influence of Shane Warne had little impact. Now Rashid might have paved the way for others to follow, like perhaps Will Beer (Sussex) or Mason Crane (Hampshire).

Playing Away described a passion among inner-city black Englishmen for cricket, but by 1990 reports emerged that youngsters in the Caribbean preferred the post-colonial American influences of Hip-Hop and basketball and that seems to have been reflected also in changing tastes among the next black, British generation. During the 1990s, the West Indian side went into a decline from which it has not yet recovered, and with their role models less impressive, youngsters turned to other stars and celebrities, not least in contemporary music. By 2015 there were very few cricketers of Afro-Caribbean origin in the county game. The best known, Michael Carberry, had to move from his native Surrey to Kent and then to Hampshire before he was given, and took his chance, in the county game. In the winter of 2013–2014 he bravely battled as an opening batsman in the Ashes disaster but was then returned to the county game where he might appear against Chesney

Hughes (born Anguilla, Derbyshire); Londoner Daniel Bell-Drummond of Kent; Chris Jordan (Barbados, Sussex); Tymal Mills (born in Yorkshire, Sussex) or the Warwickshire all-rounder Keith Barker (Manchester). Once, Hampshire fielded four black players in one county match, now there are about half-a-dozen in the whole English game.

Playing Away was funded and shown by Channel 4 in its early, 'progressive' years, which have been reigned in significantly through economic pressures. The addition of Channel 4 to the three existing British television channels came in 1982, but this percentage increase was nothing to 1989 when newspaper 'baron' Rupert Murdoch launched Sky Television. The decade also saw the popularity of the Sinclair Spectrum and Amstrad word processors, anticipating the explosion of home computing and the Internet, which would follow in the 1990s.

The popularity of television and the proliferation of channels coincided with a number of special events that added to the competition for audiences. On 29 July 1981, English cricket had to compete with the Royal Wedding of HRH Prince Charles and Lady Diana Spencer, which was celebrated with a national holiday and watched by a global audience of 750 million people. It is, however, still possible to find others – mostly men – proud to share their memory of having avoided 'the fuss' by attending a county cricket match that day. In Hampshire, some people still recall seeing Richard Hayward score a century on debut for Hampshire in a match v the new tourists Sri Lanka at Bournemouth.

A few years later on Saturday, 13 July 1985 at Trent Bridge, the Australians, replying to England's 456 (Gower 166), went from 94–1 to 366–5, effectively securing what would conclude as a draw on the following Tuesday. Edmonds and John Emburey bowled 121 overs between them with 33 maidens, taking 5–284. It was pretty dull fare for the occasional spectator but perhaps they were not watching the cricket, as that Saturday coincided with "Live Aid". It was organised to raise money to relieve the famine crisis in Ethiopia, brought to the public's attention in Britain by a BBC News broadcast, and based around live, outdoor concerts in London, Philadelphia and various European cities – organised largely through the energy of ex-punk Bob Geldof in London – and broadcast simultaneously around the world, attracting an estimated television audience of 1.9 billion across 150 nations.

Summertime popular music festivals in the UK dated back at least to the late 1950s with the Beaulieu Jazz Festivals. In the mid-1960s there were the 'Jazz & Blues' Festivals at Richmond and Windsor and then from 1968–1970 the increasingly large Isle of Wight Festivals. The Glastonbury Festival was launched in September 1970 and is now generally an annual event that sells out each year in a few hours. There are many more outdoor summer festivals today, each of them competing for audiences with cricket and other events.

With the resolution of the Packer 'crisis', the English domestic season settled into the same pattern of four competitions for a few years, but there were other visible changes. In the 1980 edition, *Wisden's* editor, Norman Preston, noted that the "preponderance" of overseas players in county cricket had persuaded the TCCB to limit them to one each per county from 1982, although he added that their arrival in 1968 had led to greater equality between the counties. Yorkshire, persisting in recruiting only their own, had endured a lengthening period without success.

Batsmen were increasingly inclined to wear helmets, with Graham Yallop the first to wear one in a Test Match in 1978. The fifth rewriting of the Laws of Cricket, with a publication in April 1980, considered banning helmets, especially for fielders, but decided against it. That view is now unimaginable. Thirty-five years later the laws are being rewritten again and English cricket has made helmets a compulsory piece of equipment for all batsmen and close fielders, other than slips.

Meanwhile, the 1980 *Playfair Cricket Annual* carried a photograph of Graham Gooch and in the background for the first time were advertising boards around the boundary. They are visible also in action photographs in the same year's *Hampshire Handbook* although not from every angle on every ground. But the change had begun, and by 1984 the Hampshire side appeared for their annual pre-season photograph for the first time sporting a sponsor's logo on their sweaters.

1980 was somewhat troubled; at home, not least, since it was the wettest English season since 1958, but beyond England Gordon Ross, in his editorial for the *Playfair Cricket Annual* suggested that in the previous year "cricket has presented a less attractive face to the world at large" having once been considered "the very model of the way sport should be played". He reported a case of a cricketer throwing a brick at a spectator; in New Zealand Michael Holding, unsuccessful in an appeal, had kicked down the stumps in anger; Colin Croft barged an umpire over; and even the MCC members were revolting as 'Dickie' Bird needed police protection in the Lord's pavilion on Saturday afternoon as the Centenary Test Match was delayed by inclement weather and light – more than 10 hours were lost on the first three days. England trailed Australia by 180 in their first innings, and challenged to chase 370 on the final day, batted to 244–3. Barry Wood, Man-of-the-Match, Kim Hughes, and Boycott scored centuries and despite the disappointments, the overall attendance averaged around 17,000 per day with takings just beyond £330,000.

In addition to that one match, the West Indies toured, and having won the first Test Match by two wickets, won the series as rain spoiled the next four matches, not one of which reached a fourth innings. Gooch, just, outscored Richards in the series but Garner with 26 wickets at 14.26 was outstanding. The weather had an impact on the County Championship too, but it was dominated by London with Middlesex leading Surrey by 13 points to take the title. They contested the Gillette Cup Final as well and again north London triumphed over their neighbours south of the river, while Northamptonshire won the other Cup Final as Essex fell just six runs short on 203–8 in 55 overs, and Warwickshire took the Sunday League title for the first time having been last the previous year.

In **1981**, *Wisden* had a new editor, John Woodcock, veteran cricket reporter of *the Times*. He looked back at previous contributions by new editors in identifying a range of issues still facing the game. These included continuing discussion of the lbw law, the absence of English leg-break bowlers, elusive fast natural pitches and English batting requiring an "injection of culture and enterprise". He was less than enthusiastic about the three floodlit matches played as an experiment in 1980, suggesting that floodlit cricket at Stamford Bridge "smacks of gimmickry" and, thus, did not publish the "meaningless" scorecards. Woodcock also noted that to "the dismay of many traditionalists" the counties at the TCCB had voted from 1981 that County Championship pitches should be fully covered against the elements. There was a request that to balance the impact on spin bowlers, pitches should be drier, but it's doubtful whether that happened very often. Woodcock spoke for those traditionalists in noting that weather, and its impact on pitches, had always been a part of English cricketing heritage, but the desire to have the County Championship resemble Test Match conditions prevailed. There was also to be an end to the restriction of 100 overs in the County Championship's first innings.

Headingley hosted one of the most extraordinary Test Matches as Botham, then Willis, took England from what seemed at first a certain defeat, to a stunning victory. The game attracted huge interest as it unfolded on the Monday and Tuesday – and productivity must surely have suffered across the country. Among the more impressive facts, it was only the second occasion on which a Test Match side won after following-on (previously England v Australia in 1894–1895), it was the closest Ashes result for more than 50 years, and it was England's first win against any side in 13 matches. While it was a triumph for Botham who scored 50 and 149* and took 7–109 in the match, it came after he had lost the captaincy. He had replaced Brearley in 1980 but failed to win a match; now Brearley returned, England won three matches in a row and with them came the Ashes. Despite this excitement in

England, *Wisden* noted, "on a broader front it was an uneasy year", and the following year, the editor's Notes opened with "politics cast a shadow across the cricket fields of the world" and deplored an on-field scuffle between Dennis Lillee and Javed Miandad.

Nottinghamshire won the **1981** County Championship, their first title in over 50 years, while Sussex, who had never won it, were runners-up. NatWest replaced Gillette as sponsors of the main limited-overs trophy and might have wondered why when two of the less fashionable counties, Derbyshire and Northamptonshire, reached the Final. In the event, it was one of the best. Northamptonshire's captain, Geoff Cook, led the way with 111 and from an opening partnership of 99 they posted 235–9 in their 60 overs, but the wickets lost would prove crucial. Derbyshire's 'foreigners' John Wright and Peter Kirsten added 123 from 41–1, but Neil Mallender took three wickets and Derbyshire required 19 for an outright victory from the last two overs. Since the penultimate one was to be bowled by the Pakistan paceman, Sarfraz Nawaz, Northamptonshire were favourites, but his six balls went for 12 runs. Among all these overseas stars, with one over to go and seven runs needed, the batsmen were Colin Tunicliffe (born Derby) and Geoff Miller (Chesterfield). Miller scored two from the first and one from the second, so Derbyshire, six down at this stage, knew that three more runs would leave them level in which case fewest wickets lost was the first tie-break. A 'dot' ball followed, then a single, so four scored and two balls remained. A single followed and with no further wickets down; Derbyshire were one run behind Northamptonshire. As soon as the ball was delivered, Miller raced for the striker's end, Tunnicliffe took off in the opposite direction, and after 120 overs of cricket, 235–6 beat 235–9 and Derbyshire had their first trophy since the 1930s.

In the B&H Cup, Surrey lost another Final. They had Somerset at 5–2 chasing 195 (Garner 5–14) but that just introduced Richards. He hit 132* and Somerset were home with seven wickets and more than 10 overs to spare. Essex won their first Sunday League title to add to the double of 1979. Colin Tunicliffe, rather enjoying his meetings with Northamptonshire, took the season's best Sunday figures, against them, 5–24.

In February **1982**, Sri Lanka played their first Test Match, losing by seven wickets to England, who played just the one Test Match there at the conclusion of their tour of India. It was a low-scoring game: Sri Lanka 218 & 175, England 223 & 171–3, with Underwood taking 8–95 in the match. The Indian tour, under the captaincy of Keith Fletcher, almost did not take place because two members of the England squad Boycott and Cook, had been to South Africa and only at the last moment did the Indian prime minister allow them to tour.

In the wake of the improved remuneration of cricketers after the Packer 'revolution', some leading world cricketers pursued the rand. English cricketers led the way as the first 'rebel' tourists to buck the ban on South Africa and visit that country. This was in March 1982 when Graham Gooch led 11 county players, all but one having also played for England. There was outrage at their actions and the participants were banned from international cricket for three years. Only Gooch and Emburey would return to a significant Test Match career while Boycott, who had flown home early from India, never played for England again. He had returned, once again citing "physical and mental tiredness", but recovered soon enough to jet off to South Africa. The South Africans arranged further tours during the decade by a Sri Lankan side (1982–1983), West Indians 1982–1983 and 1983–1984, Australians 1985–1986 and 1986–1987 and, finally, another English side under Mike Gatting in 1989–1990. Once again the players received three-year bans. In 1991, South Africa was readmitted to international cricket and they competed in the 1992 World Cup.

England returned from the tour of India and Sri Lanka and appointed another new captain, Bob Willis, after the brief tenancy of Fletcher. Brearley had benefitted to some degree by the disruption that followed the Packer years and he missed the toughest of the West Indies years, but he was one of the finest England Test Match captains, winning 58% of his 31 matches in charge. Since then, only Michael Vaughan with 51% in 51 Test Matches and Andrew Strauss with 48% in 50, have come close to Brearley's record. Brearley also led England to a World Cup Final, the best they have yet managed in the shorter form.

In the winter, five of the six Test Matches were drawn, with India taking the series 1–0 after a victory in the first low-scoring match. It was pretty dull stuff with interruptions from weather. In the summer of **1982**, India toured and England reversed the winter's result in a three-match series, while the three games against Pakistan were more interesting, and dominated by two fine all-rounders, Imran Khan and Ian Botham. England won the first Test Matches, with the new captain injured and Gower deputising, Pakistan levelled at Lord's (Mohsin Khan 200, Mudassar Nazar 6–32) and with the captain back, England won the thrilling decider. Pakistan's 275 gave them a first innings lead of just 19 but Willis and Botham put them out for 199. England needing 219 to win were led by Fowler (86) until at 168–1, Muddasar struck again and they lost five wickets for 21. At 199–7 either side might have won, but Vic Marks and Bob Taylor saw them home. The five-day attendance was 50,000.

Mike Brearley hit the winning run at Worcester that took his Middlesex side to the **1982** title and then walked off into retirement and another, equally absorbing life. In late July at Southport, Warwickshire posted 523–4 declared but lost to Lancashire, for whom Graeme Fowler scored centuries in both innings – and both with a runner. Sussex, first masters of the shorter form, won the Sunday League for the first time and Somerset won the B&H Cup again in an even less competitive Final than 1981. They dismissed Nottinghamshire for 130 in the 51st over and reached the target for the loss of Peter Denning with more than 20 overs to spare. There was only time for Richards to reach a half-century this year and Vic Marks with 2–24 took the Gold Award. About six weeks later there was a replica in the NatWest Final as Surrey won, at last, their 159–1 in the 35th over passing Warwickshire's 158 all out. The thriller between Northamptonshire and Derbyshire was the jewel in a rather dusty crown of recent 'one day' Finals, which showed up the limitations of sometimes well-named limited-overs cricket in matches lacking any competitive edge.

During the 1980s, Hampshire became the last of the 17 counties to reach a Lord's Final and the 'prizes' in county cricket continued to be spread among most of the counties: Derbyshire (one trophy); Essex (7); Hampshire (2); Lancashire (2); Leicestershire (1); Middlesex (8); Northamptonshire (1); Nottinghamshire (4); Somerset (3); Surrey (1); Sussex (2); Warwickshire (2); Worcestershire (4) and Yorkshire (2). The three counties without success in that decade have all won trophies since: Glamorgan (4), Gloucestershire (8) and Kent (1).

In **1982**, seven of the top 10 batsmen and nine of the first 11 bowlers in the averages were overseas players, which continued to exercise many minds – as did the fact that on covered pitches batsmen dominated bowlers to an extent not seen for 50 years. There was again much talk of changes to the structure of English county cricket, including a proposal to reduce the 24 three-day matches to 16 midweek games of four days each. *Wisden* suggested that this would reduce the amount of cricket for members "who form the backbone of every county club" and might be a case of "advocating change for change's sake". A decade later it would be a fact. Meanwhile, the Test and County Cricket Board (TCCB), which as its name suggests was responsible for the professional game, took greater control of English cricket whose governing body, the Cricket Council, was concerned for English cricket at all levels, including 25,000 clubs and 150,000 players at those clubs. *Wisden*, reporting on the issue of control in English cricket, noted the extent to which marketing men had influenced change in Australian cricket and added, "Beware the small, executive sub-committee of businessmen, to whom the charm of cricket is little more than a technicality …"

In the winter of 1982–1983, the Ashes series included a thriller in Melbourne when England's victory by three runs equalled the narrowest runs margin of victory in Test Match history – and that after all four innings were intriguingly close: England 284 & 294, Australia 287 & 288. There were no centuries but eight half-centuries and four more in the 40s, while Cowans (6–77) was the only bowler to take five or more wickets. In every respect it was an even match with a high proportion of players contributing although, oddly, the least successful batsmen were the two stylists Gower and Greg Chappell. The end was very tense as Border and Thomson added 70 for the final wicket. They closed the fourth day at 255–9 and added 33 more before Thomson edged Botham to slip and Miller held the catch. This was cricket at its best, although sadly a group of drunken English supporters waving the Union Flag had invaded the field in the first Test Match and grappled with Australian fielders. Test Match sides were expected to bowl 96 overs per day, a modest target but generally beyond 21st century teams.

In *Wisden*, Philip Carling, who had moved from Chief Executive of Nottinghamshire to secretary of Glamorgan, wrote about county cricket's struggle to survive. He recorded the significant impact from the 1960s, of limited-overs cricket and sponsorship, with a reminder that the latter is not "altruism". In the past 20 years the new competitions had spread rewards among all counties but also increased expectations of success among supporters. Counties responded by signing international overseas cricketers and their remuneration led to increased expectations among English county players that, in turn, created an urgent need for improved memberships and attendances. At the end of 1982, Hampshire reported that Membership fell to 4,858, having been 8,331 in 1977. One notable change for them was the decline in their subscribing cricket clubs around the county, from 217 to 121 in the same period. Full membership was now £23 with life membership £350 and the accounts showed a deficit of almost £80,000. Ground advertising revenue was hit when the firm responsible went into liquidation.

Carling traced the impact of Gillette's initial sponsorship of the knock-out cup increasing from £6,500 in 1963 to a value of £250,000, which the original sponsors declined. At this point NatWest took on that competition alongside John Player, Benson & Hedges, Schweppes and the initial support for the England team from Cornhill Insurance. By the early 1980s the TCCB was handling an income of around £3m. Meanwhile, Carling reported counties making increasing use of their grounds in a variety of ways beyond cricket including extended ground advertising, which benefitted from televised matches. As a consequence, in the Ashes summer of 1981 almost every county recorded a profit but we can see from the example of Hampshire (above) that this was not easy to sustain and it soon went into reverse with many counties. For Carling, this inconsistency was a sign of "poor-county budgeting", and he called for cricket to be "flexible, adaptable and financially more far-seeing". In the context of 1981 successes, the counties increased the number of County Championship matches from 1983 but Carling suggested that 12 months later they would not have done that – a clear reflection of the knee-jerk decisions that lead to change following change following change. For Carling the answer was to reduce the slow procedures of the committee system in favour of "a real executive".

In his 1983 edition, *Wisden's* editor had warned that cricket was declining in the state schools, although his traditional section on "Schools Cricket" still offered 45 pages about the (boys') public schools. The report included a focus on the major schools representative matches which featured a few future county cricketers and John Stephenson who would be a 'One-Test Wonder', but not one of those players, benefitting from the best resources in their school years would move significantly into the international arena. It was different in the following year as the Southern Schools included Nasser Hussain, while Michael Atherton captained the Rest.

Having provided £1m of sponsorship since 1977, **1983** was Schweppes' last season funding the County Championship. Prudential Assurance sponsored the World Cup in 1983 but that, too, was their last involvement so new sponsors had to be sought. The search was successful and their replacements were Britannic Assurance and Texaco. Gordon Ross, editing the *Playfair Cricket Annual,* observed that the latter in particular "could not have come at a more important time with the first-class counties facing ever increasing administrative costs". Charles Palmer, chairman of the TCCB, welcomed the new deal describing the "worthy history" and "legacy" of the County Championship, which he added, "we must always cherish". He described it "demanding the highest technical skills" which breed England's Test Match cricketers. People still say such things while shunting it to the season's bookends, producing batsmen and seamer-friendly pitches and seeking to reduce the number of matches that stood at 24 in 1983.

It came as no surprise that the third World Cup, again in England in **1983,** was dominated by the West Indies. England went well until the unlucky 13th match of the tournament when they posted 234 v New Zealand and had their opponents 3–2 and 151–6, but they lost by two wickets. In 1983 there were 24 matches *before* India beat England and West Indies beat Pakistan in the two semi-finals. In the Final, Roberts (3–32) Marshall (2–24) and Holding (2–26) put India out for just 183 and after the early loss of Greenidge, the West Indies moved to 50–1 with Haynes and Richards looking set – then Madan Lal broke the partnership dismissing both men, and five Indian bowlers shared wickets as the firm favourites fell to 76–6. A partnership of 43 between Jeffery Dujon and Marshall gave them hope but India won eventually by 43 runs. That triumph transformed the game in India, creating a huge passion for limited-overs cricket, which remains to this day and now embraces T20, in particular.

The World Cup brought some cheer to English cricket in **1983,** and it needed it. The season started with monsoon conditions, and after the difficulties of 1982, brought fears that some counties could not recover financially. By early June, Gloucestershire had not completed a whole day's play at home, but one week later the visiting nations arrived, the sun accompanied them, and by-and-large it remained. Most counties had reasonable financial years albeit receiving up to 40% of their income from the TCCB. The World Cup brought some wonderful all-rounders to England, in particular Ian Botham, Kapil Dev, Richard Hadlee and Imran Khan. Hadlee was a key member of the New Zealand side that played Test Matches after the limited-overs tournament and they enjoyed their first victory over England in this country. They were not the only touring side in this period to complain that counties were not fielding their strongest sides in matches against them. During the season, Sir Donald Bradman suggested that umpires might benefit from assistance from television technology.

In **1983**, Essex benefitted from the England bans on South African tourists Gooch and Lever to win the County Championship. With pitches covered, things were supposed to be in favour of batsmen but at the end of May at Chelmsford, Essex dismissed Surrey for 14 (Norbert Phillip 6–4) although a second innings century by Surrey's captain, Roger Knight, saved the game. In the title race, Essex finished ahead of Middlesex, this success being revenge for the B&H Cup Final in which Middlesex beat Essex, Somerset won the NatWest Trophy and Yorkshire, without any success since 1969, won the Sunday League. They were not however cheered by this, and engaged in a civil war, sacking their captain Boycott. In the County Championship, forfeits and cheap bowling for declarations were increasingly common – Steve O'Shaunessy scored a century in 35 minutes for Lancashire against the bowling of Gower (9–0–102–0) and James Whitaker (8–1–87–0), but Lancashire, unhappy with the contrivance, refused to declare and the game ended in a farce.

In the winter of 1983–1984, England played and lost to New Zealand and Pakistan (plus a brief visit to Fiji) after which time their captain, Bob Willis played a few county games in **1984**, retired, and was replaced by David Gower against the West Indies. At the start of the international season in May in the first ODI at Manchester, England reduced the West Indies to 102–7 with not one of the seven reaching double figures, but Richards was still there and added 59 with Eldine Baptiste for the eighth wicket. When

Baptiste was dismissed, Holding and Richards added a further 111 for the final wicket without being parted. Richards finished 189* from 170 balls in a total of 272–9 (55 overs). It was an incredible effort with 21 x fours and five x sixes. Setting the pattern for the summer, a demoralised England side lost by 104 runs.

West Indies won the first Test Match at Edgbaston by an innings with England's new opener Andy Lloyd knocked out of Test cricket on the first day on his home ground. Fowler (106), Lamb (110) and Botham (8–103) did their best at Lord's enabling England to lead by 41 and Gower to set West Indies 342 to win in less than the last day. Greenidge then smashed 214* (241 balls) and they got there in on the first ball of the 67th over by nine wickets. England had not lost a Test Match after declaring their second innings since 1948 and many followers ranked these West Indians alongside Bradman's 'Invincibles'. There was an Allan Lamb century at Leeds, and with West Indies winning by just eight wickets the results seemed to be getting closer. It was a mere 'blip' as they reverted to an innings victory at Old Trafford with another double century for Greenidge. Lamb scored another century but Paul Terry, in his second Test Match, had his arm broken and followed Andy Lloyd back to the relative peace of the county game. Pat Pocock returned to the England side after an interval of 86 matches and took four wickets. At the Oval, West Indies won by 172 runs and became the first touring side ever to win all five Test Matches of a series in England. Some of their supporters celebrated this as a 'Blackwash'. In his two matches, Pocock recorded a pair of 'pairs' – only the second time in English Test history and the first in that century.

Essex won the Sunday League and the County Championship (again) – the latter was the first sponsored by Brittanic Assurance. It finished in high drama with two balls remaining. Nottinghamshire 293–9 required four runs to beat Somerset and pip Essex, Mike Bore hit high and long and Richard Ollis held the catch that made him a hero in the east. The B&H Cup Final was almost inevitably one-sided: Warwickshire 139 losing to Lancashire 140–4 in the 43rd over. The NatWest Final was significantly better with a last-ball victory for Middlesex, chasing Kent's total of 232–6. Earlier in the season Yorkshire became the first first-class side to lose to a Minor County in the NatWest Trophy, beaten by Shropshire. To add to the indignity, they were also the first to lose in such circumstances in the Gillette Cup (to Durham) while the two other triumphs by the 'minnows' had been by Lincolnshire (v Glamorgan) and Hertfordshire (v Essex). The Minor Counties did not generally find things easy however, and Warwickshire's 392–5 against Oxfordshire was the highest in the 60-overs competition with Kanhai's 206 the record individual innings. With fine weather in **1984** every game finished on the scheduled day.

Despite the superb performances by the West Indies side there were many expressions of concern about the use of short-pitched bowling. Whenever an English commentator raised the point, Australians in the vicinity tended to look back to the 1930s, suggesting that England started it. In the 1985 *Wisden,* the Australian-born English-based journalist, Murray Hedgecock, wrote generally of the "turbulent" 1980s. Among the comments by the editor was one that may bring surprise, even to those who watched cricket regularly in 1984: the players had not welcomed an attempt to introduce a *minimum* of 117 overs in each day of the County Championship. As a consequence, representations from the county captains had it reduced to 112 per day alongside a series of fines – 112! How is it we have allowed that to fall by a further 16 overs (one whole hour) per day? In 1985, the editor was disappointed by the revised target as 117 overs per day meant just 18 per hour from 11am–6.30pm. Now, counties play, in theory, from 11am–6pm although it is often until 6.30pm (at the least) when play ends. For *Wisden's* editor, much of the fault lay with the proliferation of English "trundlers" and the decline of spin bowlers.

English counties might have sought to emulate their West Indian conquerors and field genuine fast bowlers. A sponsored attempt to discover a new generation was launched in the summer under the direction of Ted Dexter and Bob Willis but little came of it and, by-and-large, for a variety of reasons Englishmen don't bowl fast. In the dry summer of 1984, English batsmen generally profited – at least until they moved up to the Test Match arena.

Gower retained the England captaincy with Gatting as his deputy for the renewed Ashes battle in **1985**. The visiting Australians participated in a significant experiment, playing eight matches against the counties over four-days. If successful, the lobby to increase County Championship days would strengthen its case. The Australians failed to win back the Ashes and departed having lost nine of their previous 14 Test Matches. Back at home they then met New Zealand and lost by an innings. They may have still been suffering from the disruption of the Packer years but more significantly they had lost players as a result of the rebel tours to South Africa. They, too, were unhappy that some counties fielded less than their strongest sides in some matches against them, but that was an aspect of the new 'reality' in which counties were more concerned with winning one of the four trophies while the tourists, who now appeared regularly in county sides and on television, lacked the mystique and draw of 30 and more years ago. One of the features of the successful England side was their fastest scoring rate ever in an Ashes series – just better than 3.5 per over. England's success helped the income at the TCCB whose takings for the year approached £2.5m. As a consequence, the counties enjoyed a healthy share-out and most were in profit over the year.

The series was played in good spirit, but elsewhere the New Zealand captain nearly took his team from the field in protest at Pakistan's umpires. Meanwhile at home, the TCCB's Disciplinary Committee regularly met to discuss the behaviour in county cricket of players, including former Test Match captains Botham, Fletcher and Imran Khan. There were concerns, too, about crowd behaviour, particularly related to drinking, and as a consequence licensing times on some grounds were restricted. Botham's behaviour was often 'larger than life' prone to exposure from an increasingly voracious and sensational-ist tabloid media and not always to the satisfaction of cricket's authorities. Nonetheless, in the winter he recovered from a knee operation by walking from John O'Groats to Land's End to raise £600,000 for charity.

1985 was his last season as Somerset's captain (and 1986 would be his last as a Somerset player). He passed 1,000 runs in the County Championship but did not play that often, and they finished last. Middlesex won the title for the third time in six years. Hampshire, under Mark Nicholas, stayed in contention to the penultimate match when, with Northamptonshire nine wickets down, Roger Harper dispatched the final ball for six to win the match. Had the wicket fallen Hampshire *might* have won the title, but Middlesex had the stronger all-round bowling attack and following the acrimonious departure of Jesty at the end of 1984, Hampshire did not field one Hampshire-born cricketer all season. Essex dominated the limited-overs competitions, winning the Sunday League and the NatWest Trophy – the latter by one run, dismissing Nottinghamshire's, Derek Randall, from the final ball. Leicestershire won an unusually close B&H Cup Final against Essex with Peter Willey, 86* and 1–41, taking the Gold Award.

The editor of *Wisden* expressed concern that after five seasons, the covering regulations were producing increasingly uniform and batsman-friendly pitches, adding that only once before **1985**, in 1928, had 19 batsmen averaged more than 50, while 1985 was the *first* season in which only four regular bowlers averaged under 20 runs per wicket: Richard Ellison (Kent), Hadlee (Nottinghamshire), Marshall (Hampshire) and Gary Sainsbury (Gloucestershire). Bill Frindall took over editing the *Playfair Cricket Annual* following the death of Gordon Ross and the new man praised, in particular, his predecessor's role in helping to establish the Gillette Cup, including the idea of awards for the Man-of-the-Match.

Just before he died, Ross had written his last piece for publication, which Frindall included in the new annual. Ross confirmed that "of course" he loved Test cricket but added

> I enjoy Lord's more when Middlesex are playing a three-day County game … when there is the peace … that we used to know, when you can drift around the old place chatting to players, umpires, scorers, groundsmen, administrators, friends, acquaintances, even perfect strangers.

Ross recalled this deep sense of peaceful well-being also on a particular morning walking across Diglis Bridge to the ground at Worcester, picturing the hordes of commuters who at the same time would be pouring over London's bridges on another day to work "in a much less appealing way" than his duty of reporting the county cricket for *the Times*.

Since Ross was born in the first world war, grew up during the General Strike (1926) and economic depression of the 1930s and was in his 20s through the second world war, there was perhaps a certain sentimentality in his reference to the peace of the past, but in respect of cricket, and particularly English school, club and county cricket, we can perhaps understand what he meant. His last day was spent watching a match at Lord's in one hopes those familiar and friendly surroundings. However, there was none of his "peace" in the winter of 1985–1986. The England team arrived in India to learn of the assassination of Mrs Indira Gandhi and a few weeks later, Britain's Deputy High Commissioner in Bombay was murdered on the day after he had entertained the England team.

The Indians found a new star in Mohammad Azharuddin who scored three centuries in his first three Test Matches, and India also won a so-called "World Championship of Cricket" in Australia to celebrate the 150th anniversary of the founding of the state of Victoria. In September 1985, India also brought great cheer to Sri Lanka being the first side to lose to them in Sri Lanka's 14th Test Match. Sri Lanka also played hosts to a tour by an England 'B' side, which should have also visited Zimbabwe and Bangladesh until those two countries cancelled the visit because some players selected had playing and/ or coaching links with South Africa. There had been one England 'B' match v Pakistan in 1982 but this was their first tour, and this side would eventually be renamed England 'A' and then England Lions with a greater focus on young cricketers. Mark Nicholas captained this first touring side, with other players including Bill Athey, Martyn Moxon, Derek Pringle, Jonathan Agnew, Nick Cook, Steven Rhodes and Chris Smith.

For the third time in four seasons, Essex won the County Championship in **1986** (with Gloucestershire yet again runners-up) but there were still other 'champions'. Sussex won their fourth 60-over title, chasing down Lancashire's 242–8 with 10 balls to spare and at last there was an exciting B&H Cup Final although again not particularly high-scoring. Middlesex reached 199–7 in

55 overs and Kent fell just two runs short when, on a dark, drizzling evening, Graham Dilley failed to hit the last ball for six. Emburey took no wickets but conceded just 17 runs in his 11 overs to add to 28 runs and a fine catch and received the Gold Award. Hampshire clinched their third Sunday League title in a similarly tight match at the Oval, albeit with one game to spare. That was the end of John Player's Sunday sponsorship with the days of the cigarette companies' money under increasing threat – next up, Refuge Assurance. Geoff Boycott played his last first-class match for Yorkshire v Northamptonshire at Scarborough. It was a dull draw but in his only innings he was perhaps appropriately run out, having reached what David Green called a "painstaking" 61.

In **1986** Ian Botham played in just one Test Match, against New Zealand at the Oval, but he took wickets in successive overs to equal and then pass Dennis Lillee's record of 355 Test Match wickets. Perhaps he should have played more as New Zealand won a series in England for the first time. An almost wholly white Zimbabwe side retained the ICC Trophy (won in 1982) by beating Holland in the Lord's Final. India beat England in the Lord's Test Match in the same year and there was general concern at the standard of English cricket, already way behind the West Indians.

The TCCB enquiry into the playing standards in English Test Match and county cricket, known as the Palmer Report, suggested that the decline in batting standards was mainly the fault of limited-overs cricket. The problem, as *Wisden* observed, was that it is possible to set up an enquiry on the basis of a run of disappointing results, but by the time a committee has been formed, met, gathered information and reported, things may seem different. In October 1986, England had set off to Australia having lost 11 Test Matches since their last victory. When Gatting's team returned from Australia, they had retained the Ashes, won by Gower in 1985, and things seemed somewhat better. Australian cricket, interestingly, seemed to be suffering from a weakened domestic competition because most of their leading players were involved in one Test Match series after another, and others were ineligible after participating in rebel tours of South Africa. Despite the relative success of India and New Zealand, the Australians remained the popular draw. In 1985, over 93,000 had watched them at Lord's but one year later around 69,000 watched New Zealand and 57,509 watched India. Edgbaston drew just 42,750 over the five days, realising almost £250,000 in a very interesting match against India. The game was drawn with both sides making 390 in the first innings so that after England were dismissed for 235, India reached 174–5, just 62 short with five wickets in hand. Perhaps there would have been a winner but for the 48 minutes stoppage for bad light and rain in the final session.

During the winter of 1986–1987 Somerset were involved in a very public and acrimonious dispute, having decided to dispense with the services of West Indians, Richards and Garner, in favour of New Zealander, Martin Crowe. Botham was furious and laid considerable blame at the door of the somewhat remote captain Peter Roebuck. In **1987**, Crowe played for Somerset, Richards and Garner waited for the next tour of England, and Botham departed for Worcestershire, along with his 1981 Headingley partner Graham Dilley, who came from Kent. Crowe scored 1,627 runs in the County Championship at 67.79 and Somerset rose a few places in the table. Not everyone at Worcester was delighted by Botham's arrival, and his County Championship figures were modest but at the season's end, a capacity crowd celebrated Worcestershire's triumph in the Sunday League as they beat Northamptonshire by nine wickets (Botham 2–34 and 61). The B&H Cup seemed to have changed its fortunes as there was another Lord's thriller when Yorkshire 244–6 in 55 overs, beat Northamptonshire 244–7 by losing one wicket fewer – Jim Love simply blocked the final ball. Yorkshire were the fourth side now to have won all four competitions, after Essex, Lancashire and Kent although others have done so since and now, of course, there is a T20 to add. Northamptonshire endured a second Lord's defeat, this time to Nottinghamshire, which stretched over the Saturday and Monday. The rain which bedevilled the summer reduced the match to 50 overs from which Northamptonshire scored 228–3 and at 38–4 and 146–6, Nottinghamshire were struggling but Hadlee with 70* took them home by three wickets.

Nottinghamshire were the team of the season as they also won the County Championship, four points ahead of Lancashire, after which Hadlee and Clive Rice departed. For one season, English county cricket reverted to uncovered pitches during the hours of play, hoping that this would provide greater opportunities for spin bowlers while requiring batsmen to develop new techniques. It was a wet summer but the experiment was not a great success, partly because, to help the spinners rain needs to be followed by hot sun and that was rarely the case. Hampshire's spinner Rajesh Maru took 66 wickets at just under 30 each, but their quicker bowlers Tim Tremlett, Marshall and Steven Andrew all finished ahead of him in the averages because, as he observed, the regulations allowed for full covering of bowlers' run-ups, so every time the rain made the pitch lively, Mark Nicholas would turn to Marshall first, and usually another seamer with him. Throughout the season only two spinners, Eddie Hemmings and Jack Simmons, passed 50 wickets at fewer than 25 apiece. The experiment was abandoned and uncovered wickets are almost certainly a thing of the past.

In the summer of **1987**, HRH Duke of Edinburgh opened the new Mound Stand at Lord's, as the MCC celebrated their bicentenary with a drawn match between their side and the Rest of the World. The stars came out and there were centuries for (almost) all the Gs: Greenidge, Gooch, Gatting and Gavaskar – Gower with 8 & 40 missed out and only Malcolm Marshall managed three wickets in an innings. Imran Khan led Pakistan to a grumpy 1–0 series victory in a five match series over England who gave debuts to Neil Fairbrother and David Capel although both disappeared after one match. It was a wet summer and three full days were lost at Lord's for the first time in 33 years, when Pakistan were also the visitors. When the new England Team manager, Mickey Stewart, criticised Pakistan's perceived time-wasting tactics at a press conference, the visitors objected to being called "cheats" in public. The TCCB also refused the Pakistani's request to replace two English umpires David Constant and Ken Palmer. The ill feeling persisted for some years with occasional explosions, the next during the return series the following winter. This last issue would lead eventually to the introduction of neutral umpires in Test Matches.

In November 1987, England reached another World Cup Final but were unable to reproduce their dominance over Australia in the longer form, and the latter became World Champions. In those years England's counties played three domestic competitions, over 40, 55 and 60 overs, whereas the World Cup was 50 overs per side. Australia reached 253–5 (David Boon 75) with England falling just eight runs short of victory (Athey 58). Capel and Fairbrother both returned as England then moved on to Pakistan to try again to win a Test Match against them in 1987 but they failed, losing the first by an innings and drawing the next two. The second match was an awful affair. England made 292 (Chris Broad 116) and midway through the last over on day two, Pakistan were 106–5 when, as Hemmings moved in to bowl, captain Gatting moved a fielder. Umpire Shakoor Rana invoked Law 42 (unfair play) and the two had a clear altercation on the field with Gatting pointing an accusing finger more than once and claiming that he had informed the batsman. There was no further play that day and the umpire refused to resume on day three without an apology. The Foreign Office and TCCB intervened to prevent the cancellation of the tour. They threatened Gatting with the loss of the captaincy if he did not apologise.

Rana who had worn a Pakistan sweater while officiating, had been at the centre of previous confrontations with the Indian captain Gavaskar (when matches between India and Pakistan resumed a decade earlier) and Jeremy Coney, captain of New Zealand, in 1984. He said of Gatting, "In Pakistan many men have been killed for the sort of insults he threw at me. He's lucky I didn't beat him." He was appointed for the third and final Test Match until it became apparent that England would not play if he stood. The third day of the second Test Match was simply lost and the match drawn, as was the third and final game although not before leg-spinner Abdul Qadir took his 30ᵗʰ wicket in the series.

In the *Playfair Cricket Annual,* Bill Frindall described "the odorous memories of recent events in Pakistan" and suggested that the home side's Board "deserves to be expelled from the ICC" for its "blatant manipulation of groundsmen, umpires and captain". But he was highly critical of English players too, notably Broad who had refused to leave the crease after being given out, and Gatting for his part in the incident with Rana. He suggested that "such shameful episodes" were the inevitable consequence "when winning and money becomes more important than the game itself". Graeme Wright was the new editor of *Wisden.* Looking back to **1987** and noting an increasing egalitarianism in society, he expressed concern that English cricket lacked clear leadership, observing "any game made competitive by nationalism or commercialism can blind the spectator to those aspects of sport – enjoyment and entertainment – which are as important as winning". But we have seen that over the previous 25 years most counties felt able to compete for trophies in most seasons while the balance of power in Test Match and ODI cricket shifted regularly. So often in the modern world, winning *was* everything. This was even the case off the field with a dispute between the TCCB and their hosts, the MCC, leading internally to disquiet expressed by the MCC members over poor communication and decision-making.

In pursuing his anxieties about standards of behaviour, Wright, perhaps with half an eye on the British prime minister Margaret Thatcher argued, "never has cricket been more in need of firm leadership". He also went beyond cricket to identify concerns about increasingly "violent attitudes" by what he described as "otherwise law-abiding citizens, and suggested "tolerance has given way to a short-fused temper" as in the recent on-field incidents involving England cricketers. But if English cricket was putting winning and rewards before "the game itself", why was that surprising in the 1980s? These years were characterised so often as the 'greed is good' decade, with its stress on the individual, and when suddenly it seemed there might be no such thing as society. That last observation was reported from an interview with the prime minister in October 1987, just one month before the England team arrived in Pakistan. More extensively, she said that people who expect governments to solve their problems are "Casting their problem on society" but adding that she believed "there is no such thing as society", only "individual" men, women, and families. Post-Packer, the best cricketers in the most "individual" of games enjoyed increasing star status and better financial rewards.

It is again worth asserting that sport does not simply reflect the dominant attitudes and values of the society, it helps to form them. The UK in the

1980s and cricket in the 1980s were part and parcel of the same thing. If the dominant attitudes were not yet clear, in the week that England played the third and final Test Match in Karachi, Hollywood released the blockbuster movie *Wall Street*. While Oliver Stone's film warned against personal and corporate greed, it is entirely plausible that the anti-hero Gilbert Gekko (Michael Douglas) offered a role model to those who sought huge wealth and its attendant 'rewards'.

In this context, cricket was well suited to the emphasis on individualism and wealth (greed?). It is a team game, of course, with many opportunities for sides to achieve great things by 'pulling together', but it is surely also the most individual of team sports since every crucial moment of action centres on the gladiatorial contest between batsman and bowler and only subsequently, perhaps, one or two more fielders before the next sequence. Like other team sports, the stars will attract most column inches and receive the highest rewards. However, over the previous 20 years since overseas cricketers had arrived in significant numbers in county cricket, individual players at the highest level had been able to go beyond the relatively modest salaries of county players (and the rather less modest tax-free benefits) through other means, including the Packer circus and the South African Rebel Tours. Could these participants invoke a sense of pride in pulling on a county or country sweater and cap if, like Mr Gekko, they were in it principally for the money, and for themselves?

One of the consequences of the problems with on-field dissent was the move towards neutral umpires in international cricket. In November 1986, the Pakistan captain Imran Khan pressed his authorities to invite two Indian umpires to officiate in a Test Match against West Indies in Lahore, and the ICC responded fairly quickly to this initiative. By 1992 an experiment led to one neutral umpire standing in every Test Match. In 2002 India's tour of West Indies was the first in which two neutrals officiated and this is now the accepted practice.

Graeme Wright reported on sponsorship of £550,000 from the Milk Marketing Board to introduce Kwik Cricket into English primary schools and the colts sections of clubs. Since that was nearly 30 years ago, has there been any significant evaluation on its success in encouraging people to engage long-term in cricket, as players, officials or spectators – particularly given recent reports of declining participation in the recreational game?

There was now a limit on overseas players of one per county *unless* signed before 1979. This seemed like a positive move to encourage English talent although South Africans like Allan Lamb, Robin Smith and Graeme Hick had qualified for England. Gordon Greenidge, one of those 'extra' eligible overseas players, toured with the West Indies in 1988 but did not then return to Hampshire. One consequence of the new restriction was that counties looked to sign English players developed by their competitors and so the TCCB introduced an 'Extraordinary Registration' system, limiting such signings to one per year and two in five years.

There was bad weather in the first Test Match v West Indies in **1988** and England managed a draw, but lost the next four in the series. In late August they played another single Test Match v Sri Lanka at Lord's and won the match. During that summer, England used 29 players in the Test Matches (and five more in the ODIs) – and all this under no fewer than four captains, Gatting, Emburey, Chris Cowdrey and Gooch. In 1989, 13 of the 29 players in the Ashes series played in just one match. England captain Mike Gatting having survived the altercation with Shakoor Rana in Pakistan lost the role after a tabloid accusation of inappropriate behaviour in a hotel during the First Test Match. Gatting denied the charge but perhaps the TCCB had the excuse it was looking for.

In **1988,** with pitches fully covered again, the County Championship changed further with the partial introduction of some four-day matches. In the 1989 *Wisden,* the editor reported the "developing argument" in favour of 16 four-day County Championship matches, which would be fully implemented in 1993. There were three key arguments in its favour. The first was to bring the County Championship closer to Test Match cricket; the second was to eliminate the 'non-bowling' that enabled declarations and the pursuit of victory on the third day. To a large extent these aims have been met, but the third, that pitches would wear and encourage spin bowlers, has rarely occurred. On the contrary, pitches, the inspectors that visit them, and the penalties that sometimes follow, have generally led to caution and flatter, batsmen-friendly strips. There has also been a significant decline in the number, hence, a variety of grounds used by almost all counties.

Sussex are one county that have tried to maintain their 'outgrounds' although in the autumn of 2015 they announced they might cease to play at Arundel and Horsham and when the fixtures appeared, Horsham had indeed gone. A rare exception is Middlesex. In 1960, after the briefest of forays to Hornsey, they returned as they had always done, to Lord's for every County Championship match. Then, 55 seasons later in 2014, they used three grounds although their position is complicated by the fact that they are tenants of the MCC at the 'Home of Cricket'. Overall in 1960, the 17 counties visited 79 grounds, an average of 4.6 grounds per county and just over three matches per ground. In 2014, the 18 counties used 30 grounds with an average of 1.66 home grounds per county and therefore almost five matches on each ground.

In the 1960 County Championship, Essex and Glamorgan used eight grounds each; by 2014 this was down to two and three, respectively. Kent and Yorkshire went from seven to two, and Somerset from six to one. In 1960 the counties who travelled least, tended to be those with Test Match grounds – in addition to Middlesex, Nottinghamshire went once to Worksop, Surrey once to Guildford (as in 2014) and Warwickshire played twice in Coventry and once at Nuneaton. These days, they are increasingly the *Birmingham* Bears, playing in the city. Today, eight sides use just one County Championship ground: newcomers Durham, Hampshire, Leicestershire, Northamptonshire, Nottinghamshire, Somerset, Warwickshire and Worcestershire. Only Glamorgan, Middlesex and Sussex used three grounds in 2015 and Sussex will use just two in 2016.

Apart from fewer fixtures, the obvious reason for this reduction is that many counties have invested heavily in ground development and need to maximise income on those grounds. It is also much more difficult now to stage matches on outgrounds because of the stringent demands on pitch quality but also in particular the agreements with companies who advertise at and/or sponsor games. Any shift of home ground requires the advertising boards to be removed and re-assembled, which is necessarily a time-consuming event. When Hampshire took themselves to the Isle of Wight between 1956–1962 there were no advertising boards and thus no such requirements. In recent years they have considered taking a game to the island at the recently constructed Newclose Ground, but this is an expensive proposition and the ground is somewhat complicated to reach by public transport. A single limited-overs match might be possible but then comes the matter of removals there-and-back. In 2012 Hampshire did arranged a T20 warm-up there against a PCA Masters XI. It looked an attractive fixture – the large Marquee and lunch was arranged – but it rained all day and the only 'entertainment' was Lou Vincent 'surfing' across the flooded pitch.

In **1988**, Hampshire's first ever four-day County Championship match began against Surrey at Southampton on 21 April. On the first day, Cardigan Connor (4–71) helped dismiss Surrey for 246 but Sylvester Clarke had two wickets as Hampshire slipped to 44–3 overnight. On the next (second) morning, Nick Peters on debut, took 4–47, Hampshire collapsed to 91 all out, followed on and were bowled out again for 198 – and that only thanks to an eighth wicket partnership of 92 by Tremlett and Steve Jefferies (Greig 6–56). Surrey won the game on that second evening by nine wickets, the match having lasted less than half of its scheduled four days! Hampshire then travelled to Canterbury and beat Kent (230 & 99) by seven wickets despite a first innings deficit of 60 runs. At last, a couple of top-order batsmen (Chris Smith and Nicholas) worked out how to play four-day cricket, although this match was over by lunch on day three.

Worcestershire certainly learned how to play over four days and won the (Britannic Assurance) County Championship, which was still played over 22 matches, to which they added the Sunday League. In one of their first four-day matches, at Taunton, Hick scored 405* from 469 balls – Somerset losing by an innings, managed just 414–20 in the match. It was nearly a treble for Worcestershire, but Middlesex beat them in the **1988** Gillette Cup Final. NatWest had sponsored the senior limited-overs cup from 1981 and while Middlesex won it three times in the 1980s, seven other sides also triumphed, while eight teams won the B&H Cup including Hampshire in 1988. They were the last of the 17 counties to reach a Lord's Final, and having got there, they went back in 1991 and 1992 – also successful visits. They were also one of eight counties who won the Sunday League, still played over 16 40-overs weekend matches. In 1989, Lancashire were the first county to win both Lord's Finals in the same season – and both by large margins – but they still could not win the County Championship.

Essex and Middlesex each won three County Championships in the 1980s but there were also two titles for Nottinghamshire, and Worcestershire who made it a double in **1989**. Sadly, this was under somewhat contro-versial circumstances: it was the first year of the 25-point penalty for poor pitches and Essex finished just six points behind the County Champions having been fined for a Southend pitch over which they claimed no control. Nottinghamshire finished 11th but also lost 25 points for a pitch at Trent Bridge that had sometimes attracted 'lively' observations in the days of Hadlee and Rice – a long way from Neville Cardus's observations about summer afternoons before the war. Lancashire, the first winners in 1969, won the Sunday League again 20 years later, while Bruce French and Eddie Hemmings took Nottinghamshire to a thrilling last ball victory in the B&H Cup Final against Essex. Middlesex were back 'at home' for the NatWest Final but lost to Warwickshire with two balls to spare. For the winners, no one took more than one wicket and no one reached a half-century, but Warwickshire were warming up to dominate county cricket in the early 1990s.

At the end of the decade, Rupert Murdoch launched Sky TV and on 24 February 1990, in Kingston Jamaica, the company began the first television broadcast of an overseas England Test Match. England's opening bowlers, Gladstone Small and Devon Malcolm, were both born in the West Indies while their top-scorers Allan Lamb and Robin Smith were South Africans, and Nasser Hussain was born in Madras. England's number three was Alec Stewart while his father, Mickey, was present as England's first full-time Manager, a post he had taken on in 1986. From 1992–1996 he became the Director of Coaching at the ECB.

In the Test Matches it was back to the Ashes and back to the BBC, which split its television coverage between its two channels with Tony Lewis, Richie Benaud, Jack Bannister, Alan Knott and Ray Illingworth taking viewers through the play. In the first innings of the series, Australia imposed 601–7 declared and beat Gower's side by 210 runs. They won at Lord's by six wickets then rain held up Australia's charge at Headingley where Angus Fraser on debut took 4–63. The frustration was short-lived for the visitors who won the fourth Test Match by nine wickets and the fifth Test Match by an innings and 180 runs, after a first day score of 301–0. Poor England (in both senses) had to face a sixth match and called up Alan Igglesden of Kent and John Stephenson of Essex. Australia became the first Test Match side to pass 400 in eight successive matches but rain helped England to survive. The whole series was watched by just over a-third-of-a-million spectators with record receipts of £4.25m but on the field, English cricket was in a bad way as the decade came to an end.

Chapter Six: the 1990s

Margaret Thatcher was prime minister from May 1979 until the penultimate month of 1990, when the cricket loving John Major replaced her after a Conservative Party 'coup'. Thatcher and her three successive Governments brought a particular style of Conservatism to the country and neither it, nor the party, has ever been quite the same since. Sandbrook describes how Thatcher's election as party leader divided the party with the 'old guard', upper class and public school/Oxbridge educated more likely to vote for her challengers, while Thatcher attracted support from the more right-wing, meritocratic supporters. When she won, he said Thatcher expressed no sympathy for "the Conservative establishment" who she felt "fought me unscrupulously all the way".

Across the country, the difficult winter of 1979 had led to Margaret Thatcher's first election victory. By her second success, Britain had fought the Falklands war, which began in 1982, and then the Government fought the miners who were on strike for a year. In 1985 they returned to work with no deal agreed, the industry declined, and in 2015 the last deep mine in Britain closed for good. The number of stoppages for strikes across the country also reduced significantly through Thatcher's premiership. She won a third election in 1987 and survived a challenge within her party in 1989, but in late 1990 she was challenged again and resigned. Thatcher was the first prime minister to lead Britain for a whole decade since the 1790s but she left Downing Street tearfully. One of the key moments in her eventual demise was the resignation speech by one of her former ministers, Geoffrey Howe, and at one time a great ally, who had pushed the Government's central 'monetarist' economic strategy, which led to the rise of the de-regulated city and a culture of greed parodied on television by Harry Enfield's character 'Loadsamoney'.

In his resignation speech to the House of Commons, Howe mentioned Thatcher's successor, John Major, as he used a cricketing metaphor to attack his leader's approach to Britain's negotiations with her European partners, suggesting that it resembled:

> Sending your opening batsmen to the crease, only for them to find as the first balls are being bowled, that their bats have been broken before the game by the team captain.

It is a matter of conjecture whether any contemporary politician would contemplate a cricketing reference in such a significant speech to Parliament. It seems unlikely, and if not, is perhaps one more piece of evidence that cricket is no longer embedded in the everyday life of the mass population. Around that time, Howe was not the only Conservative politician to invoke the game, and In 1990, the party chairman Norman Tebbit (in)famously told the *Los Angeles Times*

> A large proportion of Britain's Asian population fail to pass the cricket test. Which side do they cheer for? It's an interesting test. Are you still harking back to where you came from, or where you are?

Three years later, John Major, by then prime minister, sought to reassure Eurosceptics across the country with a speech in which he asserted that in 50 years time England would still be a country celebrating its traditions including among other things old maids on bicycles, warm beer and "long shadows on county grounds". We are now halfway through his 50 years, the 'Battle of Europe' is being fought once again and perhaps the "long shadows on county grounds" are partly from the floodlights at T20 matches and partly the metaphorical shadows of an uncertain future for the game Major loves.

One year before Thatcher resigned, western democracies had welcomed the fall of the Berlin Wall with the hope that this might lead to improved relationships with the Russians and a more generally peaceful future. In 1989, academic Francis Fukuyama published his essay "The End of History" which, while somewhat misunderstood, suggested the ultimate triumph of liberal western democracy as *the* mode of government. We know now, of course, that it was rather a fanciful hope. The New Zealanders, and then the Indians, toured England and in August 1990 as the Indians were playing the Second Test Match, Britain sent troops as part of a Coalition to protect Saudi Arabia against the invading forces of Iraq in what is known as the 'first' Gulf war. More hopefully, and with greater immediate implications for world cricket, Nelson Mandela was freed in February 1990 at the start of the rebuilding of South Africa.

As with the Conservative Party, the cricket committees that ran the English game began to reflect the sense of Britain as a growing middle-class meritocracy. By the mid-1990s, the Hampshire County Cricket Club committee no longer had members from Her Majesty's armed forces but included two GPs, a Dentist, Lawyers, Accountants, a University Lecturer, a Journalist and their former batsman Barry Reed. Across the country, the 'professionals' were increasingly in control of the day-to-day, on-field business of English cricket. Men like Mickey Stewart, Ray Illingworth and David Lloyd managed England, while the captains included Graham Gooch and Alec Stewart. At Essex, Keith Fletcher had handed the captaincy to Gooch who had also survived a poor start in Test Match cricket and the controversy of the Rebel tour to South Africa to captain England, replacing Gower for the tour to the West Indies in the first months of **1990**. At Jamaica in February, Gooch led his side with debutants Nasser Hussain and Alec Stewart to England's first victory against the West Indies since 1974. The second match never started, the third was drawn with Devon Malcolm taking 10 wickets in the match, then West Indies won the last two matches and the series with centuries from Carlisle Best, Greenidge and Haynes (two) while Curtly Ambrose with a best of 8–45 was the natural successor to the great pacemen of the previous decades.

Back in England, Gooch led the team to victory by 1–0 in the first series against New Zealand; then against India at Lord's, Gooch dominated with innings of 333 and 123. In the circumstances, centuries for Lamb and Robin Smith were almost forgotten, but Kapil Dev did hit four consecutive sixes in a show of defiance. The remaining two Test Matches were drawn with Gooch adding 116, 7, 85 and 88. He averaged 125.33 – surprisingly way behind Robin Smith's 180.5.

England's final Test Match in West Indies took place in April, otherwise only a single Test Match between New Zealand and Australia occurred in March **1990** after which, outside England, there were no further Test Matches until Karachi on 10 October, and the only ODIs took place in the same English season. This meant that other than the 1990 touring sides, counties could approach any international cricketers to appear in their sides throughout the season. As a result, Mark Waugh played 21 County Championship matches at Essex and others included: Viv Richards (18, Glamorgan); Courtney Walsh (19, Gloucestershire); Malcolm Marshall (18, Hampshire); Desmond Haynes (22, Middlesex); Curtly Ambrose (14, Northamptonshire); Jimmy Cook (22, Somerset) and Waqar Younis (14, Surrey). English county sides rarely sign players of that quality or for that length of time any more.

Jimmy Cook was a South African opening batsmen, still with no certain prospect of playing Test Match cricket. He scored eight centuries in the County Championship in 1990 with a best of 313* and 2,432 runs at 76.00. It was that kind of summer – the constant threat of pitch penalty points, flatter seams on the ball and sunny weather – and the batsmen had fun. Graham Gooch averaged 99 for Essex and scored more runs in total than Cook. Middlesex won the County Championship with their top five all well past 1,000 runs and Haynes over 2,000. Derbyshire won the Sunday League for the first time and Lancashire beat Northamptonshire in a one-sided NatWest Final (De Freitas 5–26) as well as the B&H Cup against Worcestershire.

Gooch was missing with a poisoned hand as England, under Allan Lamb, met Australia at Brisbane in November 1990. They bowled Australia out for 152 to take a lead of 42 but still lost by 10 wickets. Gooch then returned and Tufnell made his debut but Australia won again, followed by two draws and another victory for Australia in the final Test Match at the start of February. England had failed to win a Test Match in Australia for the first time since 1958–1959.

Looking back on the **1991** series against West Indies, Bill Frindall (*Playfair Cricket Annual*) described it as "one of the most enthralling in living memory". Gooch's 154* in the First Test Match at Headingley was a smaller score than Lord's 1990 but some judges placed it in the highest echelons of Test Match innings. The all-conquering West Indies arrived in England after a 2–1 series victory in Australia and when England's first innings of the series ended on 198, it seemed that Marshall, Ambrose, Walsh and Patterson would continue the success of previous tours. But De Freitas took 4–34 and despite Richards' 73, England led by 25. Ambrose (6–52) blew away the English top order *except* for Gooch who stood firm, and England's 252 set a victory target of 278. De Freitas took four more wickets and England won by 115 runs. The series then swung to-and-fro, ending 2–2 and with England at last believing they could compete with the tourists. At Headingley, England gave debuts to the two most frustrating batsmen of the decade, Graeme Hick and Mark Ramprakash, but in nine Test Matches between them neither reached 50, while Gooch and Smith again dominated the batting.

The County Championship season of **1991** lasted longer than ever and after 22 matches Essex were Champions again, while different teams won all four domestic trophies: Nottinghamshire were Sunday League Champions ahead of Lancashire who also lost the B&H Cup Final to Worcestershire, while on a beautiful September day at Lord's, Hampshire beat Surrey by four wickets in the twilight with two balls to spare to take the 60-over NatWest Trophy for the first time.

In November 1991, South Africa returned to the international arena with a limited-overs match v India. In April **1992** they played their first Test Match in more than two decades, in the West Indies, which for obvious reasons was also the first match between the two countries. Needing 201 to win, they reached 123–2 but six wickets for Ambrose won the match for the home side. Sadly, a local boycott by those not yet content with the situation in South Africa kept the attendance at 6,500 on the five days. For different and harder to interpret reasons, in the autumn of 1992 South Africa played their first Test Match at home but the attendance was very poor. The overall scoring rate was below two runs an over but that does not explain a small crowd on the first day.

In January 1992 at Sydney, Australia drew the third Test Match of the series with India. They gave a debut to a young leg-spinner, Shane Warne, whose figures in the only Indian innings were 45–7–150–1. In the next match his aggregate figures were 0–78 and he did not play in the final match. England toured New Zealand from January 1992, posting 580 to win by an innings in the first game. Their debutant, Dermot Reeve, was the first Hong Kong-born Test Match cricketer. They won the second match with ease and drew the third.

In **1992** Pakistan beat England 2–1 in an often tense and unpleasant series in which England's young batsmen struggled again against the impressive Wasim Akram and Waqar Younis. Despite the dispiriting incidents during the season, *Wisden's* editor suggested an "obsession" at Lord's with avoiding fuss, while adding

> Those of us close to the game know that cricket is run by very nice, hard working, intelligent and in many cases forward-thinking people. They seem entirely unaware that they sometimes give the impression to those further away of having served an apprenticeship under one of the less enlightened Romanovs.

During the winter of 1992–1993 Hick enjoyed a more successful tour of Sri Lanka and India, although his teammates were less impressive. India's spinners took them to a 3–0 victory, winning each Test Match in the series. *Wisden* suggested England's tour was "well up with the worst of all time" and the selectors' chairman, Ted Dexter, and captain, Gooch, were soon gone, although the latest professional manager Keith Fletcher survived. Northamptonshire beat Leicestershire to win the **1992** NatWest Trophy; Middlesex won the Sunday League; Essex won the County Championship; and rain forced Hampshire to a second day at Lord's before they won the B&H Trophy against Kent. Yorkshire did not win anything in 1992 but the cricket world changed forever in the county after the committee voted 18–1 to invite Craig McDermott to be their first overseas player, 24 years after the other counties had taken advantage of the new regulations. Fred Trueman called it a "bloody disgrace" and McDermott withdrew at the 11th hour with a groin injury, so Sachin Tendulkar came instead and proved to be as enchanting off the field as he would become as awesome on it.

Apart from that significant local initiative, for some years, and after many structural changes, the English cricket season had settled into something of a routine. The counties continued to compete for the four trophies with the original two knock-out cups, the Sunday League and the County Championship. There were variations over the years as to which 'extra' sides played in the Gillette/NatWest and B&H Cup competitions, but on the whole this was a relatively stable period with most counties winning trophies, at least occasionally. England were in a pattern of Test Match series, hosting one or two countries each year, touring during the winter and also playing a gradually growing number of ODIs, with regular World Cups.

Wisden's editor was now Matthew Engel who regretted the end of the tradition of announcing England's Test Match side on a Sunday morning. He wondered, too, whether the fact that cricket trousers were less flannels and rather more "resembling sandpaper", explained why cricketers "are so keen to play as little as possible". More than 20 years later the 2015 PCA survey did not report on clothing but their members still wish to play less. More cheerfully, Engel praised the attraction of the game "that works on so many levels" and he described the various ways in which spectators engage with it, from those who "think they know what is going on" to those contentedly detached, even at key moments. Cricket, he added, "can appeal to the athlete and the aesthete alike; it can veer between lyric poetry, differential calculus and Thai kick-boxing". But while it offers more range and depth than any other sports he reminded us of its fragility. It is always "in a crisis" and for Engel in 1992 that crisis was "acute", not actually because of the unpleasant on-field antics but "because of a clear yet insoluble problem by turning itself into two separate sports". This seems such an important point that is worth emphasising: *"Cricket at the highest level has acquired a unique and insoluble problem by turning itself into two separate sports."*

By 2015, that problem far from being resolved, had been exacerbated – cricket at the highest levels (plural), including the women's game, has turned itself now into **three** separate sports and even at club and league level it is usually two, with all 2015's debates about the future structure of English cricket failing to address the problem. As a problem, it is certainly "unique" among major sports, especially team sports but does it have to be insoluble? Is the problem for cricket that it looks around the world of sport and cannot see an alternative model, when perhaps that model is to be found elsewhere, not in sport but in the competing world of entertainment? The music industry, for example, does not consider the impact of 'pop' music a reason to dismantle or ignore all other forms. In terms of entertainment, Engel feared there was not much to be found in too many of the Test Matches in the previous 12 months, describing Zimbabwe's inaugural Test Match v India as "screamingly dull".

Since 1988, some of the County Championship matches had been played over four days and in **1993** came the next major change as the competition changed completely to that format. Engel suggested it was "much admired by those who sit in offices and plan cricket" but he believed "much disliked by those who still go and watch it, especially at Festival Weeks". In one sense the idea that the County Championship has changed from three to four-day cricket is somewhat misleading because of the low expectation and slower delivery of overs per hour. In terms of the county cricket of many years ago, the 96 overs per day over four days is the equivalent of, at most, 10 sessions, not 12. Engel suggested that the TCCB had "ground down" opponents to the new format by having County Championship matches played on pitches that offered relatively little help to the bowlers, thereby increasing the degree of boredom, and demand for contrivance in the three-day game. But whatever Engel or the regular spectators thought, the change took place and so, from **1993**, the county scene was in *every* respect different from the way it had been in 1962 – the last year when there was only the three-day County Championship. There were also 18 teams, following the admittance of Durham in 1992.

In that first year of four-day matches, just 48 of the 153 games were drawn – around 30%, whereas in 1987, the last year of all three-day matches, there were 85 draws in 187 games (45%). Incidentally, in 1980 just before pitches were covered, there were 112 draws in 187 matches (60%) whereas we might have expected those pitches to lead to more results. The introduction of four-day matches for all County Championship games in the 1990s led to a significant reduction in drawn games in that first decade. Just less than 37% of matches in that decade were drawn and with the exception of the severely truncated 1940s, that was the lowest percentage since the 1920s. It was also significantly lower than the all-time highest figure of 53% in the 1980s. In the 21st century the figure has risen slightly to the low 40s, while scoring rates are higher than ever, and better than three runs per over.

In **1993**, Middlesex were first winners of the longer County Championship. In order to accommodate the extra day, the competition was reduced by five matches, to 17 each side, all in one division. The *Playfair Cricket Annual* complained that the authorities should have considered reducing the number of limited-overs fixtures by cutting the Sunday League completely as it no longer held the mass appeal of its early years. On the contrary, they increased it to a 50-over contest and to the annual's horror, approved the wearing of "gaudy" coloured clothes. *Playfair* suggested that scarlet should have been worn by all 18 sides to show the clearest case yet of cricket prostituting itself. In *Wisden* the editor feared that the colours would change regularly to exploit the replica shirt market.

1993 was significant in various other ways. Australia toured again and in the first Test Match at Manchester, Peter Such took six wickets to dismiss Australia for 289, after which Merv Hughes had Atherton caught behind at 71–1 bringing Gatting to the crease. He had scored just four when he pushed tentatively at a ball around leg-stump and shared the general astonishment as his off bail was removed. Blonde-haired Shane Warne had bowled what was perhaps the ball of the century, or at least the televised ball of the century, and Australia were on their way to four victories in the first five Test Matches. Gooch top-scored in both innings of that first match with 65 and 133 but in the second innings was dismissed handled ball and England lost by 179 runs. In the third match, Gooch dropped down to number five to accommodate a new opening partner for Atherton, Somerset's Mark Lathwell. He scored 20, 33, 0 and 25 in his two Test Matches before disappearing from international cricket – and fairly soon from the county game. On his final appearance, Australia compiled 653–4 declared with two centurions, plus 200* from captain Border.

Gooch resumed opening in the fifth match of the series but his partner, Atherton, took over the captaincy. Australia still won and retained the Ashes, although in the sixth Test Match at the Oval there was some relief. Among the run scorers, Hick made 80 and Ramprakash 64, and in his second Test Match as captain Atherton had a victory. David Boon and Mark Waugh both finished the series with over 500 runs, as did Atherton, while Gooch accumulated 673. But while Warne had 34 wickets (25.79) and Hughes 31 (27.25), only Such with 16 (33.81), had double figures in the wickets column for England, who chose 12 specialist bowlers in the six-match series against Australia's six. Despite disappointment in England, *Wisden's* editor struck an optimistic note, suggesting that at home and in Australia and India, crowds had enjoyed some exciting and high quality Test Match cricket, with Warne the "most talked-about player of the year".

England's Women won their World Cup and there would be further competitions in 1997, 2000, 2005, 2009, and 2013. Meanwhile, the ICC separated from the MCC although the latter retains responsibility for the Laws of the game since the ICC has little interest in cricket beneath the international level. *Wisden's* editor noted the arrival of neutral (or "third country") umpires but considered the idea of helping them with video technology a "disaster". Whether cricket-lovers agree with that view, many will support his deep disappointment at the increasing habit of successful batsmen waving their bats only (or initially) at their team-mates. As he pointed out, nobody expects actors taking a curtain call to bow to the wings.

In another structural change in **1993** and 1994 the B&H Cup became a straight knock-out competition and Derbyshire were winners in the first of those years. Meanwhile, its senior partner, the Gillette Cup/NatWest Trophy, celebrated its 30th anniversary and in September the NatWest Final produced a suitable match to mark the occasion. Sussex, the first winners of the competition, reached another final, but they endured a traumatic week culminating in that match at Lord's. First at Portsmouth on 29 August they posted 312–8 in the new 50-over Sunday League (Alan Wells 127) only to see Hampshire beat them with one ball to spare – Paul Terry and Robin Smith both reaching three figures. On the four days from Tuesday at Hove, they scored 591 & 312–3 declared with centuries from Alan Wells, Keith Greenfield, John North and Neil Lenham, yet Essex beat them by seven wickets, scoring 493–4 declared and 412–3 – Paul Pritchard made a double century and Stephenson and Hussain three figures. On the next day, the Saturday, Sussex batted first at Lord's and reached 321–6 in their 60 overs. Warwickshire lost both openers at 18 but Paul Smith, Dermot Reeve (ex-Sussex) and Asif Din (104) took them to a last ball victory and a record aggregate for a Lord's Final. In the first final in 1963, Sussex (168) beat Worcestershire (154) in a 65-over match – a total of 322 runs in 123.4 overs. In 1993 the aggregate was almost exactly double, 643 from120 overs, while in the course of one week Sussex, in four innings, amassed 1,536 runs for the loss of 27 wickets, yet lost all three matches!

At the end of the **1993** season a number of major players retired from English county cricket including Ian Botham (briefly with Durham), Viv Richards, Malcolm Marshall, David Gower, Neil Foster, Chris Tavaré and Derek Randall – few that could compete with them play regularly in today's County Championship. One of the best loved of the cricket commentators, Brian Johnston also died in 1993.

In his editorial notes in *Wisden,* Engel was scathing about the development of young cricketers. He pointed out that there were "few enough gifted young cricketers" and the system in place to develop them is complicated and often competitive between associations and organisations. Meanwhile, he feared that "millions of other youngsters never even pick up a cricket bat". He blamed the dangerous streets, the schools and the counties who were "doing everything wrong". He warned that "the roots of the problem" ran very deep.

There was yet more change in **1994** when, after one unpopular year what *Wisden* described as the "hopeless compromise" of the 50-over competition, the Sunday League reverted to its original 40 overs and was won by Warwickshire who were the dominant team of this period, winning six trophies from 1993–1995 and another in 1997. In 1994 alone, Dermot Reeve's somewhat unconventional team won three trophies, losing out only to Worcestershire in the NatWest Final when Hick and Tom Moody added 198 undefeated for the third wicket. It was a good year in the West midlands. In Test Match cricket, South Africa's rehabilitation continued with their first tour of England for almost 30 years. The series was drawn 1–1 after England had beaten New Zealand by a single victory, and against the South Africans, rather like Colin Bland some 30 years before, much of the interest centred on the wonderful fielding of Jonty Rhodes. Photographs seemed to expose England's captain Michael Atherton using dirt from his pocket to change the state of the ball, which he denied, while in New Zealand, a Pakistan player was hit by a bottle thrown by a spectator.

In the winter of 1994–1995, the Flower brothers, Andy and Grant Flower, both made centuries as Zimbabwe won a fine innings victory against Pakistan although they lost the series 2–1. England went to Australia whose new captain, Mark Taylor, led them to large runs victories in the first two Test Matches. The third match was drawn, securing the Ashes. England won the fourth but then lost the fifth to go down 3–1. Michael Slater (623) and Graham Thorpe (444) were the leading scorers, but McDermott (32 wickets) and Warne (27) were well ahead of England's best bowler, Darren Gough, with 20 wickets at 21.25. *Wisden's* editor suggested that with these series as one-sided as they had ever been, the urn should travel to Australia and he wondered whether it was relevant that so many of England's recent undera-chieving players "were either born overseas and/or spent their formative years as citizens of other countries". He added that he had "never seen an England team as dismal and demoralised" as that which was on the field during day four of the Melbourne Test Matches – apparently the answer was a shift to a two-divisional County Championship. The counties discussed and rejected the idea in December 1994. "Maybe" thought *Wisden's* editor, 1994 would be the year of 'Fantasy Cricket' by which he meant not the latest daft idea from the TCCB but the new game taking a grip of the sports pages of certain newspapers. He participated in *the Daily Telegraph* version but finished outside the top 35,000.

The northern professional Ray Illingworth replaced the southern amateur Ted Dexter at the head of England's selectors. Test Match Special's scorer Bill Frindall, editing the *Playfair Cricket Annual,* looked back over the previous year at the start of the 1995 season, and had much to say in his editorial. He noted that early in 1994, England had followed one of their lowest-ever scores (46) at Trinidad with a rare victory at Barbados. There were also Brian Lara's two world records in 1994, 375 for the West Indies v England in Antigua and 501* for Warwickshire v Durham, the last of six centuries in seven innings for the county. Frindall observed that the largest annual yet published was to accommodate the continuing proliferation of Test Matches and the growing size of county staffs.

He expressed concern at growing allegations of bribery and corruption with possible links to betting in India and was very unhappy about the number of Test series looming for the England side. Meanwhile, Australia's latest Ashes triumphs led him to consider failings in the county game. Like everyone else, he argued that there was too much cricket played but proposed a pruning of the number of limited-overs competitions and suggested instead a regional four-day tournament between teams from the four 'corners' and London Counties, with semi-finals and a final. He wanted an end to counties employing players not qualified for England, an end to batting and bowling points in the first innings of the County Championship, and the Sunday League as a competition for the best amateur players.

Frindall alerted his readers to the new organisation which would succeed the TCCB in January 1997 and which would be concerned with cricket at all levels in the country – although he was not sure what that country was exactly (England? Britain?) In the event the organisation is known as the ECB, standing for the England & Wales Cricket Board (my emphasis). Frindall suggested that the new board's first job should be to take central control of all 18 county groundsmen to eliminate pitches made to order by the home side. It was a full menu of proposals, hardly any of which have been adopted, although most of the key questions about corruption, county standards, player overload and unsatisfactory pitches remain.

The **1995** English season brought the West Indies to England for an exciting six match series that ended 2–2. West Indies were not quite in decline, for with Lara, Ambrose and Walsh they posed a constant threat but neither were they the dominant force of the previous decade. England selected 21 players, giving debuts to Peter Martin, Dominic Cork (7–43 at Lords, the best England debut figures), Jason Gallian, Nick Knight, Mike Watkinson and Alan Wells. Oxford University won their match against Cambridge, still played at Lord's, but only Will Kendall (Hampshire) and Iain Sutcliffe (Lancashire) would go on to win caps at county sides. Warwickshire won the County Championship again and beat Northamptonshire (who had challenged them over four days) in the NatWest Final, Lancashire's 274–7 in the B&H Cup Final was too much for Kent despite a fine century by Aravinda de Silva but Kent had their moment, winning the Sunday League on run-rate from Warwickshire. Those two sides and Worcestershire finished level on 50 points.

Looking back on the season in his notes as Wisden's editor, Matthew Engel suggested that while it had not been the greatest of years it was "wonderfully rich and satisfying" albeit lacking the ultimate reward of England winning the Test Match series. The pitches were not always satisfactory with Edgbaston too bowler-friendly and the Oval quite the reverse. It is an odd thought from today, that the West Indies had arrived in England from a series defeat against Australia, which was their first in no fewer than 15 series. The other worry was the general absence of West Indies supporters from the Test Matches, perhaps because tickets now had to be bought months ahead.

Engel suggested that the problem might spread and perhaps particularly affect the likelihood of young people attending.

Engel reminded readers of the somewhat playful way in which the cricket world reacted to the bets posted and collected by Marsh and Lillee at Headingley in 1981. It was no longer a laughing matter with accusations that Salim Malik had tried to bribe Australians Mark Waugh, Tim May and Shane Warne. Whatever the truth, there was dissatisfaction with the response of the ICC, while Graham Halbish, Australia's Chief Executive, called it "cricket's greatest crisis for 20 years". Part of the problem as Engel pointed out is that the complexities of cricket make it ideal for betting – and very complicated in those countries to expose where betting is illegal. There was another controversy following the publication in *Wisden Cricket Monthly* of an article by Robert Henderson suggesting that black cricketers were incapable of trying fully when representing England. The players named threatened to sue, the matter was settled out of court, and Engel described Henderson's unqualified views as "piffle". It was certainly that in a variety of ways, not least the suggestion that the players failing were a matter of "biology", yet somehow being "subconscious" – a clear confusion of disciplines. Engel's disappointment was partly because of the progress that black British cricketers had made in the county game – 20 years later that optimism seems entirely misplaced.

Wisden 1996 ran an article based on interviews by Pat Murphy, asking of eight players and former players, "Has the Game Got Worse?" If that was the question put to them rather than just the headline, then as any undergraduate knows, it was a leading rather than an open question, which may have helped to determine the answers. Nonetheless, there were some interesting replies. Norman Gifford described himself as a recent "casualty" as the Sussex coach because they had not won trophies but recalled that when he started his career at Worcestershire in 1960, they "weren't expected to win anything". Geoff Cook identified pressure on players and umpires from "the need to win" and the attendant quest for cash prizes, which "reflects" contemporary society. Gifford, Cook John Emburey, and Chris Broad all felt the pitches might be better, while Gifford and John Childs wished young players discussed the game more, but along with Eddie Hemmings, admired the improved fielding. Emburey (and John Childs) thought that players' behaviour was getting "out of hand" and that the game was now "less friendly" with "too much emphasis on winning". Hemmings agreed, but celebrated the "proper wages", as well as the fitness levels, while warning against complacency among younger players. He and Broad were enthusiastic about one-day cricket for bringing the public to the game, including through television, although was opposed to action replays because of the challenge to the authority of the umpires. Broad revealed his nine-year-old son (Stuart) had cricket heroes from watching on television but he was concerned that the "corporate" people running the county game did not understand first-class cricket, while "at Lord's they just seem to sit back and rake in the money" without being "radical enough". Robin Marlar agreed that county chairmen were "not qualified to talk about" English cricket, described the disappearing TCCB as "a mess" and was not alone in worrying about the absence of good swing bowling. More generally, he criticised current techniques and attributed many of those problems to the "mediocrities" coaching in English cricket. Cook suggested that the game had become "less sentimental, it's a case of the survival of the fittest … the camaraderie isn't there any more", although Bob Woolmer felt current players were "every bit as good as they were" when he started in 1968.

Editor Matthew Engel and cricket historian Philip Bailey looked back at the 50 years of postwar cricket and discovered that Middlesex were just ahead of Surrey and then Yorkshire as the most successful county side, with West Indies as "World Champions". Twenty years on, the latter would certainly not still be the case and it may be that Surrey and Yorkshire have re-asserted their traditional supremacy although the bottom three counties in 1995, Sussex, Nottinghamshire and Durham, have generally enjoyed the 21st century. England were fourth then in the Test Match calculations, with Australia second and South Africa third – calculations based on percentage wins. That is a simple approach but it might be an interesting one to apply to each year's County Championship as they did in this table – not least because the endless changes in points available for different things made any other approach too complicated. They noted the more egalitarian period as a variety of teams won the title after Yorkshire's 1968 success but suggested that with the reduction in major international signings, the gap between the best and the rest had grown again. In 21 seasons since 1995, 10 teams have won the title, including Glamorgan only in 1997 and Leicestershire twice either side of them. Of the eight sides that have not won the title in that period, Hampshire, Middlesex and Somerset will be in the First Division in 2016.

World Cups now came on a regular basis. England contested three of the first five Finals but lost them all. Australia had beaten them by seven runs in India in 1987 after their captain Gatting was caught from an infamous reverse-sweep, and then Pakistan beat them by 22 runs in Australia in 1992. England have never reached a Final since, while in March **1996** in Pakistan, Sri Lanka with their 'pinch hitters' at the top of the order, triumphed over Australia, bringing new ideas to the game. That last World Cup competition took place after a dispute that arose because the TCCB believed it was England's turn to stage the tournament. The Test Match playing countries supported them by five votes to four but once the votes of associate countries were added, the result was reversed. AC Smith described it as "by a long way the worst meeting I have ever attended". Richard Hutton, by now the editor of *the Cricketer* magazine, suggested the danger of a very real split between an England/Australia-led group and another based around the Indian subcontinent. In the event England hosted the following tournament in 1999 – and probably wished they had not.

The limited-overs format in England was initially a game dominated by seam bowlers, but another innovation that has remained is the effective use of spin bowlers, sometimes opening the bowling. 1996 was the last time that Pakistan hosted an international tournament and for security reasons it is doubtful whether in the near future they could ever host another international competition from within their borders.

The County Championship of **1996** was organised with most matches running from Wednesday to Saturday. This was good news for the players who could play the Sunday League *after* rather than during a County Championship game, and it was good news for the then fashionable corporate groups who enjoyed a midweek day out, although the latter proved somewhat ephemeral. For its many real supporters, obliged to attend school or work, the County Championship became increasingly remote with Saturdays the forgotten day and once lost relatively few of those weekend supporters returned, so it became and remains largely a competition watched by the retired generation. The matches also began with three points now awarded for a draw, which was intended to encourage a 'Test Match' mentality in the four-day game. There was no better example of that than the innings by England's captain Michael Atherton at Johannesburg in December 1995. South Africa declared, inviting England to score 478 to win the second Test Match of that series and at 145–4 they faced defeat. Atherton then resisted Alan Donald in a heroic (and occasionally fortunate) struggle, supported by Robin Smith (44) and 'Jack' Russell (29*) – the captain reached 185* in 643 minutes and 492 balls and England closed on 351–5. Only three men had then played a longer innings for England. South Africa had their revenge however when, after four drawn matches, they won the last Test Match and the series.

Back at home, England won the first Test Match of the summer and drew the next two against India to take the first series, but they lost the first and last match against Pakistan and the series 2–0. Seven men played in just one of the summer's six Test Matches and in his editor's notes, Matthew Engel described the season as "in some respects the most depressing in memory" including the World Cup and subsequent "glum failures" in Zimbabwe in

December 1996, where the England team were lined up to shake hands with the monstrous Robert Mugabe. The inaugural Test Match between the two nations in Bulwayo ended with England 204–6 and the scores level, after which the latest England coach, David 'Bumble' Lloyd, was reported as saying "we flippin' murdered 'em". Despite these difficulties, Engel described his pleasure from days watching County Championship cricket and suggested that while all true cricket lovers are essentially conservative in that affection, the endless debates about cricket's future might be best described as setting the "sleepwalkers" against the "hysterics". He warned "the blunt fact is that cricket has become unattractive to the overwhelming majority of the population" because it is "widely perceived as elitist, exclusionist and dull". Engel believed the county cricket needed "rapid reform" and proposed fewer limited-overs games, an end to the benefit system and better payments rewarding success. Benefits have continued but in the autumn of 2015, the Chancellor, George Osborne announced plans to hit them hard with the ending of the tax-free bonus.

Leicestershire won the County Championship in **1996** with West Indian, Phil Simmons, securing what might be considered the 'modern double' of 1,186 runs and 56 wickets. Four men passed 1,000 runs and David Millns and Alan Mullally formed a potent opening pair. Lancashire posted a modest 186 in their 60 overs in the NatWest Final but Glenn Chapple took 6–18 and Essex were all out for 57 – and even that only thanks to a ninth wicket partnership of 23. Lancashire thus secured the Lord's Final 'double' having beaten Northamptonshire by 31 runs in the B&H Cup Final, Ian Austin taking 4–21. Once again there was a tie at the top of the Sunday League with Surrey beating Nottinghamshire on run-rate to secure their first Sunday title.

The Australians returned in **1997** having held the Ashes since 1989 and in the middle of eight consecutive series victories that would take them into the next century. The Australians had barely arrived when on Thursday, 1 May 1997 Tony Blair led the Labour Party to victory and Government for the first time for 18 years. It is unlikely that many cricketers voted Labour, since it is hardly their 'natural' preference, but perhaps the shift encouraged the England side who won the first Test Match by nine wickets after dismissing the visitors for 118, followed by a double century from Hussain. Many Labour supporters now look back on Blair's success as a false dawn and so it was with the cricketers. The second match was drawn but then Australia won three in a row and the Ashes were lost again. *Wisden's* editor reported the popular perception that cricket "was a tired old sport" but in the early years of the Internet he was able to report that cricket sites "were consistently among the busiest on the entire web". In addition, 'Dickie' Bird's autobiography exceeded an "extraordinary" quarter-of-a-million sales, and demand for tickets at Westminster Abbey to attend the memorial service for Denis Compton were higher than any similar event for 30 years.

The Indian businessman, Jagmohan Dalmiya, who was viewed with suspicion by some in world cricket, was elected as the first president of the ICC. There were growing rumours of match fixing around the world, and too many limited-overs internationals about whom few cared shortly after they had finished. At home, David Graveney was appointed chairman of selectors – the first since HS Altham in 1954 who had not played Test Match cricket.

Almost inevitably, and in an atmosphere that *Wisden* described as "hysterical", the reason for England's failings was attributed mainly to the County Championship. As a consequence, the newly formed ECB was required to act. It had come into being on 1 January **1997**, bringing together the work of the TCCB, NCA and the Cricket Council to govern all aspects of all cricket in England and Wales, including women's cricket after the Women's Cricket Association was incorporated in April 1998. The ECB shares its headquarters with the MCC, who still have international responsibility for the Laws of Cricket, and their first chairman Lord McLaurin came from the same role at Tesco's.

McLaurin oversaw a number of dramatic changes in English cricket, particularly county and top league cricket, before he stood down in 2002. These emanated In particular from the publication in August 1997 of *Raising the Standard.* In central Southern England, the Southern Premier League accepted the requirements, which included quality of pitch and facilities, an effective colts set-up and the playing of at least some all-day matches. The purpose was to tighten the link between amateur club and professional county cricket. Since the Hampshire Academy side – like many other academies in other leagues – competes in the top division there is a sense in which this has occurred, although, other than that, the Southern League has rather more become a home for *former* rather than prospective county cricketers, as well as others who played for the county's 2nd XI. In Kent there was an experiment with two-day league matches but many players found it hard to give a whole weekend to cricket and then return to work on Monday – and some families were less than pleased at the prospect.

In its 1998 edition, *Wisden* commented on the popular perception that the document proposed a two-division County Championship, which the "selfish and parochial counties" had rejected. That looks like a good media story but it was untrue – what they rejected was the three equal conferences model, a proposal that the editor described as "nonsense". There was one element of the proposal that resonates to this day and that is the view expressed there that the best formula for county cricket was for each county to play 14 matches. In 1997 that was 14 as against 17, while in 2015 it was 14 as against 16. No doubt once it is reduced to 14, probably in 2017, the campaign will begin for 12 as the ideal number – and after that? Elsewhere, the editor noted, the original Sunday League was now the "any-day-of-the-week" league while he warned that the slightly hidden agenda of many of the advocates of the two divisional County Championship was eventually for an elite, city-based, Test Match-ground league. The ECB were also pressing to have cricket removed from the list of sports reserved for terrestrial television. Rugby had achieved this but its viewing figures had fallen dramatically since Sky TV took over the broadcasts. The editor was also bewildered by the new system for calculating rain-affected limited-overs matches, named after its inventors, Messrs Duckworth and Lewis.

Bill Frindall suggested that one of the failings of the ECB's *Raising the Standard* was in not addressing the "feudal county benefit system" and replacing it with a proper pension system. Frindall suggested that there was no need to take the advice of some 'sages' and eliminate weaker counties, since a decent pension system would allow counties to reduce staff sizes from around 25 to perhaps 17. He was highly critical of one outcome of the document aimed at reducing limited-overs competitions, which was the replacement of the old B&H Cup with the 'Super Cup' in 1999, which was anything but 'Super'. *Wisden* called it half-hearted and suggested that some had called it the Superfluous Cup. Gloucestershire won it, beating Yorkshire at Lord's to trigger a fine run of limited-overs trophies in just a few years. The traditional B&H Cup returned in 2000 but it would not survive long.

In *Wisden,* Matthew Engel made reference to the 150th anniversary of the birth of WG Grace, which was to fall on Saturday, 18 July 1998. This was a relatively free day in the domestic cricket calendar and Lord's was hosting a match between the MCC and the Rest of the World. But as the editor noted, this had nothing to do with 'WG' but was a charity memorial match to mark the tragic death of HRH Diana, Princess of Wales. Anyone who lived through that shocking event will recall the extraordinary outpouring of national and very *public* grief which is said by historians to signify that moment when the British character seemed to have changed from resolutely insular, pragmatic and unemotional to something rather the opposite. Mass events on a grand scale were increasingly common and increasingly *mediated* through television, radio, journalism, now for the first time, via the Internet, and soon as well through social media. Cricket responded to the death of Diana perhaps because every institution felt the pressure to be seen to do so, but as the editor remarked, the Memorial Fund in her name was not the charity "in most urgent need of cricket's patronage", while her connection with cricket "was somewhat remote".

Among the counties in **1997,** Glamorgan won their third County Championship, this one still sponsored by Britannic Assurance. Three batsmen who had brief Test Match careers, Steve James, Matthew Maynard and Hugh Morris scored heavily, while three international bowlers Waqar Younis, Steve Watkin and Robert Croft took more than 50 wickets each. It was the turn of the NatWest Trophy to feature one-sided games and Essex, skittled in 1996, dismissed Warwickshire for 170 and got home for the loss of captain Pritchard in the 27th over. The B&H Cup Final was not particularly thrilling as Kent 212–9 in their 50 overs lost to Surrey, 215–2 with five overs to spare. The very promising Ben Hollioake was Man-of-the-Match for his 98. Warwickshire kept collecting cups – this time, the Sunday League, two points ahead of Kent.

Bill Frindall edited the *Playfair Cricket Annual* again in 1998 but he invited Bob Woolmer, Test Match and county cricketer and international and county coach, to contribute a foreword. Woolmer began by observing that the two major changes in the game during his career had been the change from uncovered wickets and the introduction of limited-overs matches. He expressed concern about the "debilitating" effects of jet lag on the world's major players, including the increased possibility of injury. On English cricket he confessed to being "intrigued and sometimes baffled by the changes to the county system". Regular defeats to Australia, in particular, suggested once again the need for changes to the county system.

There were six Test Matches in 1997 and each county played 17 County Championship matches. Four men played in every Test Match and also played a fair amount of County Championship cricket: Atherton and Hussain (10 County Championship games), and Stewart and Thorpe (nine each). Those who played in five of the six Test Matches were Mark Butcher and Croft (13 each), Andrew Caddick (12) and John Crawley (11) and they all played in county limited-overs matches (Surrey as finalists). Some of those men played also in the three Texaco Trophy ODIs in May. England could not win the World Cup but they beat the Australians 3–0 with Michael Bevan and Adam Hollioake as the Men-of-the-Series. Duncan Fletcher as England coach would push for Central Contracts which would be introduced in 2000, increasingly freeing England's top players from the demands of County Championship cricket.

Meanwhile, Sri Lanka met Pakistan in a two Test Match series in late April by which time all competitions except the NatWest Trophy were underway in England. In mid-June Sri Lanka met the West Indies before returning home to host a series in August with India. Test Matches abroad during the English season would increase over the following years, and today they restrict significantly the availability of overseas players for whole seasons or longer careers in county cricket. By 1997 the best signing was someone like David Boon, no longer playing Test Match cricket and able to appear in all but one of Durham's County Championship matches or Stuart Law, hardly ever selected by Australia, with almost 1500 runs for Essex in every County Championship game. The alternative was perhaps best found at Hampshire where the highly promising Matthew Hayden was not yet in the Australian side. His 1,438 runs in the County Championship came at 57.52 each to which he added the highest aggregate in the country in the Axa Life Sunday League.

England travelled to Jamaica on 29 January 1998 to start a Test Match and new series. After 10 overs and one ball from Walsh and Ambrose, they were 17–3 and the two umpires, Steve Bucknor and 'Shrini' Venkataraghavan, abandoned the match on the grounds of a dangerous pitch. It was thus the shortest Test Match of any that had started. In the 56 minutes of play, the England physiotherapist had attended to injured batsmen on six occasions. West Indies won a tight second Test Match recovering from 124–5 to reach a winning target of 282–7, and England won a similarly close low-scoring match to level the series in Trinidad. In this switchback series, West Indies won the next game, while Ramprakash (154) with his first Test Match century and Thorpe 103, added a record 205 for the sixth wicket as the penultimate game was drawn. West Indies clinched the series 3–1 with an innings victory in Antigua, having dismissed England for 127.

In **1998,** Leicestershire won their second County Championship in three years, ahead of the northern red and white rose counties. Lancashire met Derbyshire in what was designed to be the last of the September cup finals, and while it was the end of 60 overs, the shift to late August was not sustained for long. It wasn't a glorious finale for the oldest limited-overs competition, as play did not commence until 4.30pm on Saturday. Michael Slater and Kim Barnett took Derbyshire to 70 before the first wicket fell and by the 37th over they were all out for 108 (Austin 3–14). On the Sunday, Lancashire romped home for the loss of Atherton in a match that lasted just 67 overs in total. The competition's highest total stood at 413–4 by Somerset v Devon in 1990 and the lowest 39 all out by Ireland v Sussex in 1985. Mike Gatting with 69 made the most appearances and, as if to confirm it was a batsman's game, Graham Gooch and Robin Smith with nine each set the record for Gold Awards. Michael Holding's 8–21 for Derbyshire at Hove in 1988 was the best bowling, there were 11 hat-tricks and Lancashire fittingly won the last Final for their record seventh Trophy. They also won the Sunday League while the B&H Cup Final was similarly one-sided with Essex 268–7 beating Leicestershire 76 all out. At his natural home, Headingley, 'Dickie'

Bird umpired a competitive match between first-class sides for the last time and, appropriately enough, the Sunday match between Yorkshire and Warwickshire required an umpire's inspection after rain. *Wisden* published a photograph of "the latest and most bizarre" cricket craze – two young men with pints of beer, dressed in drag, watching the Test Match at Edgbaston. The practice is now widespread although it has not yet been spotted in the pavilion at Lord's, which has its own colourful costumes.

The 1999 edition of *Wisden* was the first to pass 1,500 pages as the amount of cricket and cricket records continued to increase. The editor suggested that the most recent crisis concerning match-fixing had been largely ignored by the cricket world, although the Australian Board admitted that in the 'affair' of Warne, Waugh and Salim Malik, their two players "had accepted thousands of dollars from an Indian bookmaker for providing apparently innocuous information". For Matthew Engel the crisis was far more widespread and insidious and he described it as worse than the Packer affair and the biggest threat to the sport's well being since Bodyline more than 60 years before. Dalmiya, he said, had failed to offer any leadership and "should resign". In a separate article Mihir Bose examined the whole issue of betting and match-fixing, concluding that in the "complex" cricket world of 1999, "there seemed little sign of this sorry story ever ending, let alone soon".

There was rather more leadership from Colin Ingleby-Mackenzie who was president of the MCC from 1996–1998. As he made clear in his autobiography decades earlier, as a young man he greatly enjoyed the company of the ladies, so it was perhaps fitting that during his term of office that women were admitted to full membership of the MCC after a pretty determined campaign led by the president and with some clear 'guidance' from the sports minister Tony Banks. Rachel Heyhoe-Flint was the one of the first to be elected, although whether any more radical 'sisters' took the Marxist view (Groucho that is) we may never know. Matthew Engel pointed out that while *in theory* membership was open now to anyone in the country, in practice the MCC could never be more than a tiny elite since, unlike the county clubs in modern England, its membership was strictly limited, with long waiting lists.

By the time England hosted South Africa at Edgbaston in early June, Alec Stewart had replaced Atherton as captain although the latter hit another century against Donald and his fellow bowlers in an opening partnership of 179 with Butcher. After four days, England led by 289 with two wickets left but the final day was washed out. England collapsed to 110 all out at Lord's and lost by 10 wickets while at Old Trafford, South Africa's 552–5 declared was their record score against England. England finished on 369–9, scores level, as umpire Cowie declined an lbw appeal. For the first time in Test Match cricket, a speed gun measured the performances of Gough, Donald and their fellow bowlers. England's narrow escape turned the series. Angus Fraser took 10 wickets in the match as England won at Trent Bridge and England's 247–2 was their highest winning fourth innings since 1902. England clinched the series in 30 minutes exciting play on the fifth morning at Headingley, watched by 10,000 spectators who were admitted free. On the Sunday evening South Africa, needing 219 to win, recovered from 27–5 to 185–8. On the last morning they moved on to 194 but lost the last two wickets adding just one more run. Gough took 6–42 on his home ground.

Atherton had played 63 consecutive Test Matches but missed the single game against Sri Lanka at the Oval with a bad back. England opened with an innings of 445 and centuries for Hick and Crawley, yet lost by ten wickets as Muttiah Muralitharan took 16–220 in the match – the fifth best analysis in all Test Match cricket. Sri Lanka's opening bat Marvan Atapattu had scored just one run in his first six Test Match innings yet here completed 1,000 Test Match runs in 20 matches.

In the winter of 1962–1963, while the MCC (England) had toured Australia, English cricket had removed forever the distinction between amateur and professional cricketers. England, 36 years later, were 'down under' again as an equally significant change was voted through by the first-class counties, the decision to change from a single 18-team County Championship to two divisions with nine teams in each. Glamorgan were the only county to vote against the idea, while Durham and Essex abstained and the other 15 supported it. The decision was taken after significant criticism of the existing format from its chairman, Lord McLaurin. Another key change was that the BBC had lost its right to screen Test Matches, which would now be shown on Channel 4 and Sky TV. Given *Wisden's* current campaign to return cricket to terrestrial television, it is interesting to note that at the close of the last century, their editor believed it served the BBC right, because "its presentation of cricket has been (as with other sports) complacent and dreary".

In 1998–1999 England took with them to Australia Alan Mullally who had been raised there, although born in Southend. He took five wickets in his first Test Match 'back home' and the match was drawn. England's totals of 112 and 191 were inadequate at Perth and Australia took a series lead which with centuries by Langer and Slater, they extended in the third Test Match to retain the Ashes. Boxing Day was wiped out by rain and on the 27 December England were 4–2 before a century from captain Stewart took them to 270. With a deficit of 70 runs, they set Australia a target of 175, and the home team reached 130–3, claiming the extra half-hour in a day that lasted over eight hours of playing time. Astonishingly, Headley finished with 6–70, Australia lost seven wickets for 32 runs and England had a narrow victory. The fifth Test Match was Taylor's last as Australia's captain and he led his team to victory despite Gough's hat-trick – the first for England against Australia for 99 years. There was not one run out in the five Test Matches.

In **1999** it was Barry Richards' turn to provide a foreword for the *Playfair Cricket Annual* and he opened by describing yet another "tumultuous" year, specifying concerns with bribery, throwing, dissent and umpiring standards. He suggested ICC's "diversity" was preventing it from addressing bribery and betting issues and was also very concerned that litigation, evident throughout modern societies, was affecting the game at all levels, with unscrupulous lawyers only too willing to pursue cases of unintended injury even to schoolchildren, apparently playing an innocent game. The questioning of Muralitharan's action in Australia also brought legal complications and Richards expressed some sympathy for the bowler's "humiliation". He predicted that players were becoming increasingly vocal in their views as to how the game should develop, not least as more cricket from around the world was broadcast on television. The consequence would be that players would become more aware of issues beyond their own matches – although the same must surely be true of administrators, umpires and spectators. He was in favour of increased use of technology if it led to more correct decisions by umpires and while calling for better pitches he offered one fascinating thought about statistics and averages – that there should be a separate set of averages *only* for matches won.

For England, the World Cup of **1999** was quite dreadful. After they were eliminated *the Times* described it as an "ignominious defeat" and in *the Sun,* John Etheridge suggested it was "the most catastrophic day ever for English cricket". The English coach, David Lloyd, confessed England were "found wanting, when it really mattered". *Wisden* described the opening ceremony as "laughable" after which England, led by Stewart, started quite nicely, beating Sri Lanka by eight wickets and at Canterbury, Kenya by nine wickets. On the following day at Leicester, Zimbabwe beat India by three runs – the closest finish in the tournament, then at the Oval South Africa hammered England by 122 runs (Donald 4–17). They recovered to record a third win, beating Zimbabwe by seven wickets and seemed sure to qualify for the 'Super Sixes' until unexpectedly Zimbabwe beat South Africa by 48 runs. So England met India at Edgbaston needing victory but lost by 63 runs chasing what would now seem a relatively modest target of 233. To make matters worse this was the only match forced by rain into a second day. The tournament was in every respect a damp squib for the hosts.

1999 saw significant changes either enacted or looming: the County Championship would divide into two leagues from 2000; and Britannic

Assurance ended its sponsorship; the old Sunday League became a two division CGU National League won by Lancashire; and the B&H 'Super Cup' at Lord's was won by Gloucestershire. They also beat their neighbours Somerset in the Final of the NatWest Trophy, now a 50-over competition and played on 29 August. The National League was the first county competition that involved promotion and relegation and both that and the division of the County Championship for the following year brought increased competitiveness and increased controversy.

So, change there was again as the century drew to its close. The consequences of the new competitiveness were apparent immediately in this first season in two competitions, which were introducing promotion and relegation and in both cases led to tensions between Hampshire and Warwickshire. The final National League positions were decided on Sunday, 19 September, a day of unpleasant weather, which had been forecast for the day before. In the National League, Hampshire, already condemned to relegation, met Warwickshire, who needed a victory to survive. The weather was poor, but eventually an 11-over game began and the home side posted 114–4. Hampshire lost wickets regularly and when Shaun Udal was caught from the first ball of the 10th over Hampshire, 76–6, were almost certain to lose, while a *minimum* of five more balls had to be bowled to constitute a match – but at that point with rain falling, the umpires decided that they and the players would follow Udal to the pavilion. The match was declared No Result because of those missing five balls, and Warwickshire were relegated. Victory would have saved them, and there was some fury among the spectators.

This was exacerbated by what had happened over the previous four days at Derby. Hampshire played Derbyshire in the final round of County Championship matches to decide the cut-off for next season's introduction of the first and second divisions. Warwickshire were similarly mid-table but gave themselves every chance of a place in the top tier with a two-day victory over Sussex at Edgbaston, although the Sussex captain Chris Adams suggested that the pitch preparation constituted "blatant cheating" as his team were dismissed for 99 and 176. At Derby Hampshire needed a victory and Derbyshire sought bonus points to finish in the top half. After Hampshire scored 362–8 declared on the third morning at Derby, the home team reached the batting point they needed to ensure a Division One place. This came during an over from Hampshire's occasional leg-spinner Giles White, who bowled just 35.4 overs in his 14 matches that season and whose place as a bowler would be challenged the following year by the recent news that his county had signed Shane Warne.

The forecast for the final Saturday was not promising so after Derbyshire declared at 277–9 there was the unedifying sight of 'joke' declaration bowling on a penultimate day, not in response to bad weather but to a weather *forecast* which it transpired was a day out. Hampshire reached 199–5 declared in 35 overs and set Derbyshire 285 to win in four sessions – a generous target but again probably mindful of the forecast. Nixon McLean and Udal took two early wickets each and Derbyshire closed on 109–4 and in trouble. On the Saturday, three wickets went before lunch, reducing Derbyshire to 163–7 with captain Dominic Cork gone for 51. Hampshire looked on course for victory until De Freitas and Simon Lacey added 104, taking Derbyshire to within 18 runs of victory before Dimitri Mascarenhas dismissed De Freitas. Peter Hartley, once of Warwickshire, had Paul Aldred lbw at 279–9 and three runs later on a gloomy but dry afternoon held a return chance from Lacey and Hampshire, rather than Warwickshire would be in the first division next year. Warwickshire suggested unreasonable collusion and demanded an enquiry, but the umpires reported themselves content and the result stood. I watched the whole match and found the choice of White to bowl as the oddest moment, while the contrivance of the third afternoon provided dreadful cricket. This was supposed to have been eliminated by four-day matches, unless the weather had affected the game adversely but in this case it was based merely on a forecast for the following day that turned out to be wrong. Beyond that, it was never obvious to spectators whether significant negotiations and 'deals' had taken place, but it was a warning of what might happen with the added elements of pressure and expectation in two divisional county cricket.

In the Test Matches of **1999**, England captained by Hussain lost the series to New Zealand 2–1. England won the first match, then Hussain chose to bat at Lord's on the basis of another faulty weather forecast and England were skittled for 186 (from 102–2). New Zealand took a lead of 172 and won at Lord's for the first time. Thorpe deputized for Hussain who broke a finger in the field and then Butcher led England to a 'losing' draw at Old Trafford, where they were probably saved by Manchester's usual weather. There was another captain, Stewart, at the Oval as Darren Maddy and Ed Giddins made their debuts, with the latter bringing up the rear in England's famous 'tail' of Mullally, Tufnell and Giddins. They managed just nine runs between them with four dismissals but were hardly to blame for all-out scores of 153 & 162 as England now lost to New Zealand for the first time at the Oval. It was a desperately disappointing summer with which to close the century.

Any doubts about the need for yet another re-organisation evaporated after the World Cup and New Zealand series. The domestic structure was considered at fault and apparently would remain so unless and until it was remodeled along the lines of Australian or South African domestic cricket. These solutions were usually propelled by former England captains like Bob Willis or Michael Atherton, paying little apparent attention to the greater support that the English county game attracted than those other countries, and based on virtually no experience of being an 'ordinary' adult spectator of county cricket. They spoke as players, for players, and expected supporters to follow whatever they preferred. Interestingly in the years when England's Test side triumphed there seemed to be less appetite for mocking overseas arrangements, perhaps praising the English structure, or suggesting that Australia might benefit from an 18 team County Championship.

There was a change at the head of the England side with Duncan Fletcher appointed coach. He was born in Southern Rhodesia and had played for Zimbabwe although his parents and grandparents were British and he would eventually be given British citizenship. One of his main wishes was to instigate a system of Central Contracts for the best England players, allowing the coach to control how much County Championship cricket they might play. During the first few years of the new century he would do much to restore pride in the England side but it is interesting that while the structure, training and management of coaching in England has become increasingly 'sophisticated', it has proved increasingly difficult to find English coaches to lead the national side – and in many cases the same applies at the English counties.

Despite 1992's Black Wednesday and the longest recession since the 1930s, Britain had survived to welcome the new millennium. English cricket had thrived on the Victorian's creation of the rail network, but that had been savaged following Dr Richard Beeching's report in the 1960s, and 30 years later British Rail was privatised. At around the same time the Government introduced the National Lottery, which would provide funds for various worthy causes, including English cricket. For more than 30 years the counties had played on Sundays but their potential supporters had the option now of extended shopping on the 'Day of Rest' and some of cricket's earliest sponsors were outlawed as a consequence of restrictions on tobacco advertising. From 1995 the Channel Tunnel made mainland Europe more accessible while Britain's 'Empire' shrank a little more as she handed over control of Hong Kong to the Chinese, and its unity was shifting with arguments for devolution in Scotland and Wales. The world kept on changing although Cliff Richard provided an alternative sense of continuity with the last UK number one of the century "The Millennium Prayer". In the early years of the 21st century it often felt that prayer might be the only answer to a series of greater tragedies, which once again served to remind us that cricket really is 'only a game'.

Chapter Seven: the 21st Century

On Sunday, 2 January 2000, prime minister Tony Blair claimed that the country's Millennium celebrations had been a great success. He noted a "real sense of confidence and optimism" that he wished to "bottle" although HM the Queen seemed less than delighted to be clasping Blair's hand to sing "Auld Lang Syne" at the new Millennium Dome in Greenwich. On New Year's Day 10,000 paying customers were admitted to the Dome for the first time. Blair was three years into a decade as prime minister and would win further General Elections in 2001 and 2005. The population of the UK was just short of 60 million, having been around 35 million at the start of the previous century. In theory, that offered a significant increase in the number of people who *might* play and/or watch cricket, and there were certainly more county members than in 1900 although not as many as there had been in the decades immediately following the second world war. Travelling to support county teams became more expensive as petrol prices rose to around 80p per litre, leading to the first 'Fuel Protests' in late summer of 2000. The average weekly wage was just over £400 – by 2015 it was almost £500.

All that was somewhat domestic, but any tales of parochial celebration and dissent would take a back seat during the 21st century to a succession of military interventions by western allies in the middle east and various terrorist responses including 9/11 (2001) in the USA, the London bombings of July 2005 and two separate events of slaughter in Paris in 2015. Europe faced a refugee crisis in 2015 of huge proportions and previously there was the economic crisis, which began in Britain with the nationalisation of Northern Rock in September 2007 along with the 'phone-hacking scandals which led to the closure of the *News of the World*. The sudden fashion for ephemera urging us to "Keep Calm and …" (whatever), evoked the gritty 'all in this together' spirit of the early 1940s although *the Guardian* rather spoiled the jolly sense of nostalgia by those who mostly weren't there, revealing that the original posters had been rejected by the Government and were never used until the 21st century! The whole world seemed an insecure, threatening and unstable place but top level international sport, far from offering any respite, seemed merely to mirror it. In terms of international cricket, this was exposed in the 2015 documentary, *Death of a Gentleman,* but that soon paled into relative insignificance against the corruption at the head of FIFA and the crisis in world athletics. The latter was initially around the use of illegal drugs by athletes at the 2012 British Olympics, but soon spread to familiar stories of corruption and undue influence among those running the sport. It seemed in the generally nasty 21st century, that nothing was sacred.

The old century ended with England in South Africa. In the first Test Match in November, they gave debuts to Gavin Hamilton, Chris Adams and Michael Vaughan; poor Hamilton 'bagged' a pair, took 0–63 and never played in another Test Match, while his Yorkshire team-mate, Vaughan, would become one of England's most successful captains. South Africa won the game, their 10th consecutive home victory, but there was no 11th as England drew in Port Elizabeth and again in Durban. Sadly, England's new century started with an innings defeat in Cape Town after centuries by Jacques Kallis and Daryl Cullinan.

The last Test of the series was in Pretoria and after South Africa reached 155–6 on day one, the next three days were lost to rain. On the final day, with no prospect of a result, they batted on to 248–8 when, to everyone's surprise, Hansie Cronje declared and the match referee Australian, Barry Jarman, was asked to sanction two forfeitures. England reached 251–8 to win in the 76th and final possible over which seemed a rather thrilling end to a frustrating match and for England, a disappointing series – but it was not what it seemed.

The match ended in mid-January and less than three months later police in Delhi revealed a recording of Cronje discussing match-fixing with a representative of an Indian betting syndicate. Later in the year, Cronje was banned from cricket for life. *Wisden's* new editor, Graeme Wright, suggested Cronje's "worst crime was not against cricket … but against morality and decency" in the way he "ensnared" his team-mates. Wright added that had cricket's authorities dealt properly with the Malik/Warne/Waugh affair some years earlier, that might have prevented Cronje acting as he did. In June 2002 Cronje died in a plane accident in South Africa.

Wright supported Lord McLaurin's attempts to improve the quality and image of English Test and county cricket. He suggested, however, that much of what the ECB had done at most levels of the game had been viewed with some suspicion since "change, let alone radical change, is rarely welcomed" in case "it will destroy what we hold dear". That may be true, and as we have suggested, cricket is an inherently conservative game, yet over the past 35 years there had been endless change, major and minor. Wright suggested also that sponsors no longer felt their name could be linked usefully to cricket in terms of "traditional values" and the place of the game "in English life". In more modern terms, he compared Vodafone's £12m sponsorship of English cricket with the company's simultaneous £30m sponsorship of Manchester United.

The English season of **2000** was the first in which England's centrally contracted cricketers were freed from regular appearances for their counties, while fewer top overseas professionals were able to play throughout the English season. At the end of the year, the ECB decided to replace the financial penalties for slow over rates – incurred by all but five counties – with the deduction of points. The required rate was only 16 overs per hour now, but throughout the postwar years, whatever the expectation, the cricketers usually came up short. Warwickshire who had ended the 20th century furious at their double 'relegation' did not have to wait long for honour to be satisfied. In 2000, for the first time, both the league competitions involved promotion and relegation for the top and bottom three – up to 12 of the 18 sides each season. In 2000, Warwickshire won promotion in the National League while Derbyshire and Hampshire lost their places in the County Championship's first division, along with Durham, and they were also the bottom three sides in the National League. In 2001, Warwickshire and Hampshire were both promoted in the County Championship and while Hampshire were initially a 'yo-yo' side, Warwickshire would be County Champions in 2004.

In addition to their on-field disappointments, the years 2000 and 2001 were momentous and traumatic for Hampshire as they became the first of the old counties to give up their traditional home grounds for a brand new stadium, designed to host county and international cricket. The first matches played on the Nursery and main grounds at their new Rose Bowl were 2nd XI games in June and July **2000,** after which they prepared to move fully to the ground from 2001 while embarking on a farewell 'tour' of their grounds in Basingstoke, Portsmouth and the headquarters in Southampton. For economic reasons they had played in Bournemouth for the last time in 1992, but as the moves were organized in the new century, they faced the very real prospect of bankruptcy, which was avoided only through the invest-ment of Rod Bransgrove who was briefly chairman of the old County Cricket Club committee. The restructuring of the business transformed them from that members' club into a plc. On the field they would return to Basingstoke for a couple of matches a few years later but at present they are one of the counties playing all home matches on one ground – and the only county playing on a 21st century ground.

Surrey retained the County Championship in **2000,** and Northamptonshire were the first team to win the new second division. Gloucestershire secured a limited-overs 'treble', as they beat Glamorgan in the Final of the B&H Cup,

Warwickshire in the NatWest Final and also won the National League, now sponsored by Norwich Union.

England played against Zimbabwe at Lord's in mid-May **2000** – the earliest a Test Match had ever been played in this country. The visitors were dismissed for 83 and while Heath Streak took 6–87, England won by a massive innings and 207 runs. Murray Goodwin's century helped Zimbabwe to draw the second game at Trent Bridge but he and Neil Johnson immediately declared their decision to retire from international cricket and emigrate; they would play for Sussex and Hampshire. The West Indies arrived next and at Edgbaston beat England by an innings in what was the 1,500[th] Test Match ever played. Graeme Hick 'bagged' his first pair in first-class cricket but oddly, given the margin of victory, there were no West Indian centurions.

At Lord's, West Indies reached the end of day one on 267–9. The last wicket fell without addition on the next morning and in an extraordinary second day, England were dismissed for 134, West Indies for 54 (Caddick 5–16) and England closed on 0–0. On the next day they pursued 188 to win, while Walsh took six wickets. At 149–7 they were struggling but Cork hit 33* and England were home. Marcus Trescothick made his debut in the drawn third game but the West Indies collapsed again at Leeds (61 all out – Caddick 5–14) where England won by an innings. Hussain made a pair at the Oval, but had the satisfaction of leading England to another victory in the match and the series – England's first series win against the West Indies in three decades.

In November **2000**, Bangladesh joined the ranks of Test playing nations with a single Test Match against India in Dhaka, which India won by nine wickets despite a debut century by Aminul Islam. A few days later England played their first Test of the winter in Lahore – a high scoring game that ended in stalemate, as eventually did the three-match series. Atherton was England's leading scorer, while Ashley Giles took most wickets. Leg-spinner, Ian Salisbury, followed Chris Schofield into the side but like most English leg-spinners, neither enjoyed much success. Australia beat the West Indies in every Test of their five-match series to confirm the shift in world power, even without Warne. In the early spring, England went to Sri Lanka and despite losing the first Test by an innings, triumphed 2–1 after dismissing their hosts for 81 in the last game. Fletcher and Hussain seemed to be turning things around. Just before the first Test Match in Sri Lanka started, the greatest batsman Sir Donald Bradman died in Australia.

England had enjoyed an encouraging time in recent series, but they could not compete with the Australians in 2001. They lost the series 4–1 with the bowling of McGrath and Warne particularly irresistible. The main England players who appeared in all five matches played relatively few County

Championship games as central contracts took increasing effect. They were Atherton (four County Championship matches), Caddick (two), Gough (two), Stewart (five) and Trescothick (three). The one exception was Butcher who played 10 matches for Surrey, but he earned ECB contracts only for Test Matches, not the ODIs. Butcher had a moment of real glory at Headingley with a superb 173* in England's only victory as they scored 315–4 in the final innings. Nasser Hussain missed two of the Test Matches but played in just one County Championship match for Essex.

Despite the frequent absence of Gough, Yorkshire won the County Championship in 2001 for the first time in 33 years as Darren Lehman, not required by Australia, made a major contribution, including a record 252 in the 'roses' match. Sussex were Division Two Champions, Surrey beat Gloucestershire in the B&H Cup Final at Lord's, and Kent won the National League. The late Cup Final, was back to the first day of September, sponsored by Cheltenham & Gloucester (C&G) and with 50 overs per side as Somerset triumphed, beating Leicestershire by 41 runs.

While Australia were beating England in **2001**, there were English summer Tests elsewhere between Zimbabwe and the West Indies, Sri Lanka and India with Pakistan and Bangladesh once again reducing the availability of top overseas players to county sides. In early September, Zimbabwe played two games against South Africa. In December 2001, Hussain's England lost the first Test of the series in India by 10 wickets but drew the next two. In the last match they had extended a first innings lead of 98 by 33 without loss, but the rain washed-out all but 16 overs on the final two days. In March, a century from the captain, 200* from Thorpe and 7–63 by Matthew Hoggard took them to victory in Christchurch, despite a magnificent double century by Nathan Astle in a New Zealand fourth innings of 451. The second Test was drawn but New Zealand squared the series in Auckland – only Hussain with 82, passing 50 for the visitors. New Zealand batted under floodlights (with a red ball) until 8pm on the fourth evening, scoring 216 in 41.2 overs.

Having enjoyed the stability of a whole two years of the two divisional County Championship and Central Contracts, the editor of *Wisden*, in his notes for the 2002 edition, was bored with the *status quo* and proposed that "the time is approaching to reform the first-class county structure as opposed to merely meddling with the cricket and the fixture list", although he was content with the prospect of some meddling, too. He identified English county cricket as a "Victorian institution that has resisted reform". The counties had, for the most part formed in the Victorian era but it is quite difficult to find any evidence from the 19th century of a two divisional, four-day County Championship on covered wickets (with pitch penalties) contested by a fully professional 'workforce' – including significant numbers from overseas – who also played each other over 40 or perhaps 45, 50, 55, 60 and, even briefly, 65-overs while wearing coloured clothing, sometimes under floodlights with a white ball. There were no Lord's Cup Finals then, either, nor did so many county matches take place at each county's headquarters. But one of the few unchanging aspects of the English game is that no one involved in it professionally believes anything ever changes, while those of us who watch and pay, experience endless change and do our best to adjust and remember the latest decisions. About three years after this editorial, the England captain, Michael Vaughan, in a *Sunday Times* interview, told Simon Wilde that every England captain for 20 years had sought changes but "nothing seems to happen". Well, one of the biggest changes "to happen" in English cricket would arrive around the time that Vaughan was making his bizarre complaint, and it would go on to have a huge impact on the game world-wide.

One matter of concern to the ECB was that while home Test Matches were shown still on a free-to-air channel, viewing figures had declined each year. Fewer people were watching televised cricket while the situation in the state schools was now very poor. Seeking to develop higher quality Test Match cricketers, the ECB engaged the former Australian Test cricketer Rod Marsh to launch the new English Academy system. He had been successful in a similar role in his country but yet again it seemed there were no suitable English candidates.

Wright believed that some counties were "living on borrowed time" and that there was a preference to let the "weakest" perish. He reported total county memberships in 2001 at fewer than 130,000 and proposed that life in Britain in the 21st century would be reflected better in a professional competition based on city or town teams rather than the somewhat old-fashioned counties. He added that "the grounds are already established in the cities" although this was not wholly true since the newest of the major grounds, Hampshire's Rose (Ageas) Bowl is not in Southampton but in the borough and parliamentary constituency of Eastleigh, where it sits in an environment of trees and hills, hinting at English cricket's rural and *county* origins. This was Wright's second spell as *Wisden's* editor but also his parting shot. Tim de Lisle replaced him from 2003.

The English season of **2002** opened with India playing a five Test Match series in the West Indies. In England, Sri Lanka posted 555–8 declared at Lord's and looked on course for a 10th consecutive Test Match victory as England (275) followed on, but centuries from Vaughan and Butcher took them to safety. The Sri Lankan, Thisara Perera, was reported to ICC for a suspect action. In the next Test Match it was the turn of Trescothick and Thorpe to reach three figures as England won by an innings, and in the third, it was centurions Butcher and Stewart who set up a successful second innings victory chase of 50–0 in just six dark overs. New Zealand travelled to the West Indies and Sri Lanka hosted Bangladesh before the Indians were England's second tourists. Now there was Test Match cricket worldwide, taking place most of the time.

The home side selected debutant, Simon Jones, at Lord's, where Hussain, Vaughan and John Crawley made centuries and England won by 170 runs. On the final afternoon, Agit Agarkar provided interesting resistance. Coming to the wicket with a single figure batting average he scored 109, but it was not enough. Robert Key and Steve Harmison were the debutants at Trent Bridge and Key opened with Vaughan who posted 197 of England's 617, a lead of 260. India were 99–2 at the start of the final day and a full house saw them bat to safety through a century by Raul Dravid and 90s from Tendulkar and captain, Sourav Ganguly. There were a number of doubtful bad light calls throughout the game, with England leaving the field to general derision on a bright Saturday evening on 341–5. The three top scorers for India in that Test Match all made centuries at Headingley and India, 628–8 declared, won by an innings, despite Hussain's century. Both sides passed 500 in the final Test Match at the Oval with Tendulkar reaching his 100th Test, Vaughan again just short of 200 and Dravid past it, as both the match and the series were drawn.

Vaughan's compensation was that his fellow professionals voted him the PCA's Player of the Year – the 16th Englishman to win in 33 seasons if we count Worcestershire's Neal Radford as English and Hick as overseas. The Cricket Writers selected Rikki Clarke as the 54th Young Cricketer of the Year – as with the PCA there had been joint recipients in one season. In the early years of the award (from 1950), a number of the recipients went on to significant Test careers, including May (1951), Trueman (1952), Cowdrey (1953) and Barrington (1955). In the 1960s, recipients included Boycott, Knott, Underwood, Brearley and Greig and later Botham, Gower, Hussain and Atherton (1990). But over the previous decade few of these promising youngsters chosen, including Salisbury, Lathwell, Chris Silverwood, Alex Tudor, Paul Franks and now Clarke, went on to become major figures. The exception was Andrew Flintoff in 1998 but it begged the question whether the writers were losing their touch or whether English cricket was failing to develop its most promising players in the intense arena of modern inter-national cricket. After Clarke, however, it was all change again, as he was followed by Anderson, Bell, Cook, Broad and, more recently, James Taylor, Stephen Finn, Jonny Bairstow, Joe Root and Ben Stokes, all of whom featured in Test Matches in 2015. Perhaps one crucial difference was the system of central contracts? Perhaps English cricket was getting better?

Back in **2002**, there was a 10-match triangular ODI series at eight venues (including Bristol) before India beat England in the Final at Trent Bridge. On the county scene, Surrey mourned the tragic death of Ben Hollioake, killed in a car accident in March 2002, but they were Champions for the third time in four years despite losing Stewart, Butcher, Thorpe and Tudor to England who played just 20 County Championship matches between them. Ian Ward had a magnificent summer and Saqlain Mustaq, helped by Ormond, bowled out their opponents. Essex won Division Two while Yorkshire were relegated from the top tier but beat Somerset in the C&G Trophy Final. Glamorgan won the National League and Gloucestershire Division Two, while Warwickshire beat Essex in the last-ever B&H Cup Final by five wickets with 13 overs and four balls to spare. Ian Bell with 65* took the last match award after 30 years of the competition that had been conceived as the Saturday limited-overs competition to match the Sunday League – an interesting but long-forgotten idea. Warwickshire's Cricket Board side also won the ECB's 38-County Cup Final, competed for by the Minor Counties and Cricket Board sides and Ian Westwood who top-scored with 67 went on to captain the full county side.

In **2002**, the Acfield Report, led by former Essex spinner and Olympic fencer, David Acfield, was set up as the consequence of the English county game suffering from years of "stagnation". Looking back, it is difficult to identify that stagnation given the endless tinkering with formats, competitions, player management and availability, pitches, grounds, and so on. It is almost as though there are two constants in English cricket: change, and the claim that nothing has changed. The 19th century Hampshire cricketer, Reginald Hargreaves, who married the real Alice in Wonderland (Liddell), might have felt entirely at home down the rabbit's burrow that was English cricket.

England's first task in the winter was their next battle for the Ashes. On the morning of the first Test at Brisbane, Hussain won the toss, invited Australia to bat and walked off at the close of play with Hayden 186* in a score of 364–2. Simon Jones suffered a dreadful knee injury and after bowling seven overs, was out of the tour as Australia won by 384 runs, setting a pattern for the series. They won the first four matches and retained the Ashes after just 11 days of cricket. Justin Langer, Ricky Ponting and Hayden all passed 400 runs, although Vaughan with three centuries had 633 runs in his 10 innings. Caddick took 20 wickets to equal Jason Gillespie, Australia's best bowler, but all round, Australia were far superior. Not for the first time, however, did the hosts lose the last match to centuries from Butcher and Vaughan and 7–94 by Caddick. For England, it was too little, too late.

In the New Year came the next World Cup, in Africa. It was scheduled to take place in *South* Africa but the ICC allowed Kenya and Zimbabwe to have a share. In its 2003 edition, *Wisden* suggested, "politics ran through this World Cup like the zebra-skinned logo that bedecked the stands". One consequence was that England and New Zealand refused to play matches in Zimbabwe and Kenya, respectively, and the winning points were awarded to their opponents. Meanwhile, two Zimbabwean players, Andy Flower and Henry Olonga, chose to wear black armbands on the field as a protest, "mourning the death of democracy" and the loss of human rights in their "beloved" country.

Even without issues of politics, morality and security, it was a long and complicated tournament with no fewer than 42 first-round matches leading to the Super Sixes where previously earned points were carried forward. One of the attractions of limited-overs cricket is its relative simplicity, especially for the casual supporter but too often the ICC and ECB contrive to make qualification, tie breaks and results as opaque as possible. The tournament took seven weeks to complete but in England only Sky Sports viewers could watch it. At the conclusion, no fewer than five competing sides changed their captains; Australia and India beat Sri Lanka and Kenya in the semi-finals; and after Ponting smashed 140* in 121 balls, his side took the trophy, beating India (234) by a massive 125 runs. The Champions had won all 11 of their matches, despite Warne being sent home after failing a drugs test.

One of the complications of world cricket in the 21st century is that it was unusual if a week passed with no international teams playing somewhere in some format, so that publishing schedules for annuals like *Wisden* or the *Playfair Cricket Annual* were increasingly difficult. While *Wisden's* editor commented at length and critically on the World Cup in the 2003 edition, the scores, reports and reviews were not available until the following year. There he pointed out that more than half the world's Test Matches in the first 125 years had been played in the last 25.

In the *Playfair Cricket Annual,* editor Bill Frindall observed that he was increasingly "bored' by the surfeit of ODIs and other limited-overs matches and he made one intriguing suggestion: to reward the bowler and fielding side by allowing an extra over for a bowler, each time he takes a wicket. Was it ever considered? Frindall added, "all bowlers will applaud the idea but very few are administrators".

England's international summer of **2003** was either feast or gluttony, depending on taste, with seven Test Matches and 13 ODIs. Broadly, the three elements of the current three-competition domestic pattern were fixed in 2003, with the division of the two county championships, the C&G Cup and, most significantly, the introduction of the T20 competition replacing the B&H Cup. *Wisden* suggested that this "knockabout" competition was a "valid experiment" but argued, "the circuit is still overloaded" as the National League remained with the addition of Scotland – while Loughborough University became a new university first-class side and in the autumn opened its new cricket academy.

There was general delight as Sussex won their first County Championship title. The win was increased to 14 points but the system of three up and three down was thought to be too much with two divisions of nine sides soon switching to two each. Gloucestershire clinched their sixth Lord's trophy in five years with a victory against Worcestershire. That competition was still a straight 50-over knock-out which began in earnest when a few Cricket Boards, Minor Counties and Scotland played the county sides. Gloucestershire received £53,000 for winning the trophy. In 2015 that competition has changed to three leagues involving just the 18 counties with a knock-out phase and a Lord's Final which has lost much of its glamour. It may be a salutary reminder to those who are intent on investing mainly in the T20 to reflect on how the once popular knock-out cup competitions and Sunday League have gone from being the commercial centerpieces of the county game to 'also-rans' in less than a lifetime, while the County Championship survives. There was still a National League, successor to the old Sunday league, and it was won by Surrey.

The new T20 competition began on a fine Friday evening on Sky TV from Hampshire's Rose Bowl. Shane Warne was due to be captaining Hampshire during **2003** but was found to have ingested a banned substance and missed a year's cricket from the World Cup onwards. The 2003 T20 competition was modest by current standards although it was immediately popular. The counties competed in three leagues playing five matches each, with no quarter-finals. The inaugural Finals Day was at Trent Bridge, where Warwickshire beat Leicestershire and Surrey beat Gloucestershire in the first two matches. Warwickshire's 166–3 with four balls remaining was the day's highest score but they managed only 115 in the Final and Surrey lost just one wicket cruising to victory in the 11th over – a complete non-event of the kind that can always bedevil shorter matches. James Ormond's 4–11, and 50s from Ian Ward and Ali Brown, led the way.

In early summer, England won their two Tests against Zimbabwe, the second at Chester-Le-Street, England's first new Test venue for over 100 years. There was a capacity crowd on Saturday, which proved to be the last day as although England's 416 lacked a single century, it was too much for the visitors' 94 and 253. Meanwhile, even Australia took to playing Tests during the English summer beating Bangladesh twice in Darwin by an innings, in late July. South Africa arrived in England for the latter part of the summer and topped the limited-overs triangular table, beating Zimbabwe in the last of the nine 'league' matches at the Rose Bowl – another new English international venue. In the Final at Lord's the visitors crashed to 107 all out and England won by seven wickets in the 21st over – another one-sided contest.

Graeme Smith (277) and Herschelle Gibbs (179) dominated the first Test, adding 338 for South Africa's first wicket. Vaughan replied with another century and England drew the match comfortably as Hussain handed the captaincy on to the Yorkshireman. He had a difficult start as Smith scored just 18 fewer at Lord's, passing Bradman's record innings by a visiting batsman. There were hundreds for Butcher and Hussain at Trent Bridge, and with debutant James Kirtley, taking 6–34, England squared the fascinating series. Kallis bowled South Africa to victory at Headingley only for England to draw level at the Oval. South Africa's 484 was built on Gibbs' 183 but Trescothick (219), Thorpe (124) and Flintoff (95) gave them a lead of 120. Alec Stewart retired after 133 Tests with a victory in a drawn series.

Looking back on **2003**, *Wisden's* latest editor, the returning Matthew Engel, was in a cheerful mood. The best team had won the World Cup, the sun had shone through the English season, the new T20 was a success with the public, while the ECB "has been thinking hard and creatively about the problems it faces". It was not all delight, however. At the international level, the ICC was addressing the problems of match-fixing with a "sense of urgency", while Engel referred to the five members of the self-styled "Cricket Reform Group", including Michael Atherton and Bob Willis, whose manifesto contained all kinds of proposals but principally an 'elite' group of just six county sides, playing 10 matches each season *between* the Tests to enable the England players to participate. They also wanted a clear line from various forms of minor county/club cricket and the first-class game enabling players, other than full-time professionals, to reach the top of the county game. But Engel pointed out that the counties are generally quite good at identifying such talent, adding that since those sides began meeting the first-class counties in 1964, the 'minnows' had won fewer than 5% of the 748 matches while most of the defeats "have been slaughters". He did, nonetheless, agree that county cricket "does need reform". Despite that, Engel revealed that he had returned to the post after two years in the USA realising "cricket changes so fast these days that, even after a short absence, one comes back entirely disorientated". Of course, the two things are not mutually exclusive. As with, for example, the British education and health services, it is entirely conceivable that change is endless while leaving the core systems and structures badly in need of reform. If that occurs in the most important of the country's social institutions, why should we be surprised if it happens in the sporting world?

In the winter, England beat Bangladesh 2–0 and then gave a debut to Paul Collingwood as they lost the final Test and the series to Sri Lanka, for whom Muralitharan was Man-of-the-Series with 26 wickets at 12.3 each. England's spinner Giles had 18 at just under 30 apiece but there was just one century, by Vaughan, whose average of 36.83 was easily the best. The defeat was the third heaviest in their history following Sri Lanka's massive total of 628–8 declared.

In a busy winter just before the **2004** season, England toured West Indies, winning three and drawing one of the four Tests Matches. How those tables had turned after decades of West Indian supremacy. Nonetheless, Brian Lara, who had briefly lost his world record Test Match score to Matthew Hayden, regained it at Antigua becoming the only man to reach 400 in a Test Match. In the summer of **2004**, England beat New Zealand 3–0 and in a return with West Indies on home soil won all four matches – a year's aggregate to August of played 11, won 10, drawn one.

Michael Vaughan's side were playing effective Test cricket in anticipation of another Ashes series in 2005. As in the 1960s, England had not won the Ashes through the 1990s but that period was now stretching halfway into the next decade. Harmison was England's outstanding bowler in the Caribbean, while Ashley Giles took most wickets in the home West Indies series, and no fewer than five English batsmen passed 300 runs, Flintoff, Key, Vaughan, Trescothick and Strauss. The latter had made his Test debut in the summer's first Test Match against New Zealand at Lord's, scoring 112 in the first innings and he reached 83 in the second when a poor call from Hussain saw him run out. He was only the fourth Lord's Test Match debut centurion in its history and he was playing under Trescothick as captain because Vaughan was injured just before the match. There was surfeit of ODIs with New Zealand beating the West Indies in the triangular trophy after England managed just one victory after which England beat India 2–1 in another late summer series.

That short series was a warm-up for the Champions Trophy based at the Rose Bowl, Edgbaston and the Oval. Twelve sides, including the USA and Kenya, competed in four mini leagues, after which England beat Australia and West Indies beat Pakistan in the two semi-finals. At the Oval, England posted 217 in the Final, thanks mainly to a Trescothick century and reduced West Indies to 147–8. It seemed they were heading for a first limited-overs trophy, until a ninth wicket partnership of 71* from 92 balls won the match. The competition was not an unreserved success. Spectators had to face stringent restrictions: the Rose Bowl was not yet running its access and departure smoothly; rain and cold weather was hampering; and a bizarre example of the demands of spectators came in the club house bar at Winchester's

Hursley Park, used by teams as practice facilities – one tournament sponsor from a rival company demanded that a display of KP Nuts were removed from display. 'Nuts' it certainly was, although 'KP' was, at that point, merely a 'Notts' player.

In **2004**, the county competitions were the same. Warwickshire lost Giles to England but won the County Championship despite recording only five victories, while Nottinghamshire and Hampshire, first and second in Division Two, would replicate those positions in the higher division 12 months later. Gloucestershire beat Worcestershire to win the C&G Trophy again, while Glamorgan, having won the National League in 2002, won it again in 2004 with a prize of £54,000. Leicestershire and Surrey again reached the T20 Finals Day and it was the midlands county who won the second competition, as in 2003, after a league of five matches with no quarter-finals. Darren Maddy was by far the leading run scorer, with Adam Hollioake the leading all-rounder.

In the winter, England beat South Africa 2–1 in a series that again raised hopes for the following Ashes summer. Kallis and Strauss dominated the batting, both exceeding 600 runs, while Hoggard, Flintoff and Makhaya Ntini were the leading wicket-takers. In early March, South Africa beat Zimbabwe by an innings in the kind of 'Test' that asked questions of standards and encouraged talk of two divisions. The margin of an innings and 21 runs was not the largest in history but the match was over in just two days after South Africa declared on 340–3, a lead of 286, which was more than enough. On 17 February 2005, Australia beat New Zealand by 44 runs in the first International T20 – the two sides wore retro-style clothing, the 'Kiwis' sported fake moustaches, and Ponting, despite a 55-ball innings of 98, said "it is difficult to play seriously". As if to emphasise the point, when his team met England in a T20 at the Rose Bowl that summer, they lost heavily.

So we came to England in **2005**, simply one of the greatest English cricket seasons ever, and presumably remembered clearly by all cricket lovers who witnessed it. Pietersen upset folks at Nottinghamshire and signed for Hampshire, but then won a place in the England limited-overs side in his homeland in the winter. He top-scored on Test debut in both innings of the first Ashes Test Match at Lord's but Australia recovered from 87–5 to win by 239 runs – Glenn McGrath taking 9–82 in the match. There followed the incredible match at Edgbaston where Australia, needing 282 to win, were 175–8 and 220–9 before, on that last morning, Brett Lee and Michael Kasprovich took them within two runs of a tie and three of victory when Geraint Jones held the catch that won the game.

Lee and McGrath held out for a draw at Old Trafford and then England forced Australia to follow-on at Trent Bridge. Australia made 387 in their second innings and England needed just 129 to win. They lost wickets regularly but made it by three wickets and so came to the Oval needing a draw to regain the Ashes. Warne, at slip, dropped Pietersen, whose 158 on the latest date Test cricket had ever been played in England, kept England safe, the umpires were applauded for taking the players off for bad light and the Ashes were safe. Vaughan's team were rewarded with a 'lively' day out in London, including a trip to Number 10 Downing Street to visit Tony Blair, who had won his third General Election that same year. Coincidentally, Pietersen's 158 at the Oval was exactly the same score at the same ground that fellow South African Basil D'Oliveira, scored in 1968. That earlier innings caused huge repercussions of course and, it might be suggested, led ultimately to the circumstances in which Pietersen was playing for England.

Warne's Hampshire had been promoted with Nottinghamshire in the previous year's County Championship and the two teams now competed for the big prize, but Warne, who took 40 wickets at less than 20 apiece in the Test Match series, faced another frustration. In their penultimate match it seemed that Nottinghamshire would have to accept a draw, until the Kent captain David Fulton declared on the final morning 249 behind. Nottinghamshire hit at seven runs per over, declared, and in the 53rd over bowled out Kent and won the County Championship. Warne was livid and in their final match, Hampshire scored their record 714–5 to beat Nottinghamshire at the Rose Bowl, but they finished 2.5 points behind Nottinghamshire and have not now won the County Championship for more than 40 years. There was some consolation as they won the Lord's C&G Trophy, albeit captained by Hampshire-born, Shaun Udal, as Warne was on Test Match duty.

The Ashes had followed a two-match Test series against Bangladesh, a triple tournament between England, Bangladesh and Australia and then a three-match limited-overs series between the Ashes rivals, so that the Test Match series began very late, but even with the new football season underway, cricket dominated the sports media and attracted enormous public interest. It was everything the ECB and the viewing public wanted, although before the year was out the former concluded a deal with BSkyB which gave Sky exclusive rights to live cricket in England from 2006–2009. 2006 would be the first time that home Test Matches were not shown on terrestrial television and the agreement, which has earned substantial amounts of money for English cricket, is still in place despite criticism from those who believe that it impacts badly on attracting new supporters, especially the younger ones.

During that momentous summer, the ICC left Lord's and relocated to Dubai where it remains to this day. In *Wisden*, Engel wrote extensively about the move and about the ICC but any concerns disappeared as he praised not just the English men but also England's Women who had just won their version of the Ashes, too. He assured us that there was no need to be nervous in describing the summer as "the Greatest", surpassing "every previous series in cricket history on just about any indicator you choose" adding "it was triumph for the real thing" by which he meant five-day Test cricket – "the best game in the world, at its best". Sadly, he was obliged to note that the massive increase in interest in the Test series was matched by less attention being paid to the County Championship. He pointed out, too, that while Durham had never been a members' club, Hampshire had ceased to be so in the 21st century and now the Yorkshire members of all people were about to hand control "to a self-perpetuating, six-strong junta". Elsewhere the counties remained members' clubs and Engel suggested that English cricket, not football, is therefore "the people's game" and "will maintain its strength best if it stays that way". It is not the way that things are going.

In October, Australia played against an ICC World XI and beat them by 210 runs as well as winning the three 'ODIs'. The ICC and *Wisden* could not quite agree whether the match should have Test Match status and Bill Frindall called it a "witless" result of the greed for more television income. As was the case with the Rest of the World in 1970, 'Tests' were supposed to be between nations, although in quality and statistical terms those matches were more interesting than any involving Bangladesh or Zimbabwe. By the time a decision was made nobody cared terribly. England went to Pakistan where Udal made his Test Match debut at 36 and Mohammad Yousuf played his first Test after changing his name from Yousuf Youhana. England needed 198 to win the first match but lost by 22 runs. The second Test was drawn, while Shahid Afridi was banned for deliberately scuffing the pitch but Pakistan survived without him to win the third match and the series. England went on to India after Christmas and gave debuts to Alistair Cook, Monty Panesar and Ian Blackwell, although it was a recall for veteran spinner Udal that helped them to square the series after India won the second Test. On his 37th birthday, Udal had figures of 4–14 as India, needing 313 to win, managed just 100 all out. It was Udal's final Test and somewhat reminiscent of the last time a Hampshire-born, Hampshire player, had played for England – AJL Hill who, in 1896, took 4–8 in South Africa but was never picked again. At last, and just a couple of years later, one of Hampshire's own Southampton-born, Chris Tremlett, would finally represent England in a Test Match in England. It was all too much and he soon moved to Surrey.

The two **2006** series that migrated to pay-for television were England v Sri Lanka and Pakistan. In the fourth Test at the Oval, England, who had already won the series, were bowled out for 173 and Pakistan replied with 504. England, 331 behind, made a better show in the second innings, reaching

298–4 when the umpires raised questions about the condition of the ball and awarded England five penalty runs. The Pakistan team were outraged and refused to take the field after a break for bad light. After a significant delay and discussions with match referee Mike Procter, umpire Darryl Hair removed the bails and the match was declared forfeit to England. In 2008, the ICC reversed the decision and declared the match drawn but England appealed and the original decision was upheld.

In the domestic **2006** season, the NatWest Pro40 League replaced the Totesport National League, and the competition was reduced to each side playing the others in their division, once instead of twice. Scotland were excluded and Essex were the first winners while Sussex beat Lancashire in a low-scoring C&G Final. Sussex were County Champions again. In July 2006, 19 Caribbean sides took place in the inaugural but ill-fated Stanford T20 tournament.

Wisden published its list of the leading world cricketers for each year from 1900. The first was 'Ranji' (Prince Ranjitsinhji) who counted as English, as were nine others before the first world war with three Australians and two South Africans. From 1960–1999 things were rather different. Sobers won the accolade in 1960, in total seven times (plus 1958), and his fellow West Indians were Viv Richards (x3), Malcolm Marshall (2), Brian Lara (2), Clive Lloyd, Joel Garner and Curtly Ambrose. Australia won most overall, and in this 40 years they had: Dennis Lillee (2), Shane Warne (2), Alan Davidson, Jeff Thomson, Greg Chappell, Alan Border and Steve Waugh; from South Africa, despite years in the wilderness, came: Graeme Pollock (2), Mike Procter and Barry Richards; from Pakistan: Imran Khan and Wasim Akram; from India: Kapil Dev and Sachin Tendulkar; the New Zealanders: Richard Hadlee and Martin Crowe; and from Sri Lanka, Sanath Jayasuria. There were just three single-year English nominations: Fred Trueman (1963), Ian Botham (1981) and Graham Gooch (1990) – with Andrew Flintoff appearing in 2005. The vast majority of those cricketers had appeared in English county cricket but it suggested that 'star' quality was somewhat absent from the England side in the second-half of the 20th century.

In the same edition, Roland Watson asked whether one year on from the euphoria of 2005, English cricket had missed a "once-in-a-generation chance" with a football World Cup and England disappearing from the terrestrial television channels. But he hoped not, and his article was headed "the boom goes on …", citing participation among young people and increased sales of cricket equipment. Professor Steven Barnett, however, looking specifically at the television viewing figures, identified the dramatic decline from the Ashes average peak of 34% of viewers in 2005, to fewer than 10% for the two series in 2006. In particular, he pinpointed "the decline in casual viewers".

In November 2006, 14 months after England's Ashes triumph, the two sides were competing again with Flintoff captaining England. Ponting and McGrath set the pace in the first match at Brisbane and Australia won a huge victory. By the time the series ended on 5 January they had won all five matches and with that, the Ashes, which were briefly on display in the South Australia Museum. During the series Warne became the first bowler to reach 700 Test Match wickets.

The tour of 2006–2007 was a disaster so, of course, there had to be a new investigation culminating in the Schofield Report. Just for a change, it proposed a reduction in domestic cricket but the County Championship remained as it was. There would be a change, however, as from 2010 one 40-over tournament would replace the two, the National League would be discontinued, and there would be just three competitions for the first time since 1971. Graham Thorpe (*Wisden*, 2008) was disappointed that despite the report offering much that was common sense, it lacked "any input on how to prepare players for Test cricket by making the county game more competitive and intense" adding "that lack of intensity is by far the biggest issue facing the English game". The implication, as ever, was that any solution must lie with structural change, yet in just 20 years county cricket had dispensed finally with uncovered pitches, moved from three to four days, increased limits on overseas players and introduced promotion and relegation in the first-class and limited-overs leagues. The England set-up now had its players on central contracts with an unprecedented number of backroom staff and administrators to meet their needs. If all that had failed to increase "intensity", why would another *structural* change make any difference?

Players and recent former players were invited increasingly to express opinions about the English county and Test game but they rarely, if ever, identified any problem with themselves or each other. Britain as a country had an increasingly critical and powerful media and a long tradition of biting satire that had flourished as the young 'alternative' comedians became establishment media personalities. There was a habit in the country to look to apportion blame elsewhere – particularly to blame government and the bosses – and if that was so, why would the cricketers be any different? It seemed it was always the ECB and/or the counties to blame, while the cricketers were doing their best in impossible circumstances.

In his *Wisden* editor's notes, Engel suggested that the current structure of English domestic cricket was "not merely the worst that has yet been invented but possibly the worst that could be imagined" and the "destruction of the once beautiful knock-out cup should be used as a case study of blithering administrative idiocy". He added, "a great many things have changed since 1947", but was not overly enthusiastic about the modern habit of cricketers, like Flintoff and Pietersen, adorning their bodies with tattoos. In less than 10 years since, it might be quicker for the current editor to list those *without* such decorations.

Turning to England's Australian disaster, Engel noted that Duncan Fletcher had been given considerable resources since his appointment as England's coach in 1999 and for the first six years had used them to great effect, but now things had turned sour. The appointment of Flintoff as England's new captain had been no more successful than that of Botham a quarter-of-a-century earlier, and for Engel, Fletcher's time was up: "whatever happens in the World Cup, England must have a new coach". Engel was concerned that England players hardly ever appeared in the County Championship while "other countries" players are more likely to play "lower grade cricket" – some of them, indeed, in English county cricket.

From late January **2007** to mid-May, there was a gap in Test Match cricket world-wide – the longest break since 1971–1972. It is unlikely to occur again. In its place came the latest World Cup that took place in the Caribbean. *Wisden* called it "joyless and long-winded to the point of tedium". In the semi-finals, Australia beat South Africa and Sri Lanka beat New Zealand with Australia winning the Final, which was calculated by the Duckworth-Lewis method in farcical circumstances. Adam Gilchrist scored 149 but when play was halted after 33 overs of the Sri Lanka innings, Australia thought they had won, only to be taken back to play in darkness on a ground without lights. They still won. During the tournament, the Pakistan coach and former England cricketer, Bob Woolmer, was found dead in circumstances that seemed suspicious. Jamaican police carried out an enquiry but months later a court in that country recorded an open verdict. Some of the rumours about his death identified increasing concerns with betting and match-fixing.

In **2007**, counties were awarded extra sums to enhance the fitness of their players. A couple of players who demonstrated that were Darren Gough and Mark Ramprakash, both winners of BBC's *Strictly Come Dancing*. The 2007 season saw a new Chairman at ECB, as David Morgan of Glamorgan handed over to Giles Clarke of Somerset. Sussex won their third County Championship in five years but only after an incredible finish to the season at the Oval, where Lancashire, needing 489 to beat Surrey and clinch the title, fell just 25 runs short. At Lord's in August, Durham, who were eventually runners-up in the County Championship, overwhelmed a strong Hampshire side in the Final of the Friends Provident Trophy to collect their first major trophy after 15 years as a first-class county. The match was only spoiled for them by poor weather, which extended into a second day with few of their supporters in attendance. Worcestershire won the Pro40 League and Kent beat Gloucestershire in the T20 Final. Matt Prior made his Test Match debut as England beat the West Indies in the summer's first series but lost 1–0 to India. Another South African, Kevin Pietersen, amassed more than 800 runs and four centuries in the seven Test Matches and was apparently erroneously blamed for a rather silly prank when someone scattered jellybeans around the crease as India's Zaheer Khan walked in to bat. It backfired as Khan scored 10* and then took 5–75 and India won.

In September **2007**, South Africa hosted the first T20 World Cup and 12 teams contested a somewhat complicated tournament in which England managed to beat only Bangladesh. After more than 30 years of trying, England's dismal display left them alongside Bangladesh and Zimbabwe as the only Test-playing countries never to have won a limited-overs trophy. In the semi-finals, Pakistan beat New Zealand and India beat Australia, after which India beat Pakistan in a thrilling Final. India scored 157–5 and with four balls remaining, Pakistan's last pair needed six to win. Misbah tried to scoop the next ball over fine leg but was caught and India's victory caused a reaction at home, similar to, but far more immediate, than their World Cup triumph of 1983. In less than 12 months, they would launch the T20 Indian Premier League (IPL), another step in their domination of the world game. It grew in opposition to the Indian Cricket League, a private concern which the Board of Cricket Control India (BCCI) declared an outlaw organisation, and which ceased to operate after 2009. The IPL was launched on television after a multi-million dollar auction of players with huge crowds, fireworks and other entertainments on a Friday afternoon (BST) while it was raining heavily on many English county matches. It seemed somehow symbolic. It took India five years to catch up with English county cricket and about five months to overtake it.

This is a publication about English cricket so while the English game is no more separate from the global game than it is from English culture and society, it is not appropriate to pursue the development of the IPL in any detail here, beyond stressing that its success offers a model for those who want English cricket to move in that direction. *Wisden* observed that the Indian version was "shifting the tectonic plates of the professional game as never before" with the period when players "primarily" represented their countries "suddenly" coming to an end. The ECB planned a new T20 structure from 2010 featuring two overseas sides but as the 2008 season came to a close the latest severe worldwide recession bit and those plans were just one relatively minor casualty in the whole downturn. An alternative proposal was a nine-team franchise based at the counties' international grounds. It was a threat to the other counties and to date has not occurred, but there is still time.

Wisden had another new editor in 2008, the journalist Scyld Berry. He sympathised with the threat to the smaller counties, but argued also that they should devote more resources to cricket within their boundaries rather than "relying for recruitment on public schools and the southern hemisphere". Not for the last time, he described Britain's inner cities as "mostly untrawled waters". A survey of London secondary schoolchildren found cricket in 21st place of those sports to which pupils wished to have better access.

In England, the major initial impact of the IPL was through the signing of top players in the early weeks of the county season. Meanwhile, England lost 1–0 to Sri Lanka in the winter with Test debuts for Ravi Bopara and Stuart Broad. Alistair Cook followed Bradman, Miandad and Tendulkar in posting a seventh Test century before the age of 23.

In his notes, Berry regretted the failure to implement two key recommendations of the Schofield Report that both England's Test and county cricketers should play fewer matches. He reported a research project that revealed the England team generating 80% of the ECB's revenues while the counties contributed the other 20%. The research suggested that watching England, live and on television, had become "an elite pastime", arguing that the Australians put a much higher value than the ECB on making cricket affordable and available to the 'ordinary' fan. He quoted a number of senior figures in the cricketing world including Michael Atherton who suggested, "county cricket in its present form fulfils no useful purpose whatsoever", while Nasser Hussain described the purpose of "the whole system" as the "preservation of the *status quo*". With certain cautious caveats, the editor reported a continuing decline in television viewing figures for Test Matches, although Sky was reaching a higher percentage of younger viewers. Berry paraphrased Abraham Lincoln in asserting that "government for the counties by the counties must perish from this earth", while the ECB's primary goal must be "England success".

In July **2007**, the former Glamorgan and England cricketer, Steve James, published an article in *the Daily Telegraph* revealing that almost all capped county cricketers were earning £30,000 p.a. with senior players "commanding salaries of £80,000 and above", although there were concerns that at the lower end some young players were on less than the national minimum wage that had been introduced by the Labour Government in 1998. James pointed out, however, that it is not a straightforward matter to define the hours worked by a professional cricketer. He reported that the PCA estimated that bringing together playing, travelling, training and time spent away from home equates to about 50 hours per week, which in itself raises interesting questions. In the 21st century most 'ordinary' county professionals are on 12-month salaries, yet play county cricket for only half the year. They certainly work quite hard on training and fitness through the winter but for many, this will be at their home ground. Through the season, even the rare player who appears in every match is unlikely to average as many as four days play per week or, to be generous, perhaps 120 days each calendar year. Travelling time is, of course, an issue for county cricketers but they are not unique in that and those of us who have had to commute to work and travel from work *without* that being considered part of working hours, will wonder about those calculations by a profession that claims overwork, tiredness and even "exhaustion".

In the following summer, *the Cricketer* magazine published an edition titled "The Rich List" in which some of those salary figures seemed higher. According to the magazine, England's contracted players were now earning between £1m and £3m per year, while county "yeomen" such as Robert Key, Ravi Bopara, Paul Collingwood and Chris Woakes earned between £100,000 – £150,000. Overseas players who would generally be on seasonal contracts were earning from £60,000 – £130,000, while for English T20 specialists like Luke Wright, Owais Shah, Michael Lumb and Dimitri Mascarenhas, the figure rose between £120,000 – £400,000. The magazine also identified 10 young "stars" likely to make an impact over the next 10 years. Their salaries were reported as varying between £50,000 and "well into six figures" and among those that have done well were James Taylor, Alex Hales, Jonny Bairstow, Jason Roy and Jos Buttler. The others in that category included Paul Stirling who has featured for Middlesex and Ireland, Matt Coles who has had an up-and-down few years, Tymal Mills, struggling to play more than one-day cricket and, sadly, two Hampshire players Danny Briggs and Michael Bates both now are trying to establish themselves at new counties. Briggs, they said, was "one to watch for 2015" at the end of which season, he left Hampshire, having lost his County Championship place and moved to Sussex. Michael Bates meanwhile "might be England's next wicketkeeper", but is currently without a county side after a few matches in 2015 with Somerset.

On the subject of money, in **2008** Giles Clarke and the Board began negotiating with the American billionaire Allan Stanford to establish T20 tournaments in the Caribbean, which would rival the IPL. There was a five-year deal worth nearly £13m and an additional £30m for an annual international tournament at Lord's. Unfortunately, USA investigators raided Stanford's bank in early 2009, and in March 2012, he was found guilty of various financial misdemeanours by a jury and began a sentence of up to 120 years in prison.

In January 2009, the "Bearded Wonder", Bill Frindall, died suddenly and was much missed. Although principally a statistician, he had once appeared as a bowler for Hampshire 2nd XI (in Bristol). Frindall's TMS colleague, Jonathan Agnew, took his role for one year and in the preface for the *Playfair Cricket Annual* attacked the "unmitigated disaster" of the Stanford affair. He described it as a "race for cash" and warned that if the television money disappeared "the result will be swift and disastrous". Despite this, Giles Clarke continued to attract sufficient support to retain his position at the ECB.

England's women retained the Ashes in Australia and followed this by going through 2008 undefeated and among its five Cricketers of the Year, *Wisden* nominated Claire Taylor, the first woman selected. In the **2008** English county season, Durham followed their first trophy with their first County Championship title, Essex beat Kent in the 50-over Friends Provident Trophy Final, and Sussex won the Pro40 League. The T20 Final was held for the first time at the Rose Bowl with Middlesex posting 187–6 and Kent losing a last-ball wicket to fall just three runs short.

In the Test Matches, England had beaten New Zealand in the winter (2–1) but Vaughan's side lost a home series to South Africa 2–1. At his resignation press conference, Vaughan was in tears. Pietersen then took over the leadership for the final home Test Match and the tour of India that started in November 2008 with seven ODIs and then two Test Matches, with a draw and a victory for India. In October, England also participated in the Stanford Series with a 'winner-takes-all' prize of $20m. It was a dreadful event and the end of the ECB's involvement with Stanford, whose downfall was imminent.

The former Glamorgan and England batsman, Hugh Morris, was now the Managing Director of English Cricket and on his watch captain Pietersen did not last the winter, 'jumping' before he was pushed. He had made a promising start as England's captain in the match of the home series v South Africa, scoring a century as England won by six wickets. This was followed by the two games in India but it was said that some members of the dressing room were not taken with him, while Pietersen, in turn, was critical of Peter Moores who had replaced Duncan Fletcher in April 2007. Moores was sacked and Pietersen would have followed had he not resigned, returning to the ranks. England lost four of seven Test Match series under Moores in the first of his two brief spells in charge. Now it would be Flower and Strauss as things improved somewhat, albeit not immediately. Despite the evidence of the viewing figures, ECB renewed their agreements with Sky TV, extending it initially to 2013.

England moved to the West Indies after Christmas, playing five ODIs and five Tests, finishing five months after the India tour started. The two teams had one opportunity to rest, however, when they played the shortest-ever Test Match at the new Antigua ground on 11 February. Ten years after the farce in Jamaica, England faced just 10 balls before the umpires abandoned the game because of the state of the outfield. West Indies won the series on the basis of an extraordinary victory in the First Test Match. England scored 318, West Indies replied with 392 and then Taylor recorded figures of 9–4–11–5, dismissing England for 51 in the 34th over. It was a tough Test Match baptism for Andrew Strauss in his first match as the appointed (as opposed to deputy) captain. In the final Test Match he delayed his declaration setting West Indies 236 to win in what would be 66 overs. They lost wickets regularly but closed on 114–8 and took the series.

In the 2009 *Wisden* edition, Scyld Berry, suggested that despite all kinds of problems around the globe, cricket is an "astonishing, unique game" that has "regenerated and grown … as no other sport has done". Nonetheless, the annual did pinpoint one disappointing area of decline, Dean Wilson reporting that in England at least, the game "within the Afro-Caribbean community is dying". He identified the loss to England and the county sides, but identified also the same problem in league and club cricket. Wilson echoed his editor noting "cricket is struggling to tap into the inner city areas" and since a large percentage of the black community lives there this is a particular problem – but it does not exclude inner city white families either. The 'Lambeth Boys' playing for fun 40 years earlier, were no longer evident, black or white.

2009 was a busy year in England, starting with two Test Matches against the West Indies in which England took their revenge, winning both matches. In mid-summer came the ICC World T20. England contrived to lose on the last ball to Holland but still qualified on net run-rate by beating Pakistan, whereupon the country that had 'invented' T20 cricket lost to South Africa. They won a thriller against India by three runs then posted a decent 161–6 v West Indies. But it rained and the West Indies won by the Duckworth-Lewis method, scoring 82–5. Pakistan won the Final against Sri Lanka at Lord's by eight wickets with eight balls remaining.

That was on 21 June and a couple of weeks later yet another Ashes tour began with a Test Match, at yet another ground, Cardiff. After two high scoring innings, it ended in great drama with a flurry of 12th and 13th men bringing fresh gloves every over to England's 10th wicket pair, Anderson and Panesar, as they battled successfully to avoid an innings defeat. Ponting was furious about the time wasting but most cricketers admitted that in the modern world, every side would do that. Apparently it is called 'professionalism'. The English were unusually cheered by the Welsh and went on to Lord's where, led by the captain (161), they won the next Test Match. Strauss, plus Collinwood and Cook, would pass 1,000 Test runs in the calendar year of 16 Tests, while Graham Swann (51) was England's leading wicket-taker. The third Test was drawn, Australia won the fourth at Headingley by an innings with a century from Marcus North.

So to the decider at the Oval with Australia needing a draw to retain the Ashes. England posted 332, took a lead of 172 (Broad 5–37), added 373–9 and declared. Australia had only the draw to pursue and a century from Michael Hussey gave England anxieties, but from 327–5 they fell away to 348 all out and England had the Ashes – for a little while. Meanwhile, Durham won the County Championship again, Hampshire beat Sussex in the last 50-over Lord's Final until it was brought back a few years later, while Sussex were compensated by winning both the T20 (v Somerset) and the last-ever Pro40 League – a final version of the old Sunday League.

So much excitement then, but it was not finished for Sussex and Somerset who in October went to India to participate in the Champions League T20 against the best sides from the other countries. Sussex were knocked out by the Eagles in a single over eliminator and while Somerset went through, they finished bottom of their group. In the Final, New South Wales beat Trinidad & Tobago. English champions competed for a couple more years with no success and then with the English season ending later, it all became too complicated.

Michael Atherton took over the foreword from Jonathan Agnew at *Playfair* and reflecting on the first decade of the new century, confirmed that the game had changed significantly in those 10 years. He noted that with the relative decline of Australia there was now no dominant side in Test cricket, which ensured a more competitive 'feel' but warned that "graveyard" pitches would lead to interest dwindling. He noted that another major change, the recent adoption of the Decision Review System (DRS) was encouraging umpires to give more lbws to spinners and it followed then that batsmen made less use of their pads – a thoroughly good thing – although there would remain questions about the certainty of the technology and about players using DRS tactically. Atherton warned also about the rise of franchise cricket – notably, of course, in the IPL – with the consequence that national boards were now competing for players, fixtures and spectators with "private investors" who saw cricket principally as a source of profit.

The first Test Match of the new decade and new century had started at Newlands, Cape Town on 2 January 2000 between South Africa and England, with the home side winning by an innings. It is listed in the second volume of *the Wisden Book of Test Cricket* as match number 1477 (and for England number 765). By late August 2009, the final entry in volume three was Sri

Lanka v New Zealand in Colombo, match number 1932, although there were a further 12 before the New Year so there were 467 matches in that decade, or just less than an average of 50 Test Matches per year. By comparison, the first Test Match to start in the 1950s was South Africa v Australia in Durban in late January. It was just Test Match number 320 although they had started in 1877 and by Christmas Eve 1959, when India beat Australia in Kanpur, they had reached number 483, which is 163 Tests in the decade or about one-third of the 21st century figure. In addition, of course, there were no ODIs, World Cups or T20 tournaments in the 1950s.

Interestingly, despite this considerable increase, the number of Ashes series and Ashes Test Matches were very similar across the decades and exactly the same in the two decades compared above. In the 1950s every Ashes series consisted of five matches and they took place in 1950–1951, 1953, 1954–1955, 1956, 1958–1959. There were five more series in the 1960s, again alternately home and away, so in both decades, 25 Test Matches, and in the first 10 years of the 21st century there were series in 2001, 2002–2003, 2005, 2006–2007, 2009. The last time an Ashes series had six matches was in 1997. Meanwhile, the fifth series of the current decade will take place in Australia in 2017–2018. Elsewhere, the obvious expansion has been in the number of Test-playing nations.

The first Test Match of 2010, and the next decade, was midway through England's series in South Africa where they won one and lost one, both by an innings. Then they moved to Bangladesh, winning both matches. They had been scheduled to visit Pakistan in the late winter, but on 3 March 2009 in Lahore, terrorists had attacked the Sri Lankan team bus on its way to the ground during the second Test Match of the series. The match was abandoned with Pakistan 110–0 in reply to Sri Lanka's 606, and Pakistan would eventually resume 'home' Test Matches in the United Arab Emirates. In the attack, six Sri Lankan cricketers were injured and six policemen and two civilians killed. The Sri Lankan coach Trevor Bayliss escaped injury but his assistant Paul Farbrace, once of Kent, suffered some injuries. From 2015 the pair would take charge of England after Peter Moores was sacked for a second time.

In May **2010** a surprising thing happened when England went to the Caribbean and won a limited-overs trophy, the ICC World T20. They lost just one match and even then, the West Indies had the rain to thank as England set them 192 to win and the home side 'triumphed' by chasing an eventual target of 60 in six overs for the loss of two wickets. Nonetheless, England then beat Pakistan, South Africa, New Zealand, Sri Lanka and in the Final, Australia, so they were worthy World Champions. Their stars included the captain

Collingwood, Craig Kieswetter, Lumb, Pietersen, Broad, Ryan Sidebottom, Swann and Tim Bresnan.

Back at home, England won both Test Matches v Bangladesh, by eight wickets and an innings, and then beat Pakistan 3–1. At Lord's, in the fourth Test Match of that series, Jonathan Trott scored 184 and Stuart Broad 169 as England won by an innings but the triumph was scarred when three members of the Pakistan side, Salman Butt, Mohammad Asif and Mohammad Amir, were found guilty of bet-fixing (principally bowling no-balls to order) and were banned by the ICC and also imprisoned.

In mid-summer **2010,** England played a limited-overs series against Australia *without* any Test Matches, it's difficult to recall why now, and in September they played two T20s and five 50-over matches against Pakistan and then flew to Australia for another Ashes series. That ended on 7 January 2011 with England's third victory in a 3–1 series win in what was probably the greatest triumph of Andrew Strauss's career. In the last match, Cook (189), Bell and Prior scored centuries and Tremlett took the wicket that clinched the match, series and Ashes by an innings and 83 runs. In the calendar year 2010, Cook and Trott passed 1,000 runs in the 13 Test Matches and Swann (59) was again leading wicket-taker. In the *Playfair Cricket Annual* Graham Gooch was keen to praise Andy Flower for his "vital role" as a "calm and committed" coach. Gooch believed that Flower, having played at the top level, understood "the moods of the players". Was this perhaps an implied criticism of the appointment of his predecessor who was a good county cricketer, but no more?

At home in **2010**, Nottinghamshire won the County Championship having been one of six teams to win it during the first decade of the century. Warwickshire, another of those Champions, beat Somerset at Lord's in the new CB40 Final – a hugely unpopular day/night match dominated by a century from Bell, while Hampshire won a last-ball thriller against Somerset on their own ground to take the T20 Trophy. With one ball to go, Hampshire on 172–5, were one run behind Somerset's 173–6. Sean Ervine was batting with Dan Christian, but the latter was injured and needed a runner. Groundsman, Nigel Gray, was required to paint an extra white line to help the umpires and the video screens told the crowd that Hampshire needed two to win. In fact they needed one since on scores level, Hampshire would win, whichever tie-break was fashionable that year. Oddly, nobody thought the spectators on the ground needed to know, although the television audience was better informed. Christian hit the last ball, Ervine set off, the runner set off and Christian set off. Somerset could therefore run him out but they didn't realize, and after a moment or two of wondering, the other Hampshire players took to the field in delight, the umpires called dead ball, and everyone learned a little more about the Laws of Cricket.

In February and March **2011** the next 50-over World Cup took place in India, Bangladesh and Sri Lanka. England reached the quarter-finals where they lost to Sri Lanka who then beat New Zealand. India beat Pakistan in the other semi-final and they beat Sri Lanka in the Final with their captain, MS Dohni (91*), who was Man-of-the-Match.

In the summer, the Sri Lankans and Indians toured England. England won the first Test v Sri Lanka, bowling them out for 82 in the 25th over of the second innings. The two sides drew at Lord's and then met again for the first Test Match at Hampshire's Rose Bowl, bringing to nine the current Test grounds in England – plus Bristol for ODIs. Unfortunately for Hampshire the game was ruined by rain although Southampton-born Chris Tremlett was Man-of-the-Match for his 6–48. India completed a series victory in the West Indies on 10 July and flew to England for the first Test Match at Lord's, 11 days later. They may have been tired, for they lost the series 4–0 – Bell (twice) and Cook (294) hit double centuries. By Boxing Day, the Indians were starting a new series in Australia, which they lost 4–0 while England lost Pakistan in Dubai by 10 wickets in mid-January 2012. They lost the next two also and the series ended 3–0.

In **2011** Lancashire surprised even their own supporters by winning their eighth County Championship, but the first outright since 1934. They achieved more victories than usual at home having moved their matches mainly to Liverpool, while Old Trafford underwent a facelift including a 90-degree rotation of the square. Lancashire were one of the counties recognizing the need to update and improve facilities on Victorian grounds, mindful of the competition from brand new international stadia in Durham and Hampshire. Surrey won a soggy, floodlit 40-over Final at Lord's by the D/L method with reserve days increasingly to be avoided, while Leicestershire won the T20 Cup to become (and remain to date) the only side to win three T20 trophies. Lancashire clinched the County Championship in the last match at Taunton while Somerset, runners-up in the previous year's County Championship, were beaten finalists in both competitions. Despite challenging regularly, they have won nothing since the T20 in 2005. In December 2011 the new Australian T20 competition, 'the Big Bash', took place for the first time.

In 2011 Graeme Wright published *Behind the Boundary: Cricket at a Crossroads*. It was developed from many discussions with many of the various people running English cricket, principally the chief executives and county chairman, and Wright described it as a book "about the present" while setting out "options for the future". He suggested it was to "stimulate discussion" rather than provide answers because if there are answers "the counties first have to agree on the problems". He was not at all sure that they could, but it was a remarkable book, perhaps the most significant book written about county cricket for a long time. In 2011 and the following years I spent a good deal of time in county committee rooms, press and media centres and mixing with members and supporters and I cannot remember a single discussion about it, although I recommended it frequently to people. It occurred to me then, more forcibly than before, that everyone involved in English cricket has an opinion or two (hundred?) about the game but very little talk is based on the thorough and careful scrutiny of evidence – particularly the kind of 'qualitative' data presented by Wright, and very little discussion proceeds with the assumptions that minds might change. That reluctance and resistance, of course, is very English, for we are generally too pragmatic to be bothered too much by thinking when it's easier to be certain, but while that attitude persists a thought from one of Wright's correspondents will ring worryingly true. To paraphrase it slightly: in English cricket there is, and has been, a great deal of change. How much progress there has been is another matter entirely. Given the extent of criticisms from ECB, players, commentators and others throughout 2015 one must assume not much, yet the people offering the solutions are effectively the same as the ones that made all the previous changes. As the anarchists warn, no matter who you vote for, the government always wins.

English cricket has become used to competing for television audiences and media investment with football tournaments. In 2010 England's footballers had competed in the World Cup in South Africa, suffering from the absence of DRS when a perfectly good goal by Frank Lampard was disallowed. In 2012, they competed in the UEFA Euro competition in Poland and the Ukraine, qualifying from their group but then losing to Italy on penalties after a 0–0 draw. However, cricket's real competition in **2012** came from the Olympics, based in London, but also taking place elsewhere in the country, including archery at Lord's.

The opening ceremony took place on the evening of Friday, 27 July and it was a triumph, celebrating so many aspects of British culture, and organized by the film-director, Danny Boyle, at a cost of just under £30m. It opened with the Red Arrows and with some extraordinary moments, including many references to the Industrial Revolution; nurses and doctors in a coordinated performance celebrating the NHS; Mike Oldfield performed "Tubular Bells" live; comedian Rowan Atkinson and the London Symphony Orchestra, and a broad celebration of the country's popular culture with a particular focus on its writers from Shakespeare to the present, plus much music. The ceremony had started with a rural event, including a model of Glastonbury

Tor, choirs singing "Jerusalem", "Danny Boy" and other British songs and actors as villagers at work or playing football *and cricket* – the latter in a somewhat nostalgic rural setting. The Olympics themselves were also a considerable success with many medals for British athletes. But there was no more cricket, although it is being mooted as a future Olympic sport, perhaps in a six-a-side format if India can be persuaded.

Prior to the Games there was much talk of the legacy that they would provide in encouraging British people to participate more fully in sports and activities that would improve the nation's fitness. This was particularly about young people who, as a generation, were perceived to be spending too much time indoors glued to screens of all kinds while consuming excessive quantities of sugar in almost every sort of food and drink. During the month of the Games, the culture secretary, Jeremy Hunt, described school sports provision as "patchy" although the annual *Wisden* reports suggest that this does not apply in the Independent sector. Some 15 months later the House of Lord's warned that the Olympics legacy was not being realized, blaming squabbles over major projects – notably the future of the main stadium – and a general failure to persuade more young people to participate in sports.

By early 2015, Sport England reported that fewer adults than ever were doing even moderate exercise each week with a particular decline among the worst off. The poor are, of course, 'always with us' but they have been poorer than previously since the financial crisis of 2008. The Governments of Blair, Gordon Brown and the Coalition all claimed that watching the spectacle of elite sports men and women would inspire people to get active. This is a little like assuming that watching the Glastonbury Festival on television persuades people to take up guitar playing. Very often what they see, hear and enjoy in sport or music is a performance of the highest quality, enjoyable for its own sake but actually beyond the dreams of most people. Young people are more easily inspired because they can still dream, but they may have been indirectly discouraged by the consequences of Michael Gove's decision in 2010 to cut the £162m funding for the School Sports Partnerships.

In **2012,** in addition to the Olympics and the football, cricket was competing with Bradley Wiggins' Tour de France victory and another Jubilee celebration. On the day of the Olympics opening ceremony, five County Championship matches and two tourists games began elsewhere in the country and cricket kept going through August with a mixture of County Championship and 40-over matches. Warwickshire, runners-up in 2011, won the County Championship with six victories – one more than they managed in 2004 – whereas in 2011 and 2013 the Champions won 10 games. In 2012 the six wins reflected, partly, some quite awful weather. Derbyshire were a surprise team, winning promotion to the First Division. Warwickshire were less successful in the 40-over Final at Lord's losing a last-ball thriller to Hampshire who completed a double by beating Yorkshire in the T20 Final at Cardiff by 10 runs.

The England team began **2012** by losing all three Test Matches against Pakistan although they won the ODI series. Then there were two Test Matches and a 1–1 draw in Sri Lanka. At home they beat West Indies 2–1, while the third match at Edgbaston reached no conclusion, losing days one, two and five to the rain. In the week before the Olympics started, England played the First Test Match v South Africa whose 637–2 declared with three centurions, including Hashim Amla's 311*, was sufficient to clinch an innings victory. Alviro Petersen must have been dismayed when dismissed for nought but he made up for it with 182 in the next drawn match. His near namesake 'KP' replied with 149 but was found to have been sending texts to South African players about his 'team-mates' and he was dropped from the third Test Match won by South Africa. England had started the year at number one in the world table but this series defeat ended that brief spell, while showing Test cricket was now a pretty level playing field.

By the time England took the field again in November in India, Pietersen was back and Cook was captain, scoring 176 in the first match, which was not sufficient to prevent India from winning. He made three figures again in the next match and with the prodigal reaching 186 and Panesar taking 11 wickets, England levelled the series, won the next with a third captain's century and drew the last to take the series. For Cook, as captain and batsman, it was a magnificent start taking him to 1,000 Test Match runs in the calendar year, but the complex figure of Pietersen continued to loom over England's world.

In March 2013 England started a tour of New Zealand and after trailing by 293 on the first innings, openers Cook (116) and Nick Compton (117) took them towards safety. Compton had made his debut in the series against India and when he scored another century in the next Test, it seemed that England had found a regular partner for Cook, to replace Strauss, but they had not – and when Compton was recalled in the winter of 2015–2016 it was because they still had not, although by then he was batting at number three, with debutant, Alex Hales, opening. The 2013 series ended in three drawn matches.

In **2013,** England beat New Zealand 2–0 and Australia 3–0, thereby retaining the Ashes. Joe Root had made his debut against India just before Christmas and in the first match of the summer scored 40 and 71 as England won with Broad taking 7–44 in the second New Zealand innings. Root and Cook were centurions at Leeds as England won again and then came a thrilling opening to the next Ashes series at Trent Bridge. Peter Siddle's five wickets put England out for 215 but they reduced Australia to 117–9 before last man Ashton Agar joined Phil Hughes (81*). Agar, on an 'academy' placement at Hampshire was called-up at the last minute principally as a slow-left-arm bowler but scored a remarkable 98 before Swann caught him. Australia led by 65 runs but Bell's century left them needing 311 to win. At 164–6 and 231–9 they were struggling, but James Pattinson and Siddle took them to within 15 of their target before the last wicket fell.

Bell and Root (opening) were centurions in the next Test Match at Lord's, which England won by 347 runs, Swann taking 9–122 in the match. Centuries for Michael Clarke and Pietersen left Old Trafford as a high-scoring draw but another Bell century and 11 wickets for Broad won the fourth match at Chester-Le-Street and with it the Ashes. Shane Watson and Steve Smith hit centuries in Australia's 492-9 declared but the fourth day was lost to rain and Clarke's declaration challenged England to chase 227. They reached 206–5 late on the last evening but the umpires agreed that conditions were difficult for the fielders and the match and series were over. In a matter of months, the two sides would meet again.

Durham's **2013** County Championship title was their third in six years while Lancashire were the latest yo-yo team. Champions in 2011, relegated in 2012, Division Two Champions in 2013, they would be relegated again in 2014 and return again in 2015. Derbyshire, promoted in 2012, went back after just one season and football-style, sacked Karl Krikken, the coach, who had got them there. Going up with Lancashire in 2013 were Northamptonshire who won the T20 for the first time, beating Surrey as David Willey starred with 60 and 4–9. Glamorgan had never won a Lord's Final but reached the 40-over version, now sponsored by Yorkshire Bank. With Broad and Swann in their side, Nottinghamshire beat them easily. The two Ashes stars had played two and one County Championship matches respectively. The County Championship now lasted well into September and for the first time the successful English counties did not compete in the Champions League – no English side won it during their brief involvement.

The next Ashes series began in Brisbane on 21 November, less than three months after the conclusion at the Oval. The series was a disaster from the start as England failed to reach 200 in either innings and lost by 381 runs. Root now batted down the order as Michael Carberry was the latest opener and top-scored with 40 in the first innings, but it was not enough. After falling cheaply twice, Trott flew home citing stress; England lost the second match by 218 runs and the third by 150 – Swann decided he had had enough and retired from all cricket. Australia won the fourth Test by eight wickets, and

England having selected Gary Ballance, Steve Borthwick and Boyd Rankin to make debuts in the fifth, lost that by 281 runs. Like Simon Kerrigan and Chris Woakes who had played their first Tests at the Oval, they would not be in the England side by the conclusion of the next Ashes series in 18 months time. England had selected 18 players and only Stokes with their one century and 15 wickets brought much hope. Andy Flower decided it was time to step aside, although he retained a coaching role at the ECB. He deserved a better farewell. England's leading scorers were Pietersen and Carberry but neither would play again. The following autumn Pietersen published his account of the various issues between himself and the England side and that pretty much sealed his fate in terms of Test cricket although 'Team England' handled the affair clumsily.

In the previous October before the England team travelled to Australia, Paul Downton had been appointed to succeed Hugh Morris as managing Director of English Cricket. Downton took over in February 2014 and his first major task was to recall Peter Moores to take on the role vacated by Flower. In February 2014, the ECB announced that England Women's Cricket would move towards a professional structure and during the summer they announced the names of the first 18 cricketers to be awarded Central Contracts. Sadly, the professionals' first Ashes series in 2015 in England, was unsuccessful, with an extraordinarily dull single televised Test Match at Canterbury. At the end of the season Mark Robinson left Sussex to take charge, as England's Women moved towards setting up a T20 regional franchise competition, initially based on six sides.

In April 2014 Sri Lanka beat India to become the fifth different winner of the fifth ICC T20 World Cup – surprisingly, Australia had not been among them. England won just one of their qualifying matches and failed to reach the semi-finals. In the summer of **2014**, Peter Moores had to organize the England side minus Trott, Swann, Pietersen and with various recent newcomers, to play two series, against Sri Lanka and India. The Sri Lankans came first and won the one T20 game and the ODI series 3–2. During the last match at Edgbaston, the crowd booed as Buttler was run-out for backing-up regularly outside the crease. The perpetrator, Sachithra Senanayake, had been reported earlier in the series for a suspect action; the Sri Lankan captain, Angelo Matthews, when approached by the umpires upheld the appeal, suggesting it was not Buttler's 'first offence'.

Then it was on to the two Tests. At Lord's, Joe Root's 200* was a good start in an innings of 575–9 declared and Cook was able to declare, setting Sri Lanka 390 to win. After a sound start, pacemen Anderson, Broad and Chris Jordan worked their way gradually through the order. Even so, it was not until

Anderson's burst of three wickets in three overs after tea that an England victory seemed probable, as 199–6 became 201–9, but the Sri Lankan numbers 10 and 11 hung on. The second Test Match at Leeds also went to the finish but this time Sri Lanka dismissed England, despite a fine not out century from Moeen Ali, rescuing England from 57–5 but not managing to do quite enough. There were just two balls left when Anderson fended off a short ball and was caught, Sri Lanka winning by 100 runs.

India arrived to 'contest' the first match at Nottingham, which was simply dreadful, all-round. The ICC reprimanded the ground authorities for producing the deadest of pitches, as Anderson with 81 in 130 balls was within three balls of equaling the longest innings by a Test Match number 11. India 457 and 391–9 drew with England 496 – the attendance, just under 75,000. At Lord's that went up to almost 130,000 and they witnessed India's best Test Match performance of the summer with Sharma's 7–74, proving too good for England who lost by 95 runs. Since the retention of the Ashes at the Oval the previous September, England had played nine Test Matches, losing seven and drawing two, although a century for Ballance at Lord's provided some hope. So it was on to the Ageas Bowl for that ground's second Test. Their first in 2011 had been ruined by rain; this second one enjoyed better weather but was not helped by the ECB's decision that it should be the first Test Match in England to start on a Sunday. The attendance on day one was fine, but overall numbered just under 50,000 – albeit a decent crowd outside London 50 years earlier.

For England, it was the start of a revival of sorts, a one-sided contest in which Ballance and Bell scored centuries but the first day hero was Cook, afforded a standing ovation for his 95 as the vultures were circling. India trailed by 239, England declared on 205–4 (Cook 70*) and Moeen Ali took 6–76 to lead England to victory by 266 runs. For India, Pankaj Singh recorded the worst debut figures in a Test Match: 0–179. He took a wicket, indeed two, in the next game at Manchester but India were plunging downwards now and lost by an innings. The game finished on day three with an overall attendance of 47,000. At the Oval the margin was even greater, England winning by an innings and 244 runs, Root 149*.

The first ODI at Bristol was drowned by the weather but the second at Cardiff survived it, thanks to D/L. India preferred this stuff and won by 133 runs. They won the next one at Trent Bridge by six wickets and then nine wickets at Birmingham where the 'home' crowd supported India and booed Moeen Ali for being Moeen Ali and for top scoring with 67. Having lost the series, England won the last one and also the T20 by just three runs, but ahead of the next World Cup there seemed little cause to be optimistic about England's chances.

In the county competitions, Yorkshire won the County Championship for the 31st time and the first in more than a decade, while Hampshire clinched the Division Two title for the first time on the season's last day, at Cardiff. Durham beat Warwickshire by three wickets in a low-scoring 50-over Lord's Final by which time the Birmingham Bears had beaten Lancashire in the T20 Final on their own ground. *Wisden* and the *Playfair Cricket Annual* still called them Warwickshire, but they were by their own choice, the first non-county side to win a major domestic competition in English cricket.

By the end of the 2014 season, there were many reasons to be concerned about the future wellbeing of cricket, from the effective takeover of the world game by the three most powerful nations to the decline of cricket in English state schools. But all the problems were put into perspective in November 2014 when the young Australian batsman, Phil Hughes, was hit by a short ball and despite having worn a helmet, died a couple of days later. It was an event that stunned the world of cricket.

In the aftermath of Phil Hughes' death, many words were spoken. Perhaps the finest were those by his Australian captain, Michael Clarke. Clarke referred in particular to the palpable sense he'd had of the presence of Hughes' *spirit* as he walked on the SGC just days after Hughes had died. He said "I know it is crazy but I expect any minute to take a call from him or to see his face pop around the corner. Is this what we call the spirit? If so, then his spirit is still with me. And I hope it never leaves", to which he added:

> Is this what indigenous Australians believe about a person's spirit being connected with the land upon which they walk? If so, I know they are right about the SCG. His spirit has touched it and it will be forever a sacred ground for me.

Both Clarke and Hughes had played for a short time in county cricket with Hampshire, and another Hampshire cricketer, Mark Nicholas, writing about Hughes invoked this idea of 'spirit', and looking forwards, argued for a significant shift in the way professional cricket is played in the 21st century. In a fine article, Nicholas noted Michael Clarke's words, claiming that Hughes' spirit "has brought us closer together, something I know must be him at work because it is so consistent with how he lived and worked".

Mark Nicholas praised Clarke's speech because it "opened the eyes of the game" which had "united through a cascade of love and compassion". Clarke added that Phil Hughes' spirit can now "act as a custodian of the sport we love" and Nicholas took up this theme to emphasise the challenge to the game worldwide, requiring us to "stop the rancour, stop the sledging, play the game and ignite the friendships that make it so special". Nicholas added "playing 'tough' cricket does not mean playing ugly cricket".

It did not require any significant insights for Clarke, a current Test captain, and Nicholas, a former county captain and current commentator, to acknowledge that *on the field,* all was not wholly right with the game – nor had it been for some time – and so both hoped for a better attitude among players going forward. In the heat and intensity of professional battles this is not always an easy thing for highly fit, highly charged young cricketers, although it might reasonably be expected to be easier for the weekend amateur who truly *loves* the game. But neither Clarke nor Nicholas chose to include in their remarks those who manage cricket at national and international levels. Perhaps they might have done.

The death of Phil Hughes, at the age of 25 towards the end of 2014, was no one's fault and no blame attached to the death of an admired and popular cricketer, and so the sport could find in his death, reasons to reiterate and pursue its highest ideals. Three weeks later, and after what *the Daily Telegraph* called his "dire run of form", England's overall captain, Alistair Cook, was sacked from his role in the 50-over game after a limited-overs trip to Sri Lanka which England lost 5–2. Eoin Morgan replaced him but this *was* someone's fault. The media criticism was fierce, for while this might have been the right decision, it was considered too close to the World Cup to allow for adequate planning and preparation.

After some uncertainty, Australia reconvened on 9 December and met India in the first Test since Hughes' death at Adelaide, winning a thrilling match by 48 runs. On the fourth day Varun Aaron bowled David Warner, but not for the first or last time in recent years only the television umpire on replay spotted the no ball. Warner was recalled and taunted the bowler. The Indian fielders were furious but Warner completed a century in both innings. Australia won the next Test by four wickets but Australia's new captain, Smith, and his team-mates were fined for the desultory over-rate while Ishant Sharma was penalized for a foul-mouthed send off, after the Australian captain was dismissed. The Boxing Day Test Match at Melbourne was drawn but during a fourth wicket partnership of 262, Mitchell Johnson grew frustrated and fielding a return, hurled the ball at Virat Kohli's wicket but hit the batsman instead. *Wisden* reported an "animated, angry exchange". It was about a month since Clarke's speech, but on the field, Test cricket and Australia, in particular, seemed back to normal. One year later, approaching the first anniversary of Clarke's speech, Australia beat New Zealand by 208 runs with plenty of time to spare, but on the last morning and with no chance of a run out, Mitchell Starc threw the ball at tail-ender, Mark Craig. Captain Steve Smith explained it was "frustration" but added, "He's done it a few times before and I'm going to have a word to him when we get back to the sheds." – whatever (and wherever) the "sheds" are.

In a friendlier context, Australia and New Zealand had hosted the latest World Cup, which began on St Valentine's Day 2015. There were 14 teams, 14 venues and 49 matches over a period of six weeks before the host nations met in the Final, which Australia won by seven wickets. There were some huge scores watched by more than a million spectators with average attendances in excess of 20,000 and the Final watched by more than 90,000. In the qualifying stages, England suffered heavy defeats to the two host nations before beating Scotland but then, having posted a target of 309, they contrived to lose to Sri Lanka by nine wickets. They even lost to Bangladesh and that abject performance was effectively the end of their tournament although they did manage a D/L victory over Afghanistan before flying home.

In the other 'pool', in eight of the first 10 matches, at least one side scored over 300 while South Africa twice passed 400. In the semi-finals, Australia beat India and New Zealand beat South Africa before New Zealand's 183 failed to test the Australians, who won the World Cup for the fifth time – five times more than England. The English media were unforgiving as Alistair Cook took charge for a tour to the West Indies from mid-April while the county season was getting underway. They drew the first Test Match after Jason Holder at number eight hit a fine century when an England victory seemed probable, but England won the next by nine wickets. In Barbados a Cook century gave England a score of sorts, but his latest opening partner, Trott, was in awful form and it seemed his Test Match career came to a close with 0 and 9, although England led on first innings by 68 runs. Unfortunately, in the second innings they subsided to 123 all out in the 43rd over, after which 82 from Dwayne Bravo was enough to square the series.

The match lasted just three days, ending on 3 May about the time that ECB's new chairman, Colin Graves, previously chairman of Yorkshire and also of Costcutter stores, took over from Giles Clarke who was promoted to the role of president. In the Daily Telegraph in May, Simon Briggs wrote of Clarke's "eight turbulent years", ranging from the farcical 'deals' with criminal fraudster Allan Stanford in 2008 to his embarrassing outburst at editor Lawrence Booth during the Wisden dinner at Lord's to launch the 2015 Almanack. Clarke was sitting on the same table as the editor and at some point stood up and indulged in a very public and well-documented rant in response to Booth's latest "Notes by the Editor" and a speech during the evening by the former ICC President Eclahsan Mani. The Cricket Paper reported Mani saying, "I am more concerned about the health of the game today than I have ever been." He suggested that five of the 10 major countries were in "desperate need of help" with respect to a lack of money and "not enough quality cricket". A number of British newspapers reported the *Wisden* 'editorial' with Jonathan Liew in *the Daily Telegraph* describing it as a "well-timed blast". If the view is that those in charge have created the problems in English cricket, can they be trusted to solve them? They are never short of proposals.

In that regular section, which now opens the Almanack, Booth began by suggesting that through 2014, "English cricket repeatedly lost touch ... with the basic idea that the national team belongs to us all". Among the problems he listed were the mishandling of the Pietersen issue, poor Test Match attendances outside London, "a head-in-the-sand" attitude to England's limited-overs team and a fall in the number of recreational cricketers. In total, the ECB recorded just fewer than 850,000 players but almost 600,000 of those played very occasionally or perhaps between three and 11 weeks. Just 250,000 could be considered regular club/school cricketers and despite huge investments in Chance to Shine, County Boards and the like, the number was falling. Back at the highest level, there were also the on-field results with a total of 28 defeats in all competitions in the previous year and the ludicrously late sacking of Cook as World Cup captain, while England's "power brokers indulged in mutual backslapping".

Booth saw the removal of live cricket from free-to-air television after the thrills of 2005, as a key factor in the decline of participation in the sport, and while he acknowledged that social change was another important element, he suggested that ECB had "chased the money and ... cut their cloth accordingly". On the same topic, Simon Briggs suggested that Clarke's focus on money had been successful – especially the Sky television deal providing around 50% of the Board's income – but equally so single-minded, that his legacy was for cricket in Britain to feel "more unloved ... than at any time in its history". Booth identified the particular failure to work with the British Asian community in developing the best young cricketers and wondered whether "England is just less of a cricket country than Australia".

Maybe it is. For obvious reasons it is less of an outdoors, summer sunshine country but it is not particularly less sporting. Perhaps it is simply that Britain suffers on the modern world stage from being the founder of so many major sports, the consequence of which is that it wishes to maintain its role, just as it sometimes still wishes it was a world power politically. If so, then in sport its resources are spread too thinly. If, for example, we took the major rugby-playing countries of New Zealand, Australia, France, South Africa, Scotland, Wales, Ireland, Italy and Argentina and played a 'triple crown' competition of one 'soccer', one rugby and one Test Match against each of them, it is unlikely that England would lose any of those series 3-0 and probable that they would win more series than they lose overall – even if in 2015, the French did resume their claims to having invented cricket. The same point applies to rugby and 'soccer' matches against the other Test-playing countries of India, Pakistan, Sri Lanka and the West Indies. If we add to that Britain's all-round excellence at London 2012, the particular achievements of British cycling, the supremacy of Lewis Hamilton in motor sport, the sailing successes of Ben Ainslie, the Davis Cup victory of 2015 and in the same weekend Tyson Fury winning the World Heavyweight title, it appears that we want to do everything and excel at everything, but we do not and we probably cannot. Whenever we fail it becomes a national disaster, everyone has an answer and so everything changes yet again.

In the reorganisation at the ECB, Clarke's new role as President enabled him to continue working internationally, while Colin Graves took responsibility for the domestic game. Clarke had worked on a deal for England, India and Australia to take main control of the International game, which would include the next six global events, all taking place in one of those countries – the next World Cup is due in England in 2019. In *Wisden*, Lawrence Booth warned this "take-over" was "rubber-stamping a system of governance containing even fewer checks and balances than ever before". He reported from the minutes of a meeting of the ICC's Executive Board where members were reminded of their responsibility to act in the best interests of cricket in its broadest sense. The president of the Board of Cricket Control (BCCI) in India, Narayanaswami Srinivasan, appeared in the minutes dissenting from that responsibility and stressing that he represented the BCCI. In June 2014 he became president of the ICC.

Meanwhile, his son-in-law, an official of the IPL's Chennai Super Kings, was banned for life having been indicted in a betting scandal related to that competition. His involvement was partly because Narayanaswami Srinivasan's company owned the IPL franchise for the Chennai side. In November 2015 this perceived conflict of interest and failure to address the corruption, which led to the BCCI withdrawing its support for Srinivasan. Shashank Manohar, the current BCCI president, replaced Srinivasan as the ICC president for the remainder of his two-year tenure and in doing so made highly critical comments about his predecessor suggesting, "he too is the root of all scandals". Coming as it did on the same day that WADA revealed the extent of the athletics 'doping' scandals, the news may have been somewhat hidden from the mass public but it was no trivial matter – added to the on-going crisis at FIFA, world sport seemed increasing corrupt, offering little prospect of a solution.

Back in England at the start of his period of office in May 2015, Graves was clearly dissatisfied with England's winter performances and the Ashes defeat of 12 months previously. In April, even before he took office officially, Paul Downton was sacked after just 14 months and Andrew Strauss replaced him. In May, Strauss then sacked Peter Moores who learned of this through media leaks during an abandoned ODI against Ireland – Alec Stewart suggested the ECB should be "ashamed". Meanwhile, supporters of Kevin Pietersen, usually led by Piers Morgan, were calling for his reinstatement despite the publication of his poisonous autobiography a few months earlier. Graves intervened and suggested that the batsman should play for Surrey because "if he scores a lot of runs, they can't ignore him". He did, but they did. On 10 May he finished the day 35* for Surrey v Leicestershire. He batted throughout the next day, reaching 326* at which point Andrew Strauss visited him at the ground to tell him he would not be selected for England. His innings finished on 355* when the 10th wicket fell and a couple of weeks later he scored just two runs against Lancashire, to-date, his last County Championship appearance. Strauss, and the new ECB Chief Executive, Tom Harrison, met Pietersen to tell him he would not be selected and Strauss told *the Guardian*, "Pietersen was not happy with the decision and I didn't expect him to be." Of course, during his brief period as a Sky Sports commentator, Strauss had inadvertently told the world what he actually thought of Pietersen, who announced in his *Daily Telegraph* column that he was "absolutely devastated".

The next day, Strauss held a press conference to explain his actions and approach to the future. Of Pietersen, he said "there's a massive trust issue between him and the ECB". It was not the only time that the typically plain-speaking Yorkshireman, Graves, had issued a statement that rebounded on him. Prior to England's tour of the West Indies he suggested the hosts were "mediocre" and England should win the series, which they failed to do. *The Daily Telegraph* reported comments from a number of former England captains about the Pietersen issue. Bob Willis admitted this was a rare moment when he felt sorry for Pietersen who had been "sent on a wild goose chase"; Michael Vaughan suggested not picking him for the forthcoming Ashes series would be difficult to explain to a child; while Nasser Hussain believed that after the "appalling" handling of Moores' sacking, the ECB had "shot themselves in the foot again".

In early May, Lalit Modi, the architect of the IPL, revealed a plan to create a body for world cricket to rival the ICC. Reporting the news, *the Guardian* suggested that world cricket feared a contemporary re-run of the Kerry Packer period of 35 years earlier. The project would centre on the new body's ability to sign up the world's finest players and with money apparently no problem the evidence from 'Packer', the South African rebel tours of the

1980s, and the IPL (and rival ICL) suggested that most top cricketers saw their priority as earning power over team or country loyalty. Former Australian cricketer, Tim May, who had also led the Federation of International Cricketers' Associations (FICA), told *the Times,* "There is a general dissatisfaction with the game's governance. Other bodies believe they can globalise the game in a more equitable fashion."

As Graves and Strauss assumed control at the ECB, the first priority was to replace Peter Moores. The media favourite was Jason Gillespie from Graves' county, Yorkshire, where he had done a fine job, albeit in the longer form of the game. He was watching his county beat Hampshire comprehensively at Headingley on the day of Strauss's major press conference but declined to be drawn on the question of the England role. It was interesting to note that throughout the 21st century England's most successful and/or favoured coaches were all from overseas, whereas the one Englishman, Moores, apparently failed and was sacked twice. For a long time now, English cricket through the NCA and ECB, has had in place an elaborate system of developing coaches through a series of levels and many county players prepare for their futures by attending courses and taking examinations. Yet it appears that none of these men were suitable for the main England role while a number of counties turned also to overseas coaches. In many respects it resembled the situation at England's leading football clubs. Why can't the English coach at the highest level? And if they can, why don't they?

Graves and Strauss seemed concerned to place an emphasis on improving England's performances in the shorter forms of the game but Graves had other items on his agenda. As he took over, John Westerby in *the Daily Telegraph* suggested that Graves would have to devote time and energy "to create a sense of common purpose among 18 counties with widely varying interests", adding that any attempt to create a T20 franchise along the lines of the IPL or Australia's 'Big Bash' "will be met by fierce resistance from some counties".

The same would be said about plans to change the County Championship, yet again. Among the proposals mooted early season in *the Cricket Paper* were cutting the County Championship from 16 to 12 matches, perhaps through a three-tier league structure including Scotland. Not for the last time, county chairman Rod Bransgrove was pictured and quoted:

> You can hold on to tradition but of course the world changes around it and then becomes as I call it gratuitous tradition and that's pointless and no good to anybody, it belongs in a museum.

The notion that the many great museums of this country (and elsewhere) are simply the repositories of things that are "no good to anybody" is interesting. If history and tradition offered no lessons and posed no threat to anyone, the major totalitarian regimes of the past 100 years, including most recently ISIS, would probably have spent less time and energy destroying many historic treasures of the world.

This County Championship 'tradition' of which Bransgrove spoke, was being honoured in 2015 – at least by those who agreed with this version of the dates – in its 125th anniversary, not least by a splendid book by Stephen Chalke, supported by the ECB. The current version of that tradition – setting aside any tinkering with bonus/draw/win points, the fixture list or numbers of teams promoted and relegated – had been in place for just 15 of those years, only a couple of years more than the T20 and considerably fewer years than the various knock-out cup competitions, yet apparently it was already time for another major change.

Whatever their priorities, Strauss and Graves will have been very happy to see two exciting Test Match series in the summer of 2015 against the two World Cup finalists, with England regaining the Ashes. In the 10 years since the wonderful season of 2005 – and exclusively on Sky Sports – the Ashes had changed hands in 2007 (Australia), 2009 (England), 2014 (Australia) and 2015 (England). Now there would be a little break before the next time. In the first Lord's Test Match, Ben Stokes hit the fastest Test Match century on the ground in 85 balls as Strauss surprised everyone, opting for Trevor Bayliss instead of Jason Gillespie. The intentions were clear as he came with stronger 'white ball' credentials and renewed his Sri Lankan partnership with Paul Farbrace. The Lord's match finished with a thrilling late victory for England.

In July **2015**, the ECB appointed Lord Patel of Bradford to its board hoping that the Labour Party peer would help the ECB to establish better working relationships with British-Asian cricketers and communities. Among his credentials, he had been part-time coach at the Yorkshire Cricket Academy. The ECB also announced further investment in the schools-based Chance to Shine and the appointment of Matt Dwyer to head up the initiative to improve participation in all forms and at all levels.

In mid-July, England won the first Test Match of the Ashes series by 169 runs but in *the Guardian,* Sean Ingle reported poor and declining audience figures on Sky Sports, with none of the days approaching half-a-million viewers. Australia won the next game, England won at Edgbaston and the teams moved on to Trent Bridge where for a morning at least English fans could forget everything else and simply wonder at the cricket. On that first morning, Broad's 8–15 were the third best figures ever for England against Australia, bettered only by Jim Laker's two performances at Old Trafford in 1956. 'Nelson' struck as Australia were all out in 111 balls, the shortest first innings in Test Match history, and the 14 extras marked the first occasion on which they have top-scored in an Ashes innings. Their final score was 60 all out in 18.3 overs and England won, of course, to lead 3–1. The Ashes series was very odd. In the event, England won the series 3–2 and regained the little urn but each of the matches was won and lost by a huge margin and the scheduled 25 days of cricket ended up as 18, equalling the record fewest number of days in a five-match Test Match series since we started playing five-day Test Matches just after the second world war.

The two sides went finally, as usual, to the Oval, where a group of protest-ers assembled representing the organization 'Change Cricket'. Among their numbers, expressing concerns with the management of world cricket were the conservative MP Damian Collins and journalists Jarrod Kimber and Sam Collins who had been responsible for the challenging documentary film *Death of a Gentleman*. In the following week, Simon Heffer confessed that watching the documentary had damaged his life-long love affair with cricket. In an article in *the Daily Telegraph* titled "The enemy within is killing cricket", he suggested "there is a complete absence of transparency in the interna-tional game". Heffer described Giles Clarke's performance in the film as a "bravura display of the arrogant, patronizing, utter lack of self-awareness one normally associates with the unpleasantly stupid", although he added "thoroughly objectionable people running English cricket is not a novelty". He asked in conclusion, "Is cricket now only about money?"

On 24 September in his column in *the Times,* Michael Atherton wrote about the death of the Indian, Jagmohan Dalmiya, who had masterminded India's rise to cricket supremacy between their first World Cup triumph in 1983 and the early years of the 21st century. But this was no hagiography. He asked us whether we ever wondered how cricket supporters had ended up as "consumers"; why Lord's Test Match tickets could now cost £100; how "every international cricket match is commoditised, sold and packaged like meat out of a factory"; and how ultimately the sport has become "a global business". The transformation, Atherton believed, was due principally to Dalmiya and its "end game" was "the hijacking" in 2014 of the ICC by the three leading countries who ended "the ideal that the governance of a sport should be high-minded, independent and for the benefit of all". No one would accuse Heffer or Atherton, *the Daily Telegraph* or *the Times* of being at the radical end of any political spectrum but there was a clear and growing consensus of concern at what was taking place.

Back in England in late July, following a full ECB board meeting, *the Times* suggested that there would be a proposal for two T20 domestic competitions to alleviate the anxieties of the 'smaller' counties that they would otherwise be disenfranchised by any city-based eight team contest. The Sussex Chairman, Jim May, pointed out that the current competition was working pretty well with full houses at Hove and crowds increasing by 30%, adding "we are going to need a lot of convincing"; while Warwickshire's chief executive, Colin Povey suggested "we are doing a lot right with T20 at the moment". In August *the Cricket Paper* reported Tom Harrison's view that the reduction in the County Championship to 14 games was "close to agreement" and told *the Guardian* he was warning counties that the ECB would no longer act as a "bank of last resort" because they need to be "in a position to sustain their own business". He added that the "implications" for reducing the County Championship further were not "significant", although that did not seem to be the view of its regular supporters. Many of the counties were troubled, however, and in *the Times,* Richard Hobson reported that changes which now seemed scheduled for 2016, had not been expected for at least another year. The ECB directors would hope to push the reforms through in the following week's separate meetings with chief executives and chairmen.

Meanwhile, the PCA seemed to join forces with the ECB in their moves to reduce the amount of county cricket played in England. Almost 88% of their 240 respondents to their survey wished to see a reduction in the amount of cricket played and they quoted one player's view that the quantity played was ridiculous while the travel was "exhausting", while another suggested it might even be "unsafe". The situation was complicated because while the ECB were clearly intent on introducing any reduction through the County Championship, that was the competition that players valued most, while the 50-over cup competition was least popular. Various people with a vested interest drew from the survey the conclusion that there must be a reduction in the number of County Championship fixtures but that view was not an inevitable conclusion from the survey results.

There is also the question of whether and why county cricketers are so tired, even "exhausted". When Eoin Morgan returned from the World Cup (and the IPL) in such a condition, Middlesex rested him until he was ready to resume with England. But let us take as an example the season played by Hampshire in 2015 and look first at Michael Carberry who (alone) played in every Hampshire match in every competition. That was a 24 weeks season for a man who seems now past any prospects of further international cricket and ignoring any abandoned matches, early finishes or days watching others batting, Carberry played cricket on 89 days in the English season of 2015 – an average over the 24 weeks of 3.7 days per week. After him came four other top-order batsmen – including wicketkeeper, Adam Wheater – before the first bowler in the list, Gareth Berg, who averaged exactly three days per week. Otherwise, apart from Liam Dawson (2.6) and Ervine (2.5), the regular bowlers all averaged less than two days per week across the season.

In 10 of those 24 weeks Hampshire played just one competitive match, so requiring no shifting of formats, and even when that did occur, over another 10 weeks, they only ever played two formats in one week, never all three. In the remaining four weeks (all limited-overs) they played more than one match but all in the same format. In eight of those 24 weeks they played five days cricket and in one, six days – otherwise it was four or fewer. In addition they used 23 players throughout the season and frequently, in a switch from say a County Championship match to a T20, the side, notably the bowlers, would change significantly. Travel can be an issue, albeit that they travel in a luxury coach, but in six of those weeks (25%) they had no away fixtures, while the T20 is regional with no journeys further than Cardiff or Canterbury.

In summary, the PCA survey clearly revealed that players want to play less cricket, although 83% believe the County Championship to be the "premier" competition. The change they most wish for is to see the T20 played in a block although the format for 2015 saw attendances rise by 17% so any change might be a risk. T20 seems like the answer to cricket's money worries but television viewing figures for Finals Day presented a salutary warning, as they were the lowest ever. The players seemed less enamoured with the longer limited-overs format and somewhat ambivalent about whether it should constitute 40 or 50 overs, but one interesting suggestion was to play early rounds abroad just prior to the English season in the hope that it might lure English supporters to spend a week or two in Abu Dhabi or the Caribbean. That would spread the season out, but the players definitely want fewer matches, while the members do not generally support a reduction in the County Championship.

When measuring players' workloads, it is worth remembering that the majority of players are on 12 months contracts, enabling them to work on fitness and skills for half of the year with no obligation to their paying public. Some go off in the English winter to appear in other tournaments but that is their choice. If it leaves them too tired to play county cricket perhaps they should follow Morgan's example – and perhaps they might relinquish their salary for those weeks, enabling a replacement to be signed. There is little doubt that players get tired, they always did, but in that they are no different from most other workers, nor are they unique in having to travel extensively as part of their professional obligations. Why shouldn't cricketers get tired? In the 1960s, county cricket became fully professional and a few years later the Professional Cricketers' Association was formed. But these young men at a peak of physical fitness are seeking preferential professional treatment and the sacrifice is to be made by those who pay to watch because the prospect is for them to watch less of what many enjoy – particularly in mid-summer.

As the 2015 English season drew towards its close, *the Cricket Paper* announced the almost certain reduction in County Championship matches from 2016, with the headline "D-Day looms". But D-Day was a great and carefully planned victory against the forces of fascism. *The Times* declared "ECB Plans for 14 matches are on track"; *the Daily Telegraph* announced that the county clubs would "finally support reduction to 14 matches" with a stronger 'white ball' programme; and *the Guardian* believed the counties were "prepared to back ECB plan to cut County Championship games". But they weren't. Suddenly, Nick Hoult in *the Daily Telegraph* revealed that "the counties are almost unanimous in opposition to a cut in the number of County Championship matches" and Colin Graves, having lost the first round, simply switched to winning them around over the winter in order to announce the changes he wanted to take effect from 2017. Meanwhile, Jason Gillespie told *the Guardian* that in his view the County Championship's "current format remains the best" under the headline, "Evolution not Revolution is needed in the English game".

Rod Bransgrove did not agree and went further telling *the Cricket Paper,* alongside a photograph of him with Colin Graves, that the current county schedule "is destroying cricket". His views were informed by those who, he suggested, "really know about the game", listing John Carr (ECB and former cricketer), Andrew Strauss, the county coaches and the players as those knowledgeable individuals. By implication at least then, he appeared to ignore those who pay to watch and in many cases have been watching for a lifetime. Somehow it seems, they don't "really know about the game", although since county cricket is a commercial enterprise they certainly know a great deal about being paying customers – unlike those who are Bransgrove's preferred informants. He went further, criticizing the fact that the county members and their elected committees "come first" in any decision making, despite the fact that they "make up such a small propor-tion of the *potential* market" (my emphasis). He was dismissive of members' preference to "go along to empty stadiums and have 10 seats to themselves", apparently ignoring the fact that many of those empty seats were paid for before the season started by members who may be unable to get there mid-week and indeed on days of early finishes or inclement weather. He did not specify the size or nature of the "potential market". In a certain sense it is presumably the 60 (plus) millions who inhabit the United Kingdom, although the prospect that the majority of them will ever watch cricket is pretty slight – especially given one of the key themes of this book is that cricket is no longer embedded in British society. Bransgrove said he was pleased that at Hampshire his committee is "much further along than most" because "they do get it; they accept the need for change", but there is no committee at Hampshire in the sense of the old-fashioned members' county clubs. There is a PLC and that board of directors makes the decisions; and there is, separately, a members' committee, which is rather like a football supporters' club representing supporters' views to the Directors.

In the late summer's ODI series there was much grumbling about Australia's refusal to withdraw an upheld appeal against Ben Stokes for handled-ball. On the domestic scene Yorkshire won the County Championship again and with Hampshire surviving on a nail biting last day, Sussex and Worcestershire were relegated and replaced by Lancashire and Surrey. This left Somerset alone as a non-Test ground in 2016's Division One although following recent ground developments they too were talking of Taunton becoming an international venue. Having been through the period where everyone had prizes we are now in a phase where more and more grounds want international matches. At one of them, in the Royal London Cup, Glamorgan's match with Hampshire at Cardiff was abandoned because of a dangerous pitch; the groundsman resigned and Glamorgan were fined £9,000 and two points. Gloucestershire rekindled memories of their glory days a decade or so before by winning at Lord's, while Hampshire set a record for six consecutive appearances at Finals Day but lost again in the semi-final as Lancashire triumphed over Northamptonshire.

Yorkshire were comprehensive winners of the County Championship with 11 victories in their 16 matches – a 69% success rate – which exceeded their 50% as County Champions in their title year of 1959, which we reported at the start of this book. In the second division in 2015, Surrey were County Champions with a 50% success rate but elsewhere the figures for the four-day competition in 2015 showed fewer percentage victories than in the sunny three-day season of 1959. Back then, the bottom three counties won 29% of their matches while all the others were at 36% or higher, with seven sides above 40%. In 2015, 11 of the teams were on 31% or fewer victories, with nine winning at best just a quarter of their matches, and Worcestershire, Derbyshire and Leicestershire below 20%. Maybe that signals a tougher brand of cricket, but it might equally have to do with increasingly flat pitches and bonus points favouring batting totals added to points for the draw. If the argument in favour of the T20 is based on excitement, maybe the County Championship could have a little more, too?

In the autumn of 2015, England went to the UAE and enjoyed some good passages of play against Pakistan with Cook, Root, Anderson and Broad playing at the highest level. Sadly, overall their batsmen could not resist the best spin bowlers and their three spinners were less effective than Pakistan's, so England lost 2–0. Despite this, Colin Graves appeared more troubled by England's failure in the Rugby World Cup, the first host nation to fail to qualify for the knock-out stages of that competition. Graves used this as an opportunity to stress his determination to change the structure of English cricket, telling Nick Hoult in *the Daily Telegraph* in October

> What I do not want to do in 2019 is be in a similar position with cricket to our rugby World Cup … It did wake us up and say we have to make sure as much as we can that does not happen to us in 2019. We want to reach the final of the World Cup in our own country, and to win it would be brilliant, but for that to happen we have to put cricket in the right position by getting the domestic competitions right. We have three years to do it.

It was clear that Graves had not accepted the decision of the counties a couple of months earlier and that he was willing to draw on any evidence, whether from cricket or elsewhere, to drive through his agenda. His phrase "getting domestic competitions right" was unambiguous – he wants to cut the County Championship and presumably once cut he, or perhaps the next chairman, will want to cut it again as has happened regularly over the past 50 years. Whether or not the players support this view, they have provided him with ammunition to pursue his campaign and supporters of the County Championship must face the probability that it will change again in the pursuit of "potential" audiences and to help the white ball game. As part of that plan, Graves returned to the question of county finances, suggesting the need for a significant change to the television contract when it next expires in 2019 so that the ECB can negotiate an individual television deal for the county competition. He identified the need to "generate money for the domestic game," adding that had never been done, while apparently ignoring the fact that all the international income is generated through matches played by *county* cricketers. Graves wants to get "value" for county cricket by "finding out how we can do it better from a broadcaster and spectator point of view". Since the County Championship is almost never shown on television we must wonder again about its future within such a scenario.

We must wonder too about the future for some counties in this context. Many commentators on county cricket have observed for generations that county cricket and county clubs seem doomed – we noted earlier how the years around 1960 were notably gloomy, before the significant changes of the 1960s came to the rescue. Somehow the clubs and the County Championship survive but in the autumn of 2015 came the news that Northamptonshire were in financial trouble. The BBC reported a loan of up to £250,000 from their local council and said that this was one of a number of sources to enable the club to "restructure" after their accounts showed a loss of £305,636 on a turnover of just over £3.7m. The leader of the council said that it was important to help maintain the tradition of county cricket in the county but added, "cricket is changing and that means the club must restructure off the pitch if they are to have a future on it."

After a trial lasting some weeks in London, the New Zealand Test cricketer, Chris Cairns, was acquitted of perjury in a case related to alleged match-fixing. Despite the verdict, the Cricket Paper feared the "ramifications" would "continue", while the Guardian suggested Cairns' reputation was "scorched". They also reported the warning from Angus Porter the chief executive of the PCA, that as a consequence of the verdict, cricketers will be more reluctant to offer information about such issues in the future. Porter suggested that the process "asks a lot of people and doesn't give a huge amount back".

Elsewhere, the ICC was concerned about the threat of terrorism in Bangladesh and its impact on their T20 tournament and projected tours, while Pakistan and India resumed their seemingly endless quarrels, with the prospect of Pakistan withdrawing from the next World T20 competition.

Meanwhile, cricket matches continued around the world. In October 2015, South Africa beat India 3–2 in an ODI series as the South Africans won the decider by scoring 438–4 with three centurions, for just the second time in ODI history. The highest score remains 443–9 by Sri Lanka v Holland (2006) but the three highest between two Test Match sides, are all by South Africa, 439 v West Indies a few months earlier in 2015, and 438–9 v Australia in 2006. Despite this, the South Africans, number one in the world, seemed to lose the ability to bat in Test Matches as they were skittled regularly in losing a Test Match series in India following the limited-overs matches. Australia met New Zealand in the first ever day/night Test Match with the Times asking in a headline, "Can pink balls save Test cricket?" South Africa came home but lost heavily to England in the last Test Match of 2015. The New Year would bring the remainder of that series, another T20 World Cup, and another attempt to cut the number of County Championship matches, but at least England finished 2015 on a high.

Conclusion: the Uncertain Future

I have described Graeme Wright's 2011 publication *Behind the Boundary* as the most important book written in recent years about county cricket. I could quote from it throughout this book, from the contributions of his various respondents, considering thoughts and ideas that I like, some that I don't like and others that I remain unsure about. From my perspective as an ageing county member who watches all formats but loves the County Championship, Wright enlightens us frequently about the motivations and procedures that drive English cricket, and he reveals very clearly the beliefs and values of so many of the people running that game at the county level – albeit five years ago, which, as I hope I have shown, can be a long time in English cricket.

One of his respondents was Mark Newton at Worcestershire who told Wright that "before long" someone has to say that we should "forget about" four-day cricket at county level because it, and even three-day cricket, is "too long for a modern audience". He compared it with going to the theatre, cinema or football suggesting that people don't watch a part and then leave or go back the next day to see the next part.

Alongside the economic issue, it is the obvious argument, of course. As I have said, I am writing this book very deliberately as a cricketing 'amateur' and in one sense I mean by that, that in just one context over 50+ years in a brief spell as a county committee member, was I *required* to worry about balance sheets. But professionally, I have spent my whole adult life involved in the arts and from that perspective I will suggest that Newton's point does not bear too much scrutiny. It is correct as far as it goes but only if limited to the most conventional, mainstream examples. To a very large extent, the kind of cinema and theatre that attracts a mass audience is driven by narrative. Ultimately, what we want to know is will Frodo get to the mountain, will he destroy the ring and will he save Middle Earth, and we stay until the end to see whether Humphrey Bogart gets his 'girl'. If we shift to television or radio, however, even the most popular kind, we know many people who do indeed come back week-after-week even year-after-year, to find out what happened next in *the Archers, Eastenders* or *Coronation Street* or perhaps to discover who will win the final of *Strictly Come Dancing* or the *X Factor*. Narrative closure is not an *essential* feature of all forms of entertainment and its role in first-class cricket – by definition, three or more days – is one of the more interesting and unique aspects of that form of cricket.

There is a narrative and there are endings in first-class cricket of course, especially with tight finishes and trophies, but do we think that the spectators who saw Broad take eight wickets before lunch on day one at Nottingham or those who saw Stokes' extraordinary double century in Cape Town, felt deprived if they saw only that one day? Similarly, watching County Championship cricket never hinges absolutely on the result – indeed, even in the days when there was only three-day County Championship cricket, Desmond Eagar, Hampshire's secretary, asked in the county's Handbook why people watch more first day than third day county cricket. The reasons have to do with habit and culture as much as entertainment, and also because cricket offers endless narrative sequences throughout, with spectators wondering whether that man will reach his century, whether the ball will turn for the spinner, if this partnership is a record or whether their side can get another bonus point. Cricket watchers find a variety of things in which to be interested throughout the day, and since they pay for the privilege, that is their business.

I chose the example of the Lord of the Rings precisely because the initial and huge worldwide audiences for the films came three separate times over separate years to witness the finish. In some respects it is an unfair example, a highpoint in narrative box-office cinema, but given the demise of the local cinema in favour of modern multiplex cinemas, many families will have travelled some distance to watch those three episodes – often the same young families who do not, apparently, attend the County Championship. Another example is the modern music festival – most obviously in Glastonbury – where the generally youthful audience stays for days at that single event. Potential audiences in the UK do not consist entirely, or even predominantly, of young families seeking new entertainments that last only a couple of hours, and one of the characteristics of the County Championship – which I have pointed out is probably the most popular British sport largely absent from our television screens – is that it is hardly marketed at all. Walk around the county grounds and there will always be advertising for forthcoming T20s or 50-over matches, and on some grounds, Tests and ODIs; and when those matches are staged, there will be all the paraphernalia that the marketing men believe is essential to retain the interest of the crowds: funfair rides, bars, extra food stalls and live music. That advertising is replicated on-line through the website and emails.

Then visit a County Championship match, which has hardly been 'sold' to anyone in any significant way in advance; some of the toilets will be shut, some of the bars, too. If we were to tell those young families that generally speaking their favourite films, plays and musicals would be available only on a Sunday matinee or during the day from Monday to Wednesday, how many would attend? If the football Premiership played its matches on Tuesday afternoons or the T20 was scheduled for Wednesday mornings, would they attract an audience? To a large extent, English cricket destroyed the Saturday audience for the County Championship and now uses that as an excuse to suggest it's done for. But there is an audience for it, albeit one that like much theatre and most British cinema, needs its product to be subsidised through other sources. Very few people argue that the arts and museums should exist only in a free-market economy because they know that in such a case some of the greatest achievements of civilisation would vanish.

This book has been a labour of love – the work of an amateur – and I do not know whether any professional cricket people, whether administrators, players, coaches, journalists or commentators, will read it. I have written it principally for my fellow spectators and supporters and with a view to the future, as a record for Spencer and all the young people like him who I hope will enjoy a lifetime involved in cricket, giving them as much pleasure as I have found over the decades. I am very lucky to be Hampshire's Hon Archivist and in the context of occasional talks I give in that role, and through the related Blog that I run, I have been able to explore with others the principal ideas in this book. I have found a good deal of sympathy and support for my views from my fellow members and supporters and that encouraged me to write it. I am not sure that it will in any way help to arrest the dismantling of the County Championship, but I have never had much enthusiasm for 'going quietly'.

During the summer of 2015, the latest challenge to the County Championship grew apace under the initiatives of Colin Graves and Andrew Strauss at the ECB, and it was strange to be involved at Hampshire as our chairman, Rod Bransgrove, gave his support to the proposed reduction in games. We have a good relationship but we take the opposite view on this issue. Sometimes the implication is that those who share my view are in our later years and merely obstructing progress. It might be true, although I see no strength in the argument that retirement from work equals retirement from life. Further, it is not the case that county cricket fans over the age of 65 enjoy only the County Championship. It is, however, increasingly that because of scheduling, they are the only people able to watch it on a regular basis, and there are, today, more of them to watch it than ever before. When the County Championship was extended in the 1890s, average life expectancy in this country was below 50 years, and by the 1950s when the focus of this book began, it was 65 and had extended only slightly to 68 by 1970; but today it exceeds 80 for both men and women. In 1994, Anthea Tinker recorded that at the start of the century the population over 65 years of age was under 5%, by the early 1950s it had risen to 10% and by 1989 the total had risen to nine million and was approaching 16%. The parliamentary website shows that figure today at 10 million and it is projected to double by 2050.

But that is not all. The Chartered Institute of Personnel and Development reports that in the 60 years from 1952, the working week fell by up to 10 hours per week. Holiday allowances had increased on average from 16 to a minimum of 28 days, while part-time workers increased from 4% of the workforce to 25% and the 33% of under-25s in work in 1952 had fallen to 15% in 2012. There are quite a few people 'out there' even of working age who have free time during the working week – but how hard are we working to draw them to our County Championship matches? What special offers might convert them into long-term followers? In addition, my generation might be particularly blessed in respect of spare time and money, and there are many like me (mid-late 1960s) who are retired with sufficient health, energy, time and disposable income to hope for at least another decade of cricket watching, while willingly paying for the privilege. Why, we wonder, does the ECB not welcome our support and our money?

Sadly, in too many debates about the future of cricket, we are seen as 'old and in the way', impeding the 'progressives' who wish to move the game on in pursuit of their ill-defined potential audience and ever more lucrative returns. For them, progress appears to mean an England side increasingly selected from privately educated or southern African players with a smatter-ing of Anglo-Asians on the fringes. If cricket dies in the inner cities partly as a consequence of its disappearance from our free-to-air television screens, so be it. If that view is 'progressive', it's a pretty strange view of progress.

In addition, I am bewildered by the characterisation of those of us who wish to protect the County Championship as conservative or reactionary. Does it mean that *anyone* who cares for any of our great traditions is better locked in the vaults of a museum, while the 'progressives' go on carving up the world, pursuing further short-term interests? Very few of my friends or closer acquaintances would be inclined to describe me as reactionary. I have been a professional and long-time semi-professional 'pop' musician including a spell playing in a band with the Woodstock Festival 'legend' Country Joe McDonald. I was an art teacher and in my subsequent academic career I taught about experimental cinema, popular culture and the arts. At Hampshire, my fellow Committee members will joke sometimes that I am the archetypal *Guardian* reader ('baby boomer' variety) but if adding a love of the County Championship to that menu seems contradictory, that can only be because people are inclined to believe the simple stereotypes peddled by soap operas or cheap journalism. If I do not fit the 'model' of an ageing, conservative follower of the County Championship, why should it necessarily apply to anyone else? The world is a complicated and interesting place and I find no inconsistency in my love of county cricket alongside a lifestyle that embraces the practice and pursuit of popular music, contemporary art or perhaps environmental issues.

What is consistent is my commitment to the County Championship, although it does not prevent me from being fond of the longer limited-overs matches that I have been watching for 50 years. With regard to T20, I played a club version of it on Tuesday evenings in Portsmouth more than 30 years ago, understand entirely its rationale, and have supported its introduction from the moment it was first proposed to the English county committees in the 1990s. I admire considerably the inventiveness of the players in adapting traditional skills to suit the format and like many of the ways in which that has impacted on the longer forms. I can live without it principally because of the noise and the relentless pace, which allows for little in the way of contemplation, reflection, conversation or analysis. If others, including young people, enjoy the whole package, that's fine – it has been an important and lucrative development and it is not going away.

As to the County Championship, I have suggested that I do not simply wish it to remain as it is, but neither do I wish to contemplate a season of virtually six months in which my county plays only seven home fixtures, the majority in April and September. I am not averse to change if it is productive and I have an idea that might enable our 'overworked' players to enjoy even more rest days. Based on the evidence of the past, I see no reason why players could not bowl *at least* 110 overs each day – after all, Stephen Chalke reports that in May 1947 Essex bowled 148 overs in a day v Leicestershire, while two years later Hampshire bowled 142 overs in a day v the West Indian tourists. Perhaps cricketers were just fitter then, but when I mentioned this to a former county cricketer he observed that to get the current rate up, teams would have to bowl spinners more frequently, as though that was a problem. If it is a problem, that is to the significant detriment of the game. Chalke records that in 1950, 56% of County Championship wickets fell to spinners while today it is under 20%. It is a bit like a symphony orchestra forced to discard half its violins while they give fewer concerts and the ticket prices rise.

Why can't each County Championship match be reduced from a current maximum of around 380 overs to perhaps 350 – the equivalent of the first four days of a Test Match? The games might remain scheduled over four days but with the possibility of completing them within three, leaving the fourth day as either the day to bowl a few remaining overs, a day to retrieve overs lost to the weather, or, if players are particularly active on the first three days, a 'rest' day. The abolition of first innings bonus points might help to improve the tempo of the game, and with the offer of a 'day off', I suspect that current slow over rates and profligate time-wasting would soon disappear. For example, with the introduction of a spinner imminent, any close fielder should be replaced by a substitute in order to 'pad up', rather than holding up play for some minutes.

On the matter of spinners, there are still people at Hampshire furious that a few years ago a very interesting match against Nottinghamshire ended with a points penalty because of excessive turn from the start. In contrast, I would suggest that every pitch that fails to take spin from the halfway point should incur a similar penalty, adjudicated by the umpires. Further, why not allow sides to make one team change after the first two innings? Just about the only significant on-field alteration to football and rugby over the past 50 years has been the introduction of substitutes, which has no adverse effect on those sports. If the pitch starts to turn halfway through, why not allow teams to bring in a playing substitute, hopefully a spinner (although that might be dictated by the match situation)?

All of this concerns the competition I love and the one that, despite decades of gloomy predictions, still survives. But the other implicit question running through this book is whether we can bring cricket back towards the heart of English culture? If not, is it destined to be like the Church of England merely something most people identify as essentially 'English', while generally ignoring it? And if that is so, are we, at last, living through the final years of English first-class cricket, while arguments to get the game of cricket into the USA and the Olympics reinforce its future as one of limited-overs matches, even six-a-side, and always completed in a single day?

In the summer of 2015, journalist Scyld Berry published *Cricket: the Game of Life*, covering a range of topics from a long career reporting on England and English cricket. One of the key issues was summarised in an article in *the Daily Telegraph* in August under the title: "A game now in danger of shrinking into a middle-class niche." The subtitle suggested, "cricket has failed to exploit the inner cities". Berry offered some statistics about English cricketers who had gone on to play for England with the highest proportion coming from Yorkshire, then London, then Lancashire. No surprises there perhaps, but it was fascinating to read that no fewer than 40% of England's Test Match players have had a close family member who had also played first-class cricket. The advantage is apparent.

Even more obvious is the statistic that one third of England's 667 Test Match cricketers (Berry concluded with Adil Rashid) were privately educated, whereas fewer than 10% of young people attend such establishments. Much the same statistic was rolled out during the 2012 London Olympics and it was repeated again with the New Year's Honours List of January 2016. If you attend a state school your chances of significant achievement are reduced proportionally – it is even an accusation these days made about careers in the theatre or popular music.

Berry argued that this is considerably to the detriment of young people "notably" from the "cities in the midlands and north of England" and he added with a hint of surprise "not one England male cricketer has been born in Wolverhampton". While I support Berry's broad case entirely, I was intrigued by his example (and his 'exception' of Rachel Heyhoe-Flint), suspecting he was pursuing the familiar tale of the North-South divide. But Wolverhampton is in Staffordshire, a minor county, and I would alert him to the sad fact that neither has a single England Test Match cricketer – male *or* female – been born in my home city of Portsmouth in the first-class county of Hampshire. Indeed, the facts are even more revealing. Since the second world war, just five Portsmouth-born cricketers have played for Hampshire, in chronological order: Mike Barnard, Richard McIlwaine, David Rock, Jonathan Ayling and Lawrie Prittipaul. Of those five, only Barnard and Ayling won county caps – the former enjoying a full career and also playing football for his home town club – while the career of the hugely promising Ayling was wrecked by the most unfortunate knee injury after a mid-pitch collision.

With respect to them all, that is not a terrific line-up from the most densely populated city in the UK, but the key point is that Prittipaul was educated privately at St John's College and the other four at Portsmouth Grammar School, a fee-paying Direct Grant Grammar School which went fully independent in the 1970s. The last state-school educated cricketer born in Portsmouth to enjoy a full career as a capped county professional, was wicketkeeper Neil McCorkell, and he retired 65 years ago.

The case of Lawrie Prittipaul is particularly interesting. His father came from the Caribbean to the UK and can still be seen playing the occasional club match around the city. Lawrie was a very promising player in the late 1990s, playing alongside Chris Tremlett, Derek Kenway, Jimmy Adams and others in the Hampshire 'colts' side that were national Champions. He was the last man to score a first-class century and a limited-overs half-century at Hampshire's old Southampton headquarters, and in 2000 he was the first Hampshire player to score a century at the Rose Bowl in the first match played on the main ground between Hampshire and Glamorgan 2nd XIs. But Prittipaul, along with other young batsmen like Kenway, Will Kendall and Jason Laney suffered from the unpredictable pitches in the new ground's early years, and he faded from the first-class game without fulfilling his promise.

Prittipaul went back to Southern League cricket but also began having discussions with another local man, Trevor McArdle, who was frustrated by the limited cricketing opportunities for his son and friends in the heart of Portsmouth. The clubs were doing their best but, much as Berry reports from elsewhere, the majority of the young people in the city who had regular access to cricket came, like Prittipaul, from families with cricketers or were at the fee-paying schools.

So, Prittipaul and McArdle devised and developed an introductory inner-city version of the game for young people who might otherwise never encounter it, as we are now 15 years from the last time the county side played in the city. They called it Cage Cricket and it was devised precisely to fit inside the fenced-in MUGAs (multi-use games areas) that already exist in many inner-city areas. The game is devised for six participants at any time and all of them bat, bowl, field, score and umpire. In such ways it offers both an introduction to an unfamiliar game and also helps them to develop valuable social and mathematical skills. The project won the support of Rod Bransgrove, Ian Botham and Shane Warne and enjoyed a high-profile launch at the Houses of Parliament where, despite a damp morning, a number of MPs and civil servants had a turn – indeed at one point it seemed likely that John Redwood MP might bat all morning.

The game has attracted interest across the country and abroad. Given the difficulty of providing any experience of cricket in schools today, this seems like a very positive situation and there is now a specific charitable arm of the game called Cage4All. Oddly, however, Cage Cricket has received little support from the ECB for reasons that from a distance are difficult to understand – indeed, some of the verbatim 'reports' suggest there has been at times quite strong opposition to the project and this opposition has filtered down to local organisations. Any assumption that all initiatives to promote cricket among young people are 'good things' is probably naïve. Cricket is dying in the inner cities partly because there are too many political hurdles to overcome, from the maintenance of traditional cricket fields to the influence of those who run the game, nationally, regionally and locally.

This is tragic. It is not a tragedy when England lose the Ashes or fail to win the World Cup, it is a disappointment, but it is tragic that young people in inner cities, with all the difficulties they encounter in these tough times, are denied the opportunity to engage in a contemporary, exciting and educational version of one of the country's great sporting traditions. My subject, Spencer, enjoys the support of his parents and his local club in rural north

Hampshire – he was thrilled to receive a new pair of batting gloves in his Christmas stocking – but few of his contemporaries in the big cities on the south coast of the county share that experience or anticipation.

In January 2007, Bill Gates delivered a speech to the World Economic Forum (DAVOS) in which he said "… if you're not fully utilizing half the talent in the country, you're not going to get too close to the top." He was actually addressing the issue of gender equality in industry, but the point holds good with the failure to utilise half the potential cricketing talent in this country. The ECB think that the best way for England to win the World Cup is by reducing the number of County Championship matches. The real answer is to enable and encourage every boy and girl to engage with our great game until it is once again embedded 'naturally' in the culture – the *whole* culture, for the whole population. On the way to that goal it would seem sensible to nurture rather than alienate those who are its natural supporters. I am not optimistic about the future of the County Championship but at least in writing this book I have done what I could to argue its case. I will leave the last word to one of English cricket's more 'interesting' characters and a man who is generally keen to have the final say:

> "The more the ECB changes, the more it stays the same"
> Geoff Boycott –*the Daily Telegraph,* May 2015

Forever Changes – The Key Sources

It will be clear from reading the book that my major sources have been the Editor's Notes and other articles in *Wisden* and the editorials and guest prefaces in the *Playfair Cricket Annual,* plus *the Cricket Paper* and daily newspapers. In the chapter on the 1960s, especially the early years, the *Playfair Cricket Monthly* was another regular source.

I have mentioned many books 'in passing' to exemplify particular points, for example *Pickwick Papers* or *the Female Eunuch*. These are not listed here but are easy to locate. The same point applies to the films and television programmes – only those artefacts that are referred to in detail in the text are included here.

Literature and Film

John Arlott, 1957, "A Cup of Cold Tea" published in *Lilliput Magazine. Re-published as* "Ain't Half a Bloody Game" in Peter Haining, 1986, *LBW: Laughter Before Wicket – 100 Years of Humourous Cricket Short Stories,* Allen & Unwin

LP Hartley, 1997 *The Go-Between,* Penguin Modern Classics

Citizen 63, (dir. John Boorman) BBC television September 1963

Hope and Glory (dir. John Boorman) 1987

Death of a Gentleman (dir. Sam Collins and Jarrod Kimber) 2015

The Final Test (dir. Anthony Asquith) 1953

The Go-Between (Dir. Joseph Losey) 1971

The Go-Between (Dir Pete Travis) BBC television July 2015

The Lady Vanishes (dir. Alfred Hitchcock) 1938

Playing Away (dir. Horace Ové) Channel 4 television1986

We Are the Lambeth Boys (dir. Karel Reisz) 1959

Wondrous Oblivion (dir. Paul Morrison, 2003)

Cricket

HS Altham, 1962, *A History of Cricket Volume One.* George Allen & Unwin (*This was first published in serial form in 'the Cricketer' magazine in 1926. It was published as a book and then in two volumes, the second with EW Swanton*)

JS Barker, 1963, *Summer Spectacular: West Indies v England*

Scyld Berry, 2015 *Cricket, the Game of Life: Every Reason to Celebrate,* Hodder & Stoughton.

Robert Brooke, 1991, *A History of the County Cricket Championship,* Guinness Books.

Stephen Chalke, 2015, *Summer's Crown,* Fairfield Books.

The England Cricket Board (ECB), 1997 *Raising the Standard*

David Frith, 1987, *Pageant of Cricket,* Macmillan

Simon Heffer, 1990, *The Daily Telegraph Century of County Cricket: the 100 Best Matches,* Sidgwick & Jackson

Colin Ingleby-Mackenzie, 1962, *Many a Slip,* Oldbourne Sports

Roy Marshall, 1970, *Test Outcast,* Pelham Books

Peter Oborne, 2004, *Basil D'Oliveira – Cricket and Conspiracy, the Untold Story,* Little Brown

EW Padwick 1984 (2nd edition) *A Bibliography of Cricket,* the Library Association. (*There is also a Volume Two, compiled by Stephen Eley and Peter Griffiths, 1991*)

Alan Ross, 1963, *West Indies at Lord's,* Eyre & Spottiswoode

Sir Pelham Warner, 1942, *Cricket Between the Two Wars,* London, Sporting Books

Charles Williams, 2013 *Gentlemen & Players: the Death of Amateurism in Cricket,* Phoenix

Jack Williams, 2001, *Cricket and Race,* Berg

Graeme Wright *Behind the Boundary: Cricket at a Crossroads*, A&C Black

Political, Social And Cultural History

Richard Hoggart, 1992, *The Uses of Literacy,* Penguin

David Kynaston, 2009, *Family Britain 1951–1957,* Bloomsbury. (*This is the second in a series called 'Tales of New Jerusalem', drawing on many oral histories and covering the period in Britain from 1945–1979, To date four have been published*)

Arthur Marwick, 1998, *The Sixties: Cultural Revolution in Britain, France, Italy and the United States 1958–1974,* Oxford University

Professor Colin McCabe, 1988, "Black Film in 80s Britain" in ICA Documents 7 *Black Film: British Cinema*

George Melly, 1970, *Revolt into Style: the Pop Arts,* faber & faber

Norman Moss, 2008, *Picking Up the Reins: America, Britain and the Postwar World,* the Overlook Press

Jon Savage *Teenage: the Creation of Youth 1875–1945,* Chatto & Windus

Dominic Sandbrook *Never Had It So Good; a History of Britain from Suez to the Beatles,* Little Brown

Dominic Sandbrook, *White Heat: a History of Britain in the Swinging Sixties,* Little Brown

Dominic Sandbrook, 2013, *Seasons in the Sun: the Battle for Britain 1974–1979,* Penguin Books

Anthea Tinker, "Old Age and gerontology" in James Obelkevich & Peter Catterall 1994, *Understanding Post-War British Society,* Routledge

Marion Whybrow, 2014, *A Childhood in St Ives,* Halstar

AN Wilson, 2009, *Our Times: the Age of Elizabeth II,* Arrow

Acknowledgements

This is my second book with Moyhill and David Cronin, and as with the first one – on a very different topic – it has been a pleasure from start to finish. His knowledge, professionalism and efficiency are a great help and comfort and I am very grateful to him.

For about 25 years I have been involved in Hampshire cricket beyond the business of being a member and supporter. In that time I have enjoyed the company of many friends from whom I have learned a considerable amount about the history and procedures of county cricket. In particular, Hampshire has been very lucky over the years to have so many fine historians, stretching back to John Nyren almost 200 years ago. In my time, my original 'mentor' Neil Jenkinson, plus Andrew Renshaw, Alan Edwards, Stephen Saunders and statisticians Vic Isaacs, Bob Murrell and 'Tigger' Miles have been a great help and I bless them all.

I enjoy delightful relationships with many Hampshire supporters and over the years I have benefitted from conversations with many Hampshire cricketers, in particular Alan Rayment who is the most charming and informative of companions.

In the past few years my radio commentaries and talks to some cricket societies and groups, especially Dorset and Hampshire Cricket Societies and the Portsmouth Area Supporters Group, have helped me to explore and develop the ideas in this book. The Hampshire Cricket History Blog has contributed similarly and the regular 'bloggers' have been a great encouragement. More broadly, the Association of Cricket Statisticians and Historians and Cricket Archive have revolutionised the world of cricket history in recent years.

Having decided to write for a 'real' contemporary version of me as a ten-year-old first time fan I was lucky to find Spencer and his family at East Woodhay Cricket Club. It was clearly a bit of a surprise to them and I thank them for going along with the idea. I hope it will enhance Spencer's fondness for our great game. Thinking of 1959, I'm grateful to my mum for having the good idea to pack me off to see 'Shack' taking that wicket in the first half-hour of watching county cricket. It paid off!

Finally my special thanks to my wife Lou: when we met 35 years ago I doubt whether she had ever given a moment's thought to cricket but she was wonderfully tolerant to begin with and has supported my involvement and interest in a variety of ways. She is also a very thorough proof-reader and has played a central role in the production of this book, ensuring that my passion is kept in check. Of course any errors remain entirely mine. Finally if you paid for this book, you will have contributed to the work of my friends at Cage4All and we thank you for that.

Harrison, Tom 210, 214
Harrow 22, 34, 50
Hartley, LP 14–15, 17, 229
Hartley, Peter 170
Hartley Wintney 44
Harvey, Neil 73
Hashim Amla 201
Hastings 38, 50
Havant 44, 110
Hawke, Lord 21
Hawke, Neil 81
Hayden, Matthew 165, 179, 183
Hayling Island CC 110
Haynes, Desmond 121, 132, 149
Haynes, Johnny 69
Hayward, Richard 125
Headingley 38, 52, 83–4, 106, 111,
    113, 115, 123, 127, 139, 146, 150, 158,
    165, 167, 176, 178, 182, 195, 211
Headley, Dean 36
Headley, Ron 35
Heath, Edward MP 80, 98, 103
Heath, Malcolm 26, 37, 62
Hedgecock, Murray 135
Heffer, Simon 113, 213, 230
Hemmings, Eddie 139–40, 145, 158
Henderson, Robert 158
Hendren, 'Patsy' 86
Herman, Bob 93
Herman, 'Lofty' 93
Hertfordshire 19, 134
Heyhoe, Rachel 112, 166, 226
Hick, Graeme 94, 142, 145, 150–1,
    154–5, 167, 175, 178
Higgs, Ken 43, 86, 92, 97
Highclere Castle 64
Hill, AJL 186
Hill, Clem 21
Hirst, George 21
Hitchcock, Alfred 12, 229
Hitchcock, Ray 35, 43
HM the Queen 172
Hobbs, Robin 92, 107, 124
Hobson, Richard 214
Hodd, Andrew 42
Hoggard, Matthew 176, 184
Hoggart, Richard 59, 231
Holder, Jason 207
Holder, John 122
Holder, Vanburn 94
Holding, Michael 116, 121, 126, 132, 134, 165
Holford, David 86
Holland 34, 138, 194, 219
Hollioake, Adam 164, 184

Hollioake, Ben 164, 179
Hollis, Christopher 13
Holt, Arthur 43–4
Hong Kong 151, 171
Hope and Glory 124, 229
Hornung, EW 13
Horsham 143
Horton, Henry 39, 50, 53, 62
Horton, Martin 41
Hoult, Nick 216, 218
House of Commons, the 53, 75, 147
Hove 41, 50, 55, 60, 72, 97, 116, 155, 165, 214
Howard, CG 88
Howe, Geoffrey MP 147–8
HRH Diana, Princess of Wales 163
HRH Duke of Edinburgh 139
HRH Prince Charles 125
HRH Princess Anne 112
Hughes, Chesney 124
Hughes, David 109
Hughes, Kim 126
Hughes, Merv 153–4
Hughes, Phil 202, 205–6
Hughes, Thomas 13
Hunte, Conrad 47, 76
Hunt, Jeremy MP 200
Hurd, Alan 49
Hursley Park 184
Hurst, Geoff 80
Hussain, Nasser 85, 132, 145, 149, 155, 161,
    164, 170, 175–6, 178–9, 182–3, 191, 210
Hussey, Michael 195
Hutton, Len 14, 23–4, 38, 51, 54
Hutton, Richard 42, 160

I

Ibadulla, Khalid 'Billy' 35, 83
ICC 47, 56, 58, 118, 138, 141–2, 154, 158,
    162, 168, 177, 179–80, 182, 185–7, 194,
    196–7, 203–4, 207, 209–10, 213, 219
ICC World XI 186
If 27
Igglesden, Alan 146
Ilford 87
Illingworth, Ray 37, 41–2, 65, 82, 92,
    96, 107–8, 111, 115, 146, 148, 156
Imperial Cricket Conference 47, 56
Imran Khan 129, 133, 136, 140, 142, 187
India 11, 18, 33, 38, 41, 71, 82, 92, 105,
    109, 113–17, 128–9, 132–3, 137–8, 140,
    142, 149–52, 154, 156, 159–60, 164, 168,
    175–80, 183, 186–7, 190, 193–6, 198,
    200–1, 203–4, 206–7, 209, 213, 219
Indian Cricket League 190